THE STABLE CRISIS

THE STABLE CRISIS

Two Decades
of German
Foreign Policy

WOLFRAM F. HANRIEDER
University of California,
Santa Barbara

Harper & Row, Publishers
New York, Evanston, and London

THE STABLE CRISIS: *Two Decades of German Foreign Policy*

Library of Congress Catalog Card Number: 72-109578

For Elisabeth

CONTENTS

INTRODUCTION

Throughout the twenty-year history of the Federal Republic of Germany, its major foreign policy goals—security, political and economic recovery, and reunification—have remained remarkably constant. Although these goals, and the policies with which they were pursued, have been modified in the light of failures and successes and in response to changes in international and domestic politics, the foreign policy preoccupations of West Germany are characterized by a striking continuity.

Perhaps the dominant reason for this is that the ends as well as the means of German foreign policy were imposed by international circumstances over which the Bonn Republic had practically no control. The defeat of Nazi Germany, the years of political impotence and economic deprivation during the occupation, and the Cold War not only raised the major foreign policy issues that were to preoccupy the Federal Republic, but also apparently mapped or foreclosed the paths toward their resolution. Indeed, the Federal Republic (as well as the German Democratic Republic) owes its very existence to the disagreements among the four occupying powers—disagreements which prevented the joint administration of Germany envisaged at the end of World War II, and which made control of Germany the pivot and most coveted prize of the Cold War. The Cold War struggle between two opposing alliances not only gave birth to the Federal Republic, but also imposed upon West Germany a fundamental concern with its security from external threats, a concern which has remained even after the Cold War confrontation ended in the uneasy truce of coexistence. At the same time, the goal of political and economic recovery emerged from the extremely limited and conditional independence and mobility granted the Federal Republic in 1949 (in domestic as well as in international affairs), and from the economic conditions of Germany in 1949—which were so dismal as to constitute a national emergency. The division of Germany, institutionalized in 1949 with the establishment of two German states, imposed upon the Bonn government what was (and is) its most difficult foreign policy task, the reunification of Germany—a task to which the Federal Republic is specifically committed by its constitutional document, the Basic Law. More concretely, Bonn's three major goals were designed to achieve: first, the physical integrity of West German territory against external threats; second, the restoration of sovereignty, the readmission of Germany to the society of free nations, internal political stability, and a thriving economy with its corollary social benefits; and third, the reunification of the separated entities of West Germany, East Germany, the so-called Eastern Territories (under Polish control), and the Saar, which, in their entirety, represent roughly the territorial expanse of Germany in 1937.

The relative constancy of these goals stems not only from their initial imposition by large-scale international circumstances, but also from the fact that these circumstances, even though they changed significantly during the last two decades, continued to pose formidable obstacles to Bonn's foreign policy. This is of course primarily true for the goal of reunification—only the Saar issue has been resolved in West Germany's favor. But West Germany has achieved legal sovereignty and some measure of political maneuverability on the international scene, it enjoys an enviable degree of economic prosperity and sociopolitical stability, and the integrity of its territory remains unviolated with no direct threats visible in the foreseeable future. This sharp contrast between the failure of its reunification policy and the remarkable (if partial) successes achieved by the Federal Republic in the area of security and political and economic recovery is not coincidental. It developed from the difficulty, if not impossibility, of pursuing these three sets of goals simultaneously with equal success, given the restrictive circumstances of the international system. In fact, the very success of Bonn's pro-Western security and recovery policy, through which the Federal Republic became the bulwark of Washington's containment policy in Europe in return for political and economic concessions, contributed to the polarization of power and purpose between the two Cold War blocs in central Europe and further deepened the division of Germany. Yet even here it is highly doubtful whether the Federal Republic, restrained by political and contractual commitments to the Western alliance system and faced with a hostile Eastern bloc, had a genuine choice of incompatible alternatives.

This fatalistic view of the course of West German foreign policy, which implies a foreordained historical necessity and denies West German decision-makers the possibility of having made viable choices, is of course somewhat one sided, even with respect to the formative years of the Federal Republic. For even though international factors may have limited Germany's foreign policy choices, the response of the West German people and decision-makers was shaped by impulses that came from within as well as from without the West German political system, and which inextricably tied together domestic and foreign politics.

This relationship between domestic and foreign politics—the "central mystery" as one writer has called it—has always been of special interest to political analysts, primarily because reflections about this relationship raise some of the largest questions about the nature of political processes. These questions deal not only with how a political unit seeks to manipulate a frequently hostile (or at least intractable) environment; they also touch upon internal dimensions such as sources of aspirations, prevailing value systems and their institutional manifestations, the perception of restrictions and opportunities in the international environment, the role of groups and individual decision-makers, and so forth—in other words, all the factors that determine how a political system conceives, articulates, and advances its demands on the environment. To talk about the connection between internal and external politics means to talk about all the major elements that form the patterns of power and purpose in the domestic as well as the international system.

Nothing so ambitious is intended here. Nonetheless, the connection between international and domestic politics has a special poignancy in the case of West Germany, because from the beginning most political groups in the Federal Republic assumed that foreign policy had a direct impact on the political and socio-economic makeup of the domestic order. The primary reason for this was that the political and military commitments made by the Bonn government to the Western alliance—commitments which were the precondition for the restoration of sovereignty and economic reconstruction—not only restricted the future maneuverability of Bonn's foreign policy but also set the stage for the future direction and content of West Germany's internal socio-political order. This was not simply another example of the *Primat der Aussenpolitik*—after all, the idea of the "primacy of foreign policy" assumes that foreign and domestic policy are inherently distinct—but rather an example of an inextricable meshing of domestic and foreign policy considerations.* It is striking how strongly the makers and critics of Bonn's foreign policy felt that the outcome of foreign policy issues would determine the kind of society that would ultimately prevail in Germany. Foreign policy projects were consistently evaluated in terms of the limitations and opportunities they posed for creating the social order that the interested parties were committed to establishing. For example, Kurt Schumacher, the postwar leader of the German Social Democrats, noted that "the contest over foreign policy is at the same time the contest over internal policy and the social content of the political order. . . . Foreign policy sets the limits to the possibilities of our economic and social policy."† Similarly, Chancellor Adenauer and his supporters expected that the results of foreign policy would help create the prerequisites for the socio-political and cultural values they hoped to instill in the German body politic. The consequences of this phenomenon can hardly be exaggerated: It had a decisive impact on the course of West Germany's political and socioeconomic reconstruction, it left an indelible imprint on the institutional and non-institutional channels of the political process, it characterized the nature of the political dialogue throughout the formative years of the new state, and it probably contributed (as the late Otto Kirchheimer

* See Czempiel, "Der Primat der Auswärtigen Politik."
† Schumacher, "Die Staatsgewalt."

has suggested) to the domestic stability of the Federal Republic.

The close relationship between Germany's external role and internal structure suggests that neither dimension should be neglected in a discussion of West German foreign policy—it is important to consider both external and internal dimensions of foreign policy precisely because its makers and critics apparently found it meaningless or impossible to separate them. For this reason I have allotted considerable space (in Chapter Four) to the discussion of the domestic predispositions that shaped the West German response to the formidable challenges posed by the international environment. The pursuit of the goals of security, recovery, and reunification amid important transformations of the international system are treated in the first three chapters, each of which examines the pursuit of one set of goals during the period from 1949 to 1969.

The large methodological concerns which arise from attempts to integrate external and internal dimensions of foreign policy are discussed in some detail in my *West German Foreign Policy 1949-1963: International Pressure and Domestic Response* (Stanford University Press, 1967), upon which I have also drawn heavily for the historical discussion of the Adenauer period. However, the analytical vantage point of the present study, compared with that of the earlier volume, has been shifted somewhat. Whereas the earlier book is strongly method-oriented and employs rather sharp chronological divisions (1949-1955 and 1955-1963) within which the international and domestic ramifications of German foreign policy goals are examined, the present work treats the pursuit of security, recovery, and reunification in the international environment continuously from 1949 to 1969 in the first three chapters, followed by a chronological discussion of the two decades' domestic background in the final chapter. This shift seemed desirable in order to match concrete historical "function" with the appropriate analytical form: The international (as well as the domestic) factors that impinged on West German foreign policy after the middle 1950s were much more complex than during the early years of the Adenauer period, and sharp chronological divisions would have implied nonexisting historical discontinuities, especially with respect to the gradual although far-reaching changes in the international system that affected Bonn's policies during the last decade. I have, however, retained the division of the Adenauer era into two periods in the chapter on domestic processes so as to highlight the important changes that took place in the middle 1950s in the domestic political system as a response to changing international circumstances.

THE STABLE CRISIS

CHAPTER ONE/ SECURITY

Since no West German armed forces were established until the late 1950s, the security of the Federal Republic was in the beginning entirely determined by the capabilities and intentions of the Soviet bloc and the countervailing power and purpose of the Western alliance. Nonetheless, the Bonn government's early decision to implement the goal of security by rearming in the context of the Western alliance had immediate and important consequences: it initiated Germany's increasingly important contribution to the Western defense system and it became the linchpin which held together the entire foreign policy program of the Adenauer government. West Germany's chances of achieving its foreign policy goals—security, political and economic recovery, and reunification—were directly affected (positively in the case of security and recovery, and negatively in the case of reunification) by the decision to join the Western defense system. Moreover, rearmament was the issue that linked the opportunities and restrictions of the international system with the entire aggregate of West German foreign policy goals. Without the Cold War polarization of tensions and interests, there would have been little reason for the Western powers to press for a reconstruction of Germany's military potential a few years after the end of World War II. Without the need to rearm Germany, there would have been little incentive to accommodate the West German government in its pursuit of political and economic recovery and in its attempt to unify Germany. Rearmament was the bridge between the Cold War attributes of the international system and the successes and failures of Bonn's foreign policy.

After several years of Cold War tensions, and following the creation of the North Atlantic Treaty Organization in 1949 and the outbreak of the Korean War in June 1950, the Western allies began to regard the rearmament of West Germany as indispensable to Washington's containment policy in Europe. The newly established government in Bonn, under Chancellor Konrad Adenauer, was cooperative; and the main problem was how to effectively control a West German military contingent, since Bonn's future allies wanted security from Germany as well as security for Germany. In 1950, the Western powers agreed to establish German mobile police units, and planned to incorporate German units at the lower echelons of an integrated European army. In addition, the NATO Council decided to accelerate the defense measures proposed in the North Atlantic Treaty of April 1949, and instructed the NATO Defense Committee to draw up plans for the inclusion of West German contingents in a Western defense establishment.

The question of control raised some serious problems within NATO. The United States recommended that no German unit should be larger than a division, and proposed that a NATO defense force should include ten German divisions. France, deeply apprehensive about Germany's impending rearmament, proposed the so-called Pleven Plan for a European Defense Community (EDC), a plan that was designed first to satisfy American pressures to rearm Germany, and second to extend European integration into the sphere of European defense. The French insisted on German units much smaller than divisions, and on the "complete fusion of all human and material elements" of the proposed European forces that were to be placed at the disposal of a unified Atlantic command. The United States and France also disagreed over France's repeated attempts to curtail German political influence in an international military organization and to limit German military functions to an essentially auxiliary role. After protracted negotiations, it was agreed that Germany would provide twelve divisions within a European army, although the Federal Republic itself would not become a member of NATO.

When the EDC treaty was signed in 1952 by the Federal Republic, France, Italy, and the Benelux countries, the question of German rearmament had become even more pressing. From the beginning, NATO planners had operated on the basis of three defense plans; in addition to two stopgap emergency plans, they had formulated a long-term requirements plan, which was based on the contingency of a main Soviet thrust across the North German plain, and which spelled out the force levels required to meet that threat and defend Europe in a major war. By 1952, there was a feeling of increased urgency among NATO members to put these plans into effect, since the Soviet Union had already exploded nuclear devices, and it was expected that American strategic nuclear superiority would be gradually diminishing. Thus, at the Lisbon NATO Conference of February 1952, the North Atlantic Council agreed on a force goal of 96 divisions, of which 35 to 40 were to be battle-ready on the line, the remainder to be capable of mobilization within a month after D-Day. Given these force requirements, it was not surprising that the Council members "reaffirmed the urgency, for the defense of Western Europe, of establishing at the earliest possible date a militarily effective European Defense Force, including a German contribution."[1]

The implications of the Lisbon strategy aroused misgivings in Bonn that foreshadowed the much more serious concerns voiced in later years. To be sure, the Adenauer government was fully aware of the political lever rearmament could provide for the pursuit of West German sovereignty and the attainment of Adenauer's fundamental goal—equal partnership for West Germany in a Western European union. Furthermore, the Western powers' insistence on West German rearmament presented Bonn with a chance to trade German support of the West for Allied political and economic concessions. Nonetheless, the Lisbon Plan caused some concern in Bonn because it apparently accepted the possibility of a "limited war" in Europe during which the Federal Republic, due to its forward position, would necessarily suffer the most.

As it was, the conventional force goals envisaged at Lisbon proved unrealistically ambitious. Implementation would have been costly and politically controversial, and many Europeans regarded conventional forces primarily as a trip-wire that would trigger an immediate American nuclear response if they were attacked. For this function, it seemed, a much smaller contingent would suffice, especially since the most effective trip-wire forces—American units—were already deployed at the Iron Curtain. The Atlantic alliance continued to rely largely on the American nuclear deterrent, and when the Eisenhower Administration enunciated its doctrine of "massive and instant retaliation" by means and at places of Washington's choosing, it merely added a catchy slogan to the existing and accepted deterrence posture.

The "automaticity" of an American nuclear response to a conventional provocation, which was reemphasized in the doctrine of massive retaliation, was highly attractive to Bonn; it seemed to reinforce the credibility of deterrence and reduce the likelihood that West Germany would become a battlefield in a conventional war. But Washington's "New Look" strategy of massive retaliation, which was coupled with the announcement that American standing forces would be reduced by 18 per cent over the next four years, was rapidly being called into question by the shifting power relationship between the United States and the Soviet Union. Massive retaliation depended heavily on the B-47 bomber bases overseas, which were beginning to become vulnerable to Soviet attack; in August 1953 the Soviet Union set off its first H-bomb, and during 1954 Moscow began to display a considerable number of long-range bombers. Meanwhile, NATO's Lisbon force goals were far from implementation.

The increase in Soviet power was in part balanced by the advances made by NATO. By 1954 NATO had approximately fifteen divisions under arms, and considerable progress had been made in planning and constructing an elaborate infrastructure of communications networks, fuel pipelines, port facilities, supply lines, and headquarters installations. Nonetheless, the absolute and relative increase of Soviet capabilities, particularly on the nuclear level, called for a searching reappraisal of American strategy. Throughout 1954 the Pentagon was engaged in reformulating the American deterrence posture in order to implement a credible defense strategy that would complement the doctrine of massive retaliation. This culminated in the decision to reinforce the Western forward line of defense with tactical nuclear weapons.

Both the increase in Soviet strength and the NATO powers' failure to meet the Lisbon force goals led to the announcement at the NATO Council meeting of December 1954 that the Lisbon plan would be revised: thirty standing divisions were to be deployed in the central defense sector, and these divisions would be supplied with "modern"—that is, atomic—weapons. During 1953 the United States had developed tactical "battlefield" atomic weapons that were expected to be operational and ready for deployment soon thereafter. Reliance on these tactical nuclear weapons to offset the conventional force superiority of the Soviet bloc seemed highly attractive, since it promised fiscal and manpower savings in addition to making up for America's gradual loss of its nuclear monopoly. NATO planning was now officially based on the principle that tactical nuclear weapons would be used to counter almost any type of aggression, and the NATO Council authorized the Supreme Allied Commander, Europe (SACEUR) to formulate contingency planning on that basis. Nuclear arms were designated as NATO's "sword," and conventional forces were regarded as NATO's "shield"—whose function was limited to a brief holding action.

For West German security, the implications of the shift in NATO planning were ambiguous, if not contradictory. NATO spokesmen stressed that the thirty divisions planned for the central sector would be there primarily to implement NATO's commitment to a "forward strategy" in the case of an all-out war. This calculation stemmed from the expectation that an all-out nuclear war would probably be of short duration, and thus would not provide time for the mobilization and redeployment of reserve contingents. Coupled with this assumption was the hope that a forward strategy with tactical nuclear weapons would allow the defenders to destroy the massed forces of the attacker before the attack could begin. But tactical atomic weapons can also be employed effectively by the attacker if the defender's strategy is based on holding an inflexible forward line. Since the Soviet Union also had developed tactical nuclear weapons, the advantage that NATO planners hoped to gain was already being called into question. Consequently, NATO planners assigned a second, related function to the thirty divisions—namely, to deal with minor aggression and to prevent the Soviet Union from mounting a rapid and limited surprise attack and confronting the West with a fait accompli. To do this, NATO's new forward strategy was supplemented with a doctrine of flexible defense, which called for highly mobile units to retreat and advance as battlefield conditions required, and to roll with the punch of the major Soviet thrust.

This dual purpose of NATO planning, which prepared for the contingency of defense and simultaneously tried to sustain the credibility of nuclear deterrence, met with a cautious official response in Bonn. The concept of mobile strategy and elastic defense had already stirred up a lively debate in the German press and among German military experts, because it seemed to accept the possibility that an attacker would penetrate deeply into West German territory; this would subject West Germany to being first overrun and then "liberated." But whatever misgivings government circles may have entertained in private, the political and contractual commitments that had already been made, and the attendant reward of sovereignty, hardly allowed a reversal or even a public reappraisal of the government's rearmament policy. In March 1955, Adenauer flatly argued that only membership in NATO could rule out the chance that the Federal Republic would become a battlefield in a hot war between the Soviet Union and the United States.

The Adenauer government could hardly neglect to exploit the political leverage provided by the decision to fortify NATO with battlefield nuclear weapons. Under the new strategy, West German conventional forces were needed even more than before. The twelve divisions that West Germany had agreed to provide under the Paris Agreements of October 1954 were now assigned two functions: one was to carry the major burden in defending the central sector (especially since the other NATO members had not met their share of the Lisbon force goals); the other was to provide a strong forward position of ground troops, which was required by the new strategy to force the enemy to attack in concentration so as to make tactical nuclear counterstrikes efficacious. In addition to being part and parcel of the Western ground forces, the planned German contingents had become an integral element in Washington's attempt to reinforce the American strategic nuclear position. Without having proceeded beyond the planning stage, "by the beginning of 1954, German rearmament—which had at the time of Lisbon been seen only as one component of a balanced force designed to complement the nuclear superiority of the United States—had become, in SACEUR's view, the sine qua non of a new nuclear strategy for Europe."[2]

This shifting military-strategic scene, which reflected significant changes in the East-West balance of power, was the background for the Western powers' deliberations on the European Defense Community. After intricate negotiations, the EDC treaty was signed by the Federal Republic, France, Italy, and the Benelux countries on May 27, 1952; and the connection between West German rearmament and West German sovereignty was now specifically acknowledged in contractual form. On the previous day, the occupying powers and the West German government had signed the so-called Bonn Conventions. They provided for the end of the occupation regime by abolishing the Occupation Statute and the Allied High Commission, and anticipated the restoration of German sovereignty in external and internal affairs, though with certain reservations. The Western Allies reserved the right to station troops in Germany and to decide questions involving the whole of Germany—including reunification, a final peace treaty, and Berlin. These Conventions were to go into effect at the same time as the EDC treaty. The treaty itself provided that Bonn would contribute twelve divisions to a European army and that Germany, although technically denied membership in NATO, would become a de facto member since the EDC would become a part of NATO and the North Atlantic Treaty would be extended to cover the territory of the EDC. The only major concession to French demands was the provision that German contingents would be integrated at the corps level, thus preventing German generals from commanding German national corps.

When the French National Assembly failed to ratify the EDC

treaty in August 1954,[3] the treaty structure that was to rearm the Federal Republic and restore German sovereignty collapsed. The entire Western defense system seemed threatened, and the United States hinted it might disengage from Europe because of French obstructionism. The situation appeared especially serious because plans to deploy tactical nuclear weapons on NATO's forward line in Germany were already being made, and because the new strategy assigned new and crucial functions to the proposed German contingents.

It was in the wake of these disquieting developments that British Prime Minister Anthony Eden went on his celebrated mission to Italy and the Benelux countries, with the purpose of arranging for Germany to join NATO and providing for Germany's and Italy's membership in an expanded and revived Brussels Treaty Organization. The Brussels Treaty of March 1948 between Britain, France, and the Benelux countries was little more than a mutual-defense agreement and had become practically obsolete with the establishment of NATO in 1949. However, the enlarged Brussels Treaty Organization, renamed Western European Union (WEU), obligated Britain to maintain an army on the Rhine, established supervisory organs to check on Germany's rearmament, and subordinated the proposed German contingents to NATO's command structure, thus meeting some of the French objections to German rearmament.

The outcome for the Federal Republic was a full success. Although the moderate political restrictions of the Bonn Conventions were essentially retained, Germany was to be granted full equality as a member of NATO, with the proviso that Bonn was to renounce the manufacture of atomic, biological, and chemical weapons and certain other types of arms, such as guided missiles, rockets, submarines, and other types of vessels. (In addition, an effective international control over German forces was provided through the Council of the Western European Union.) These provisions did not preclude Germany's possession or use of nuclear weapons; Bonn renounced not a nuclear strategy but rather the independent production of nuclear weapons on German territory. The Federal Republic agreed to establish a national contingent of twelve divisions, wholly under NATO command, and the members of NATO pledged in return to support the reunification of Germany with all diplomatic means, and to regard the West German government as the only legitimate spokesman for all of Germany. In October, Germany was officially invited to join NATO and the enlarged Brussels Treaty Organization. On October 23, the Federal Republic joined the Brussels Treaty Organization, and on the same day the occupying powers and West Germany signed a slightly altered version of the 1952 Bonn Conventions, which had been adjusted to take account of the new European defense structure. These so-called Paris Agreements were ratified by Germany in February 1955, and went into effect on May 5. On the same day, the Occupation Statute was revoked, and the Allied High Commissioners became ambassadors. On May 9, West Germany became a member of NATO, and in July a group of German officers took up their duties at Supreme Headquarters, Allied Powers, Europe (SHAPE).

Shortly thereafter, the changes in the power relationships between the two Cold War blocs, and their implications for West German security, were poignantly illustrated by the SHAPE atomic exercise Carte Blanche. During this exercise, which simulated 335 atomic bombings on German soil, casualties were estimated to have exceeded five million. Aside from its domestic political repercussions, Carte Blanche unmistakably pointed to the potential risks that a NATO partner would have to face now that the Soviet Union possessed nuclear weapons and delivery systems—risks that were to be avoided, according to the Bonn government, precisely by German membership in NATO. In the wake of the political uproar over Carte Blanche, the Bonn government intended to salvage the rationale for its rearmament policy by arguing that nuclear bipolarity had restored a place of decisive importance to conventional armament, and that even if nuclear war were to occur, regular forces would still be called upon to fulfill important tasks.

Although the Eisenhower Administration's "New Look" strategy stressed massive retaliation against conventional provocation, the

Pentagon's assessment of the forces that were needed for the defense of the West was not really at odds with Adenauer's. The question was not so much what forces were required as who would provide them. Admiral Arthur Radford, the Chairman of the Joint Chiefs of Staff, for example, argued for a global "balance of forces" toward which the United States would contribute its nuclear striking power while America's allies would contribute the bulk of ground forces and local naval and air power. This theme of a strategic division of labor among the Western alliance partners had already been taken up by British government spokesmen, who held that the American argument also applied to the British situation.

In Bonn, these developments were necessarily viewed with some apprehension. In Western capitals, there were already doubts whether a full-blown American response could be relied upon in light of Soviet nuclear power. A strategic division of labor, which would reduce the American conventional force level on the Continent and diminish the credibility of the American commitment, could only deepen these anxieties. At the same time, full-fledged preparations for a conventional response (which were of course enhanced by the presence of a strong American conventional force) suggested that an American nuclear response would not be automatic and might be delayed. It has been convincingly argued that the West should at that time have organized a deterrence posture to confront the Soviet Union at *all* capability levels, and that establishing sufficient conventional forces was essential for a credible strategic nuclear deterrence posture. But because of its forward position, the prospect of deterring Soviet ground forces with Western ground forces had little attraction for West Germany. Whether it was rational or not from the perspective of the overall East-West nuclear power relationship, the American plan to deploy tactical nuclear weapons in Europe—weapons which were publicized as deterrents rather than as potential instruments of defense—held significant attractions for Bonn. The Eisenhower Administration reasoned that the implicit threat of an immediate nuclear response, which was created by denying the likelihood of a conventional response, would deter a Soviet conventional attack. As long as it was reasonably credible, this deterrence posture was highly attractive to Western European powers, especially the Federal Republic. It was widely believed in Germany and elsewhere in Europe that preparation for a conventional response would increase the likelihood of war by undermining the credibility of massive retaliation, and would in fact encourage American "nuclear disengagement" from Europe. Since even a limited engagement with conventional forces would make Germany a battlefield, from Bonn's perspective it seemed better not to extend the range of retaliatory options because this seemed to weaken the "automaticity" of a nuclear response.

By 1956, the Bonn government began to reappraise its security policy. In the summer, when a bill for conscripting German soldiers was presented to the Bundestag, the government still argued for a buildup of conventional forces with determination and apparent conviction. Adenauer called the change of emphasis from conventional forces to atomic arms a mistake, and stressed the need for localizing conflicts by employing conventional responses. However, the government now shifted from arguing that German rearmament would help deter Soviet aggression to stressing that German force levels would aid in deterring nuclear war. Most likely, "this shift in emphasis corresponded to a modification of general apprehension. In the early fifties, at the beginning of the rearmament debate, German politicians had to deal with the fear of Soviet aggression. In 1955 and 1956, this fear had abated, and had been replaced by the fear of nuclear weapons."[4] In September 1956, the first indications of a change in policy became apparent. The Cabinet announced the reduction of the conscription period from eighteen to twelve months; this meant that West Germany's total force goal would be reduced from 500,000 to 325,000. In October, Franz-Josef Strauss, previously Minister of Atomic Affairs, replaced Theodor Blank as Defense Minister. In October and November, the change in the East-West power relationship was forcefully demonstrated when the West failed to come to the aid of the Hungarian revolutionaries and when Khrushchev threatened to employ missiles during the Suez crisis. At the end of the year, Adenauer and Strauss for the first time expressed an interest in obtaining tactical nuclear weapons for West Germany's armed forces.

To explain this shift in policy, Adenauer argued that a non-nuclear NATO response to a Soviet attack was no longer likely in light of the ramifications of the Radford Plan, the French transfer of troops to Algeria, British reliance on nuclear defense, and Belgium's reduction of its period of conscription. In effect, Bonn implied that the West could continue to rely on nuclear deterrence, and that Western Europe's conventional capabilities were now so depleted that NATO had no choice but to use tactical nuclear weapons to respond to a Soviet attack. (This shift in the government's military policy held domestic political attractions as well. James Richardson says, "Deprived of the strategic rationale for large ground forces, Adenauer had no incentive to struggle against the political pressure that had built up against an eighteen-month term of conscription. It would have been quixotic to have risked his Government's existence for the sake of a military contribution which, in terms of the current allied strategy, had become of marginal value.")[5]

Behind Bonn's somewhat oversimplified announcements were a persuasive strategic rationale and a fundamental lack of confidence in NATO's ground forces. The waning credibility of the American nuclear commitment and the failure of the West to intervene in Hungary seemed to provide Bonn with a strong incentive for seeking a voice in the nuclear decision-making of the Western alliance. The Bonn government began to doubt the value of a large German conventional contingent because this would provide NATO, and the Pentagon, with precisely the wider range of choices of response that seemed to undermine nuclear deterrence and increase the risk that Germany would become a battlefield in a conventional war. Such misgivings were reinforced by reductions of conventional forces in other NATO countries. These reductions further emphasized the existing functional separation between Germany's conventional force responsibilities and America's nuclear obligations to NATO—the less West Germany's allies were involved in the early stages of a Soviet attack, the less likely, or the more delayed, would be American nuclear retaliation. Because Germany could not accept a substitute for a "forward strategy," it consistently aimed to fully engage its allies at the periphery of the Eastern bloc. German co-management of nuclear weapons was expected to reinforce the Western nuclear presence at the East German border by extending Washington's nuclear commitments more unequivocally to cover the Federal Republic.

Strategic and military calculations were reinforced by political considerations. In January 1956, East Germany's armed forces were officially integrated in the Warsaw Pact military structure, and the Soviet Union subsequently began to advocate a reduction of troops and the prohibition of atomic weapons in the two parts of Germany. These proposals, antecedents of the various disengagement proposals put forth on both sides of the Iron Curtain in the middle and late 1950s, threatened to destroy the clear-cut military dividing line in central Europe which Bonn wanted as a deterrent. The proposals also held out the danger that military disengagement would be coupled with a de facto, or even de jure, recognition of East Germany. By incorporating both East and West Germany in one international agreement, Walter Ulbricht's East German regime in Pankow would have gained at least the de facto recognition that Bonn sought to deny it at all costs. A German share in nuclear control or planning now seemed to provide Bonn with a veto power in Western councils, which could preclude American military disengagement in central Europe.

The revamping of Bonn's defense policies met with little enthusiasm. NATO members criticized what they considered a crippling reduction of the German contribution to the common defense effort, and Bonn's ideas on the sharing of nuclear control were received coolly. In December 1956, the Bonn government was saved from a politically embarrassing situation when the British carried the brunt of the argument, and proposed in the NATO Council that the United States institute nuclear sharing by providing European forces with tactical nuclear warheads. In April 1957, the United States agreed to provide tactical nuclear weapons systems (with the nuclear warheads remaining under

American control), thus fully implementing the 1954 revision of NATO strategy. Later in the year, NATO planners called for the establishment and deployment of thirty divisions in NATO's central sector (Document MC 70), and Bonn began to show cautious interest in the deployment of American intermediate range ballistic missiles (IRBMs) in West Germany—which was being considered in Washington as a compensation for Soviet development of intercontinental missiles (ICBMs).

NATO's new defense strategy meant that West Germany and other European allies were becoming more and more dependent on weapons they had no control over. The warheads of the tactical nuclear weapons, which were deployed in increasing numbers with ground forces in Germany, were kept under tight American control, and Bonn was largely excluded from the planning for their use and deployment. Bonn's misgivings over the efficacy of this arrangement were shared in other European NATO capitals. France, in particular, was interested in ultimately developing her own strategic nuclear capability, which would permit her to join the special Anglo-American atomic entente as an equal partner—as de Gaulle proposed in 1958 when he called for a NATO nuclear triumvirate. After de Gaulle returned to power in 1958, France and Germany also reportedly discussed the establishment of some type of nuclear partnership between the two countries. It is not certain whether France was unwilling to share control and secrets, or whether Bonn felt the time had not come to engage in such a politically controversial venture. In any event, nothing came of the discussions.[6] The conclusion that de Gaulle drew from the changing East-West nuclear balance—namely that European nations needed independent national nuclear deterrents—could not be implemented by West Germany (even if the Bonn government had so desired) because of political and contractual restrictions and because of strategic considerations which made it seem imperative that West Germany's defense posture would remain closely tied to American strategic nuclear capabilities. At the same time, Bonn feared the trend toward expansion of the nuclear club, since it was fracturing the NATO alliance and thus undermining the basis of West German security.

The logical middle course between independent capabilities and no control sharing at all was a tightly integrated nuclear alliance with equal control sharing. West Germany now aimed to increase her military and political influence not so much on the basis of a "special understanding" with the United States, or through the quest for an independent nuclear arsenal, but rather by stressing the need for the political and military integration of the alliance and for a larger German share in the control of nuclear weapons. In the fall of 1960, the Bonn government began to express cautious interest in an integrated NATO force de frappe as an alternative to the national force de frappe favored by de Gaulle. By 1962, Bonn's interest in obtaining a voice in nuclear councils (which met with strong domestic and international opposition) was somewhat modified, and concentrated primarily on German participation in nuclear planning rather than on joint nuclear control.

Bonn's interest in joint nuclear management was shared in other European capitals, and during the late 1950s and early 1960s numerous proposals for a jointly controlled NATO force (or at least for consultation and common planning) were put forth in Europe. This posed a delicate problem for American policy. The Eisenhower Administration had consistently sought to prevent nuclear proliferation, and Washington would only concede the establishment of nuclear control arrangements that would allow NATO members to decide jointly about use, reserving a veto for the United States. (For example, Britain. Turkey, and Italy had accepted Jupiter nuclear missiles in 1957, under an arrangement whereby the United States retained custody of the warheads and both the United States and the recipient country could veto their use.) After several other proposals had proved abortive, in December 1960 the United States offered NATO five submarines with eighty Polaris missiles, to be delivered by 1963—provided that the NATO powers agreed on a multilateral control scheme. But in view of the impending change of administration in Washington and the need for Congressional approval—which would most likely mean that warheads would remain in

American custody—the NATO Council issued a noncommittal communiqué in response to the American proposal.

The ongoing NATO debate about the relative role of nuclear and conventional forces became even more heated when the Kennedy Administration began a thorough revamping of American strategy. Soon after taking office, President John F. Kennedy repeated rather half-heartedly Eisenhower's December 1960 offer to provide five submarines for a NATO nuclear force, with the important proviso that NATO's conventional force level (22 divisions at the time) would have to be raised to thirty divisions prior to any joint nuclear arrangement. More important, whereas the Eisenhower proposal had been put forth in the context of massive nuclear retaliation, the Kennedy proposal was related to a more flexible American strategic doctrine, which was designed to multiply Washington's strategic and tactical options and which required a conventional force build-up. The new administration was intent on reversing the trend toward reliance on strategic and tactical nuclear weapons that had characterized NATO planning during the Eisenhower Administration, and began to stress a more flexible and credible "graduated" scale of responses to a corresponding array of contingencies. Based on Defense Secretary Robert S. McNamara's maxim that "one cannot fashion a credible deterrent out of an uncredible action," the West was to be fully prepared on all capability levels in order to avoid the dilemma involved in choosing either a nuclear strike with the attendant risk of a Soviet counterstrike, or the politically disastrous consequences of doing nothing at all. In short, the Kennedy Administration wanted to provide a credible retaliatory response to every possible level of provocation. By 1962, President Kennedy and Secretary McNamara had presented a fully articulated and partially implemented "doctrine of flexibility," which involved contingency planning that tacitly admitted the feasibility and acceptability of a limited conventional war in Europe. In December 1962, McNamara suggested that because of the shifting nuclear balance of power, nuclear arms had become NATO's shield and conventional arms NATO's sword (thus completely reversing the strategic principles of the Radford Plan), and implied that a nuclear strike countering a conventional attack might be "delayed."

Even though Washington argued that far from diminishing the credibility of the American nuclear deterrent the build-up of conventional forces would enhance it, European NATO capitals were not reassured. First of all, the thirty divisions demanded by Washington did not create a force strong enough for a viable local defense strategy, yet it seemed to render a nuclear counterstrike less credible—which was one reason why NATO had not established the projected thirty divisions earlier. The European NATO members agreed with Washington that in the light of the waning American capability to conduct a counterforce strategy, NATO's deterrence posture should be strengthened; but the most credible response to a conventional attack, a response with conventional forces, held little attraction for Europeans because it meant total, if non-nuclear, war. Because of its forward position, this held especially true for West Germany, and the possibility of a "conventional pause" (during which Washington would determine whether nuclear retaliation was appropriate) necessarily made Bonn nervous. Henry Kissinger may have been right in 1962 when he said, "Those Europeans who believe that an emphasis on local defense reduces the credibility of the deterrent are confusing cause and effect"; but he also noted the ambiguity of Washington's strategic doctrine, which did not envisage a conventional force build-up sufficient to meet a Soviet challenge on any level of violence (for that thirty divisions were not nearly enough), but instead "justified the build-up of conventional forces in a more technical sense, as providing a capability for a last warning before *implementing* a counterforce strategy." This posture made Washington's assertions "that an increase in the shield forces was designed to make a counterforce strike more likely . . . appear as a subterfuge for our reluctance to face nuclear war. The need for flexibilty of response in Europe cannot be used to justify a counterforce strategy but to reduce our reliance on it."[7]

Changes in the deployment and tactical disposition of NATO's defenses added to Bonn's security concerns. The emphasis of

NATO's defense planning during the Kennedy Administration gradually began to shift to a tactical doctrine of "fluid defense" and mobility, with designated but not otherwise prepared defense positions. This defense doctrine required not only time to assess the opponent's major thrusts and to direct counterforces to critical sectors of the front, but also space—and both commodities would be crucial for Germany in case of an attack, because time and space would determine the extent of destruction on German territory. The Kennedy Administration also tried to strengthen the credibility of the nuclear deterrent by stressing the feasibility of controlling nuclear war and of preventing "spasmic," irrational nuclear exchanges. Again, this created a conflict of interest in the alliance because the European powers believed that they could gain most by "emphasizing the uncontrollable nature of nuclear war, in order to preserve the credibility of such deterrent power as [was] available on the continent."[8] Furthermore, the Cuban missile crisis and the test ban treaty strongly pointed to a Soviet-American common interest on nuclear questions. To many Europeans the test ban treaty, following the Allies' exclusion from Washington's deliberations on the Cuban confrontation, indicated that in the case of a major European crisis the two nuclear superpowers might settle the issue bilaterally, and that Washington would complement the Pentagon's doctrine of strategic flexibility with political-diplomatic flexibility.

During the last years of the Adenauer government, and throughout the Erhard Administration (1963-1966), Bonn increasingly sought to implement its security goal by insisting on participation in a proposed Western multilateral nuclear force (MLF). As already noted, proposals for a jointly controlled NATO nuclear force were put forth in Europe in the late 1950s, and elicited only perfunctory responses in Washington. But the Skybolt controversy of December 1962 triggered a series of events which made it appear as if the United States should respond to such proposals somewhat more earnestly.

Great Britain had planned to use the Skybolt, a two-stage ballistic missile to be carried by raiding bombers, as a "standoff weapon" that would provide a nuclear striking power, without ground-to-ground missiles, by prolonging the life of Britain's V-bombers which were becoming increasingly vulnerable to anti-aircraft missiles. When the United States decided in November 1962 to scrap the Skybolt development program after extensive cost-effectiveness evaluations, it meant in effect that Britain would have to either abandon plans for an independent nuclear capability because of lack of an adequate delivery system or carry on the development independently at exorbitant costs.

During a meeting between President Kennedy and British Prime Minister Harold Macmillan at Nassau in December 1962, an agreement was reached which provided that the United States would sell Britain Polaris submarine missiles, on the condition that Britain would assign such Polaris-equipped submarines to a NATO command, whenever established, as the nucleus of a NATO atomic force. An "escape clause" provided that the British government could unilaterally dispose over its contribution to this force in case "supreme national interests" were at stake. This arrangement was highly satisfactory to the British because it prolonged the life of Britain's independent nuclear deterrent. It was much less attractive to Paris and Bonn, however. The Nassau agreement was widely perceived—notably by de Gaulle—to have further cemented the "special relationship" between the United States and Britain; and although France was offered Polaris missiles on the same terms as Britain, de Gaulle rejected both the immediate Polaris arrangement of the Nassau agreement and the ultimate NATO force—in part because France had neither the submarines nor the warheads to make use of the Polaris missiles, and in part because de Gaulle was not interested in helping Washington cement the Western alliance on the basis of an Anglo-American nuclear axis.

Bonn's reaction was mixed. The Germans felt that they had been excluded from the deliberations as well as from the resulting agreement, and they were not reassured by the ambivalent strategic-military implications of the Nassau arrangement. At the same time, there was some hope that Bonn would gain a voice in nuclear decision-making—a hope that was raised in part by the language of the agreement which toned down its bilateral features and stressed its potential for multilateral nuclear control. The Nassau agreement—an exercise in "masterly ambiguity," as Arthur Schlesinger, Jr. called it[9]—had two components, and each had a somewhat different implication for Bonn's strategic interests. The "American" component (paragraph seven) looked toward the establishment under a multilateral authority in NATO of a mixed-manned seaborne nuclear force—consisting of the British contribution of four or five Polaris submarines, an equal or larger American contribution, a French contingent, and a contingent of NATO-owned surface ships to be manned and financed by the non-nuclear NATO members willing to join in the arrangement. However, paragraph six, drafted by the British, called for a more immediate solution, by setting up a NATO multinational force—equipped with R.A.F. bombers and American submarines—under a NATO nuclear command in which non-nuclear powers would participate. The American component of the agreement, with its provision for the mixed-manned staffing of surface ships, in a sense merely underlined the distinction between nuclear and non-nuclear NATO powers because it retained the specifically national contingent of American and British submarines. The British component, with its emphasis on joint planning and control, appeared to be more pragmatic, and held somewhat greater attractions for Bonn because it implied more influence (at less cost) over the deployment and use of nuclear weapons.[10] With either alternative, however, the United States would have retained a veto over use.

Aside from its unfortunate political connection with the Nassau agreement, the entire MLF idea suffered from serious military inadequacies. Most fundamentally, the various proposals for a joint nuclear NATO force stemmed from the perceived need to offset the large number of medium-range ballistic missiles that the Soviet Union had aimed at Western Europe. Although General Lauris Norstad, NATO's Supreme Allied Commander in Europe (SACEUR), had several pretargeted nuclear weapons systems at his disposal, which covered some of the missiles deployed in Western Russia, this target coverage was not complete. Since the Kennedy Administration did not wish to establish NATO as a fourth nuclear power, as SACEUR had suggested since 1959, this "targeting gap" had been filled by a force of American Polaris submarines stationed off the coasts of Europe. In other words, NATO's defense planning had to rely on non-NATO forces situated outside the Continent and not subject to NATO control. In order to reinforce the credibility of a Western nuclear response to a Soviet attack, the MLF proposal envisaged that the American standoff force would be augmented by a multilaterally controlled force of 25 surface ships and about two hundred missiles, under NATO command and staffed internationally through mixed manning. The military adequacy of surface deployment at sea, however, was widely questioned by European and American experts. Aside from the fact that the United States would have retained a veto over use (which made it difficult to see how the MLF scheme could enhance the credibility of a Western nuclear response) America's own reliance on submarines rather than on the less expensive surface vessels clearly implied that the latter were inferior in Washington's view. In fact, the MLF was not intended by the Kennedy Administration to serve a strictly military function, and was considered by the President to be "something of a fake."[11]

The political value of the MLF idea was even more doubtful. From the beginning of the Kennedy Administration, some of the "Europeanists" in the State Department and in the White House warmly supported an MLF scheme because they hoped it would become an effective device to counteract the disarray of NATO and to promote the Grand Design. Arthur Schlesinger says,

> Though it served no strictly military function (some military men looked much askance on the idea of mixed-manning and the Joint Chiefs of Staff never liked the MLF), it appealed to advocates of strategic interdependence as a means of preserving the unity of the deterrent and at the same time of giving NATO allies a nuclear role. . . . The MLF [also] attracted advocates of economic partnership because it brought new and urgent pressure on the European governments to move toward federation. The reason for this was that the only body to which we would possibly yield our nuclear veto was the government of

a united Western Europe. So long as the American veto remained, the MLF could never seem much more than a rather transparent public relations attempt to meet a supposed European demand for nuclear equality.[12]

Even though the Bonn government had shown an early interest in the collective nuclear force concept, and later became its only enthusiastic European supporter, American support for the MLF was designed not to satisfy but to forestall West Germany's alleged desire to become a nuclear power. Following French rejection both of the Nassau agreement and of Britain's application to join the Common Market, and after the signing of the Franco-German cooperation treaty of 1963, Washington began to view the MLF primarily as a stratagem to prevent a possible nuclear pact between Paris and Bonn. In short, much of the initial support for the MLF came from Washington rather than from Europe, and was based on the expectation that the MLF, with its built-in American veto, might revitalize NATO and prevent nuclear proliferation by preserving the Western alliance's "nuclear centralization." At best, it was hoped, the MLF idea would genuinely further integration and, failing that, it would at least temporarily paper over the fissures of the Western alliance.

Far from being a harmless palliative, however, the MLF proposal turned out to be a troublesome liability for American policy. It further cooled Franco-American relations, and it jeopardized an arms control agreement between the United States and the Soviet Union, since Moscow from the beginning castigated the entire MLF scheme as a device to place nuclear weapons in the hands of a "revanchist" regime in West Germany. Neither did the MLF succeed in symbolizing American-European interdependence or in furthering the integration of Europe. The military-strategic shortcomings of an American-dominated joint force could hardly foster a feeling of "interdependence" in Europe;* and Franco-German relations, which were strained

* Schlesinger, referring to McNamara's use of the term "interdependence" in his Ann Arbor speech of June 1962, notes that this "mellifluous" term was

throughout the years of the Erhard Administration, were further burdened by the divisive issue of the MLF, because de Gaulle wanted to establish a European defense structure (based perhaps on the economic foundations and the membership of the Common Market) and was adamantly opposed to German participation in nuclear decision-making, which would tie Bonn more closely to the United States.

Although Germany was presumably the beneficiary of the project, German-American relations suffered as a result of the MLF. In the first place, after Bonn had committed itself fully to an MLF scheme—so much so that for a time in 1964 it looked as if Bonn and Washington would proceed with it bilaterally*—the scrapping of the proposal by the Johnson Administration in 1965 caused Chancellor Ludwig Erhard considerable embarrassment on both the domestic and the international political scene. This was especially serious since Erhard, in the face of strong French objections, had consistently supported American policy (on NATO and the Atlantic Community, on Vietnam, and by responding to Washington's call for higher conventional troop levels for central Europe) and had relied heavily on Johnson's readiness to reciprocate by supporting the MLF. The demise of the MLF, coupled with Johnson's refusal in the fall of 1966 to accept a reduction of German offset purchases for U.S. troops

"misleading because what McNamara meant at bottom was precisely the *dependence* of western security on a nuclear deterrent under American control." *A Thousand Days,* p. 776, emphasis in original.

(Complete titles, authors' names, and publication data for works cited in short form in footnotes can be found in the Bibliography, pp. 205–215.)

* This was more appearance than reality. President Johnson and Chancellor Erhard reportedly had signed an agreement in June 1964 that by January 1965 at the latest, the MLF agreement was to be executed by the powers willing to accede to it, with the implication that this arrangement could conceivably be limited to the United States and Germany. In the light of the objections voiced against it by other NATO members, the Soviet Union, and American officials (including the U.S. disarmament negotiator at Geneva), it is unlikely that this possibility was very seriously considered by the President. See *Der Spiegel,* 42/1964, pp. 33–34.

stationed in Germany,* thus dealt a serious blow to Erhard's personal prestige. It added to the foreign and domestic policy problems which already beset the Bonn government, and, by providing additional ammunition for the domestic opposition to Erhard, contributed to the forced resignation of the Erhard Administration late in 1966.

Second, tensions developed between fundamental American interests and the major political purposes that Bonn sought to advance through nuclear control sharing. Throughout, an important reason for Bonn's interest in the MLF (in addition to security concerns) was the bargaining leverage it might provide

---

* Cost-sharing for American troops stationed in Germany had been a point of contention for a number of years because Washington wanted the Germans to continue easing the American balance-of-payments deficit through arms purchases in the United States, while the Germans insisted that they already had an adequate stock of military equipment. (During 1961-64 West Germany purchased $2.5 billion worth of American arms and munitions.) The issue aroused a good deal of annoyance on both sides, with the Americans threatening troop withdrawals and with one German commentator suggesting that Secretary McNamara "appears to many as a tireless arms merchant with shockingly high-pressure sales techniques." (Sommer, "Bonn Changes Course," p. 483.) The issue was finally resolved during the early months of the Grand Coalition in the spring of 1967 with a compromise (previously proposed to Johnson by Erhard) which called for German-American monetary cooperation rather than for continuing German weapons purchases to offset the dollar cost of American troops. The new approach provided that Germany would not convert into gold the dollars earned from American troop spending in Germany (the central bank of West Germany in any case followed a general policy of not cashing in dollars for gold) and that Germany would purchase medium-term securities in the United States, thus relieving the American balance of payments position. See Mendershausen, *Troop Stationing in Germany*.

A similar problem existed with respect to the 50,000 man British Army of the Rhine (BAOR) to whose maintenance Britain was committed by the WEU agreement. In March 1967, the British government again threatened Bonn with "massive BAOR withdrawals" unless the Germans would soon make substantial commitments to offset the cost. For the year 1968, the Germans agreed to purchase British equipment equivalent to two-thirds of the foreign exchange costs Britain incurred by maintaining the BAOR. See Hallett, "Britain and the Future of Germany"; *Der Spiegel*, 28/1965, pp. 19–22.

to help reunify Germany, perhaps in the context of disarmament or arms control negotiations. Although it was widely acknowledged in West Germany that a united Germany almost certainly would have to be a non-nuclear one, there was also some hope that if Bonn renounced nuclear control the Soviets would make concessions on the German question. Foreign Minister Gerhard Schröder made this explicit in the summer of 1965, when he declared that Germany would renounce nuclear capabilities only if the Soviets would not obstruct German reunification. This anticipated leverage, which was probably illusory to begin with, obviously required continued and forthright American support for the MLF—especially since de Gaulle had indicated that German participation in the MLF would stand in the way of a "European solution" to the German question (the only kind of solution he would support), because it would tie Bonn too closely to Washington. In other words, in pushing for the MLF the Federal Republic ran the danger of becoming diplomatically isolated on its unification policy without gaining, on the military-strategic level, more than a token of joint nuclear control.

This kind of support President Johnson was unwilling to provide. It was precisely the implied anti-Soviet dimension of Bonn's MLF policy that forced the Johnson Administration to scrap the project, because two of Washington's most cherished foreign policy goals—a detente with the Soviet Union and an arms control agreement—required the Kremlin's cooperation. Negotiations for a nuclear nonproliferation treaty were already well under way, and the Soviet Union had repeatedly made it clear that Washington would have to choose between the treaty and the MLF. The German government, however, insisted on the establishment of a NATO nuclear force prior to a nonproliferation agreement.* Throughout 1965, the MLF issue and the proposals

* Basically, the nonproliferation treaty was intended by the sponsoring powers —the United States, the Soviet Union, and Britain—to restrain lesser powers from acquiring nuclear weapons and thus prevent their use in regional conflicts which might escalate into a global nuclear holocaust. The treaty, which was finally concluded among the sponsors in the early summer of 1968, was

for a nonproliferation treaty were closely related. In January 1965, a "secret" report was submitted to President Johnson by a special panel headed by Roswell L. Gilpatric, former Deputy Secretary of Defense, which reportedly urged the President to drop the MLF idea so that work on the nonproliferation treaty would progress. The subsequent renewal of American initiative in the Geneva disarmament conference led, in the summer of 1965, to an intense German campaign to ensure that the United States would not trade the MLF for Soviet support on the nonproliferation treaty.

Although Washington sought to reassure the Germans that the Gilpatric proposal had not become American policy, all indications pointed in that direction. Since the early 1960s, American security concerns had generally shifted from the regional level to the global level of the Soviet-American strategic balance.[13] At the same time, the United States was trying to expand regional nonproliferation efforts to the global level—which appeared especially pertinent after China had exploded nuclear devices. Furthermore, an agreement with the Soviet Union on nonproliferation could be expected to nurture Soviet-American cooperation at a time when the escalation of the Vietnam conflict had strained relations considerably. Indeed, here lies the true significance of the Vietnam war for West German foreign policy. For it is not at all unlikely that the White House tacitly or explicitly compensated the Russians for their relative restraint on Vietnam with assurances that West Germany would be denied access to joint nuclear control. The staunch support of Erhard

---

the result of six years of negotiations at the Geneva disarmament conference, and reflected a genuine common interest of the sponsoring parties to forestall the destabilizing effects expected from further proliferation of nuclear capabilities. (France and China had indicated that they would not accede to the treaty.) To insure the security of non-nuclear ratifying states during the 25-year life span of the treaty, the sponsoring powers pledged themselves to act through the UN Security Council, and they also agreed (in Article VI) to pursue in good faith negotiations on arms control and nuclear disarmament. For a rather skeptical assessment of the security pledge, see Beaton, "Kernwaffen-Sperrvertrag."

and Schröder for America's involvement in Vietnam thus bears a certain ironic quality.

Sacrificing the MLF was relatively easy for the Johnson Administration, since neither Britain nor France wanted to see Germany admitted to nuclear policy making, and since most NATO members had shown no real interest in acceding to an MLF arrangement. Understandably, however, the Germans felt that their deep-seated suspicions about a possible Soviet-American deal at the expense of the German reunification question were confirmed by Washington's about-face on the MLF. Moreover, the other aspect of Bonn's interest in the MLF—that of security—became even more pressing after de Gaulle had announced French withdrawal from the integrated NATO command in February 1966.* NATO's "forward defense strategy," which had always appeared rather impracticable, was now further undermined by the loss of French troops, soil, and airspace.† This

---

* In his news conference of February 21, 1966, General de Gaulle announced that France would claim control of all foreign bases on its soil by April 4, 1969, and a subsequent memorandum demanded the withdrawal of all NATO command organizations. While France remained nominally a member of the alliance, it severed its operational connections with NATO, and NATO headquarters was subsequently moved from Paris to Brussels. De Gaulle's decision was not altogether unexpected. He had always been strongly critical of NATO's integrative features, and the French had signaled their intention to withdraw in the early summer of 1965 when they cancelled French participation in the NATO staff exercise "Fallex 66." In response to that cancellation, Secretary McNamara proposed the establishment of a four or five member NATO "select committee" for nuclear planning (which later became the NATO Nuclear Planning Group) whose intended function was at least in part to overcome French obstructionism within the alliance and to integrate the French force de frappe with NATO strategy. France declined to participate in either committee. For discussions of the background see Furniss, "De Gaulle's France"; and Goodman, "De Gaulle's NATO Policy."

† See Hunt, *NATO Without France;* and Amme, *NATO Without France*.

Actually, during most of NATO's life span the concept of "forward defense" had never been much more than a palliative slogan. When first enunciated by General Eisenhower in 1951, it meant the "fall-back" of NATO troops to the Rhine; only by 1963 was NATO sufficiently prepared to implement its first-line defense plan on West Germany's borders with the Soviet

made it seem imperative for West Germany to gain a voice in nuclear councils, especially since Washington spokesmen implied that the French withdrawal might compel NATO to resort to nuclear arms in a major conflict earlier than otherwise anticipated because "we are removing a part of a defense in depth which is useful." As one commentator noted, persons making such statements "could not have had in mind how the Germans might respond to such a remark. For it means simply that West Germany could be considered expendable before nuclear weapons were used."[14] Nor were the Germans reassured by the token proposals for joint nuclear consultations that the Pentagon put forth during 1966. In February, when Secretary McNamara met in Washington with the defense ministers of Britain, Germany, Italy, and Turkey to decide on ways to grant non-nuclear members broader participation in nuclear planning, West Germany and Italy indicated that they welcomed the opportunity to participate in such planning (primarily because it seemed to ensure the early use of nuclear weapons through explicit contingency planning), but that they could not regard it as a substitute for an Allied nuclear force and that they would oppose the nonproliferation treaty if it precluded the creation of such a force. In the spring, amid reports that Washington had definitely shelved the idea of an Atlantic nuclear force (which were still being denied officially), the five defense ministers met again in London to assess the consequences of the French withdrawal. They agreed to establish a permanent forum for consultation on the use of

bloc. Even then, shortage of troops and lack of space for maneuver threw serious doubts on the efficacy of the forward defense principle. (See *Der Spiegel,* 33/1966, pp. 30-39, especially the interview with General Kielmansegg, commander of NATO's central sector). Nonetheless, the French withdrawal from the command structure of the alliance weakened NATO even further, since joint strategic planning between NATO and France lapsed almost completely, as was reflected in remarks by the French chief-of-staff General Ailleret proposing that France build a nuclear defense system against "all points of the compass." (See Ailleret, "Directed Defense," translated in *Survival,* February 1968, pp. 38–43; and the comment by Alfred Grosser, in the same issue of *Survival,* pp. 43–44, 53.)

nuclear weapons (subsequently established in December as the NATO Nuclear Planning Group); and they reportedly discussed the efficacy of a system of graduated responses to different kinds of aggression—which prompted the Pentagon to issue an official denial that a shift to an automatic nuclear response had been considered.

Throughout 1966, the Soviets were emphasizing that any German "association" with nuclear weapons (except consultative arrangements) would stand in the way of the nonproliferation treaty, while the Germans were just as adamant in insisting on participation in a nuclear force. In March, Bonn's Defense Minister, Kai-Uwe von Hassel, called for the "cooperative physical ownership" of a nuclear weapons system, by which he meant that "a joint weapons system for the Atlantic alliance would be set up under joint finance, joint responsibility, joint ownership, joint agreement on its principles—with American participation and with the veto and the final decision remaining in the hands of the American president;"[15] and in June, a few days after McNamara had come out in favor of a permanent NATO committee on nuclear planning, Erhard again called for German participation in a NATO nuclear force. It was becoming increasingly clear, however, that many Western leaders began to view German attempts to gain a nuclear voice with a good deal of impatience, since the nonproliferation treaty seemed to be in jeopardy, and since there was little enthusiasm to begin with about a German finger on the nuclear trigger.

Against this background of German apprehensions, it is not surprising that the idea of a nonproliferation pact had met with a cold reception in Bonn from the very beginning. Considering the far-reaching repercussions of such an arrangement for German foreign policy, the Bonn government was probably justified in complaining that it had been insufficiently consulted; and the unfortunate connection between the MLF episode and American nonproliferation efforts was hardly designed to put to rest German fears of a Soviet-American deal made over the heads of the German government. The Erhard Administration's opposition to a nonproliferation arrangement stemmed primarily from Bonn's determination to keep open four major options for German foreign policy:

> The first was the chance to use a total renunciation of nuclear weapons as a bargaining counter in future negotiations with Moscow on German unity; (indeed, the Foreign Office toyed with the idea of signing a nonproliferation pledge only with the Western allies). The second was the possibility of taking part in an allied nuclear force on the basis of co-ownership. The third was participation in alliance arrangements for nuclear planning and crisis management—on the principle that permanent renunciation of nuclear weapons must be compensated for by permanent participation in a reliable system of nuclear deterrence. The fourth was the creation of a European nuclear force.[16]

All of these options would have been seriously diminished by the proposed arms control pact.

In light of his experiences with Washington, Erhard must have viewed the likelihood of gaining German co-ownership of nuclear weapons as remote. But the connections perceived between the nonproliferation treaty and the possibility of forcing some progress on the reunification question goes a long way toward explaining the Bonn government's reluctance to accede to an arms control arrangement. Reservations about a nonproliferation arrangement stemmed not so much from a desire to own nuclear weapons but from the reluctance to be deprived of the threat of acquiring them.[17] In light of the widespread apprehensions about a German finger on the nuclear trigger, the value of Bonn's insistence on retaining this threat was doubtful. But the Germans were understandably reluctant to relinquish an opportunity to extract concessions on the reunification issue, since they had so little bargaining leverage on this question in the past and since it was clear that all along the Russians' main purpose in negotiating the treaty was to deny West Germany nuclear arms. It is highly significant, however, that German recalcitrance on the nonproliferation treaty was directed at the United States as well as the Soviet Union; many Germans viewed Washington's insistence that West Germany accede to the treaty without gaining any concessions on unification as a further indication that Washington had shelved the German question, perhaps indefinitely.

There were other objections to the treaty. The Germans argued, for example, that the treaty would hamper European scientists and engineers in their work on the peaceful applications of atomic energy, thus favoring the military nuclear powers in commercial competition for building nuclear power plants, that certain inspection features of the treaty would engender industrial espionage, and that the treaty would impede European integration by undermining the importance and past achievements of Euratom. None of these objections, however, were as serious and fundamental as those that stemmed from the political and strategic-military implications the treaty provisions held for Bonn's overall foreign policy program.

The Grand Coalition government that replaced the Erhard Administration in December 1966, when the CDU's Kurt Georg Kiesinger became chancellor and the SPD's Willy Brandt became vice-chancellor and foreign minister, soon voiced deep misgivings about the nonproliferation treaty. Although their uneasiness stemmed in large part from the same calculations that had made the treaty idea unattractive to the Erhard government, there were some significant shifts in emphasis and direction. Most noticeably perhaps, the new government tended to play down the importance of the first two options Erhard had clung to so insistently: the linkage between nuclear self-denial and progress on the German question, and the hope of obtaining nuclear co-ownership within the context of an allied nuclear force. There were at least three reasons for this. First, the new government favored a more assertive Realpolitik, especially vis-à-vis the United States—and since it saw that the Johnson Administration was unwilling to arrange an allied force, Bonn could not pursue an obvious lost cause without sacrificing its realistic and assertive stance. Second, the Kiesinger-Brandt coalition wanted to mend relations between Paris and Bonn, and could not have done so if Bonn persisted in a course of action de Gaulle adamantly opposed. Third, the new government was determined to initiate a more flexible and realistic policy toward Eastern Europe, in the hope that a rapprochement would ease the way to German unity.

An attempt to extract concessions on German reunification in return for nuclear abstinence, of dubious value to begin with, would have imposed an additional handicap on the rapprochement strategy, which faced enough obstacles as it was.[18]

This does not mean that the new administration in Bonn was unaware of, or indifferent to, the implications that a nonproliferation agreement held for German reunification and for the issue of joint ownership of an allied Atlantic nuclear force. But in its public reactions, the government's persisting objections focused primarily on the implications of such an agreement for the creation of a European nuclear force and for German participation in joint nuclear planning. Bonn obtained written assurances from Washington that the nonproliferation treaty, although precluding the formation of a NATO nuclear force, would not prevent the formation of a European nuclear force in the event that a politically united Europe would come into being; and the government was also careful to stress that West Germany's participation in NATO's Nuclear Planning Group should not be regarded as a substitute for a German role in a European nuclear force.[19]

Both aspects gained new significance when Washington's doctrine of flexible response, operative for the United States since the days of the Kennedy Administration, became official and explicit NATO policy in May 1967. This was especially perturbing since the plausibility of a flexible response had become even more tenuous with French withdrawal from NATO's integrated command structure.* By December, NATO planners had formu-

---

* This led to major American efforts to produce smaller, "cleaner," and more accurate tactical nuclear weapons to make them more appropriate for use in Europe in the face of reduced force levels and reduced room of maneuver; and Bonn now demanded a German veto over the firing of American tactical nuclear weapons from German soil. A United Nations panel of nuclear experts, however, reported to Secretary General Thant that the destruction suffered in Europe from a tactical nuclear war would differ only insignificantly from the effects of a strategic nuclear exchange. (*The New York Times,* October 25, 1967, 9:1). For some German views on NATO's flexible response doctrine, see Baudissin, "NATO-Strategie"; and Nau, "Die Sicherheitspolitik." See also, Mendershausen, "West Germany's Defense Problem."

lated three possible conflict "phases" through which a NATO response to an attack would have to pass before a full-fledged American nuclear strike would be unleashed (Document MC 14/III). The first phase envisaged a NATO response limited in conflict area and limited to conventional forces. The second provided three options for escalating, calculated to impress upon the opponent the full measure of NATO's determination: enlarging of conflict area, employment of more conventional troops, and selective tactical nuclear strikes on specific targets such as heavy troop concentrations. The third phase envisaged nuclear war in central Europe. This contingency scenario was coupled with the decision to reduce the American, British, and Belgian ground forces stationed in Germany by approximately 75,000 men, on the assumption that the American airlift capacity would provide adequate compensation. Clearly, Bonn could not be expected to show great enthusiasm for renouncing a voice in nuclear decision-making at a time when Germany's vulnerability was officially underlined by NATO policy.*

German security concerns, and the government's misgivings about the nonproliferation treaty, were further strengthened by the Soviet invasion of Czechoslovakia in August 1968. The West Germans felt directly threatened by the increased strength and proximity of Soviet power across their borders, and they were hardly reassured by Russian attempts to justify the invasion with strongly worded statements claiming that a revanchist Germany had been a major driving force behind the "deviationism" of the

* The Grand Coalition government was seriously divided over the treaty issue, with Foreign Minister Brandt favoring German accession and with Chancellor Kiesinger insisting on a delay until after the September 1969 elections. Finance Minister and CSU chief Franz-Josef Strauss, an outspoken critic of the nonproliferation treaty—he called it a "Versailles of cosmic proportions"—maintained that the treaty would endanger NATO, the EEC, and Germany's "equal partnership" with the United States, and would deprive Bonn of leverage on the German question. In early 1969, several prominent CSU members close to Strauss lobbied in the United States Congress against American ratification of the treaty, causing a good deal of consternation in the White House.

Dubcek regime. Although the Grand Coalition had jettisoned the old demands for direct nuclear co-ownership and co-determination, Foreign Minister Brandt declared after the invasion that Germany would sign the treaty only if it would impose disarmament obligations on the nuclear powers, and would not endanger the security of Germany, delay the integration of Europe, or inhibit the peaceful application of nuclear energy. Most other NATO members also expressed concern. NATO's non-nuclear forces had been cut back for several years, particularly on the forward line in Germany, and the invasion of Czechoslovakia called into question the prevailing Western assumption that post-Stalinist Soviet leadership had become too sophisticated to resort to large-scale force in the furtherance of political aims. In the aftermath of the invasion, which had also demonstrated the Russians' skill in deploying twenty divisions swiftly, efficiently, and relatively secretly, NATO initiated a thorough reappraisal of its military preparedness, which culminated in the Brussels meeting of NATO foreign and defense secretaries in November 1968.[20]

The Brussels conference yielded only insignificant military results, which did not substantially improve NATO's conventional force strength in relation to that of the Soviet bloc. Germany made plans to provide more financing for its understaffed non-commissioned officer corps; Belgium agreed to raise its standing troop level; Britain promised to transfer ships and aircraft from Southeast Asia; and other members made similar gestures toward improving NATO's mobilization capability. The political results of the meeting were not much more impressive. The conference communiqué warned the Soviet Union and its four partners in the Czechoslovakian venture (Poland, East Germany, Hungary, and Bulgaria) that any Soviet intervention directly or indirectly affecting the situation in Europe or in the Mediterranean would create an "international crisis with grave consequences." Although NATO could not extend its protective umbrella to, say, Rumania, Austria, or Yugoslavia, the communiqué stated in effect that NATO would not ignore a threat developing in areas contiguous to member countries. This so-called "Harmel Doctrine" (named after Pierre Harmel, the Belgian foreign minister) clearly did not look toward military intervention, but rather seemed to stress measures of "preventive displomacy" such as diplomatic and military warnings. In any case, the Harmel Doctrine was not nearly as efficacious and credible (in light of the events in Czechoslovakia) as its Soviet counterpart, the so-called Brezhnev Doctrine, also enunciated in the wake of the Soviet invasion, which asserted the right of Soviet intervention throughout the "Socialist Commonwealth" to stave off "counter-revolutionary" machinations.

The much less publicized Bonn meeting of the seven-nation NATO Nuclear Planning Group in October was politically somewhat more significant than the Brussels conference. During this meeting, the Planning Group members assigned to Britain (as the leading European nuclear power) and West Germany (as the West European country with the largest conventional power) the task of drawing up defense guidelines for the alliance. The clear implication that a specifically "European" approach to defense planning was in the making received the official blessing of Washington, and was well-received in London and Bonn. The British viewed their defense planning role as an opportunity to further establish their credentials in Europe and to outflank de Gaulle's veto of their membership in the Common Market. Germany, whose efforts to aid Britain's entry into the Common Market had been repeatedly rebuffed by de Gaulle, was anxious to cement relations with London and to participate in a project that promised to give Bonn a stronger voice in overall defense planning for Europe.*

---

* De Gaulle had himself tried for several years to convert the Germans to a European security system under French leadership, but the implied exclusion of NATO and the United States found little support in Bonn for military as well as political reasons. (For example, in 1964 de Gaulle was reported to have asked the Erhard government for a German industrial-financial contribution to the force de frappe so that the program could be completed by 1970, while insisting on sole French control). The whole question was raised again as part of the "Christopher Soames Affair" of February 1969 which marked a low point in British-French relations. Soames, the British ambassa-

The general question of European security arrangements was affected by the Soviet invasion in yet another way. During the previous few years various proposals for European East-West security pacts and other military detente measures had been put forth in Western and Eastern Europe. They ranged from suggestions for the mutual reduction of force levels to demands for the dissolution of NATO and the Warsaw Pact.[21] These proposals—which were not entirely dissimilar in intent and format from those of the 1950s—seemed to reflect a limited European consensus within both blocs that the relevance of NATO and the Warsaw Pact was diminishing as a consequence of changing political and strategic circumstances, and that a formalized military detente would be mutually advantageous.[22] Several of these proposals not only stressed the desirability of creating immediate arrangements for the *control* and *management* of conflict situations, but pointed out opportunities for the final *resolution* of conflict. In other words, military security arrangements were expected to facilitate a political reconciliation through increased East-West contacts and cooperative economic and diplomatic endeavors, thus holding out the hope that the unresolved political problems of Europe (such as the division of Germany and the unsettled frontier questions) would become more manageable.[23]

Ever since the 1950s, these two distinct aspects and purposes of a European arms control arrangement—the military aspect, conflict control, and the political aspect, conflict resolution—had posed a painful dilemma for Bonn. Although conflict control and crisis management were even more important to Germany than to

---

dor to France, had reported to his government a conversation with de Gaulle during which the general suggested new British-French approaches to European questions such as replacing the Common Market with a wider and looser economic-political organization of Western European nations, with an inner directorate (consisting of Britain, France, Germany, and Italy) which would also form the nucleus of a European defense system to replace NATO. When the British disclosed the substance of the conversation to their allies in the Western European Union, French spokesmen denied that the conversation had been accurately reported.

its allies because of Germany's forward position, the Bonn government invariably felt obliged to reject proposals for a European arms control system because such proposals seemed to portend not a genuine resolution of outstanding conflicts but the legitimization of the status quo in central Europe, including the division of Germany. The East-bloc proposals of the middle 1960s could also be interpreted in this light. Beginning with the 23rd Party Congress, the Soviet Union and her allies renewed their proposals for a European security pact as an alternative to the Warsaw Pact, but their concept of "European security" clearly looked toward the dissolution of NATO and the withdrawal of the United States from Europe, as well as the legitimization of the East German regime.[24] Moreover, as Pierre Hassner has pointed out,

> From the Soviet Union's point of view, there is a striking parallel between the proposal for a nonproliferation treaty and the proposal for a European security system. The first is meant as a bilateral enterprise with the United States against their non-nuclear friends and allies; the second as a continental enterprise with the Europeans against the United States. In both cases, however, the opponent against whom the project is really directed is Germany.[25]

Even so, Bonn's Grand Coalition was willing to reverse the Adenauer and Erhard governments' position that progress on reunification would have to precede an East-West detente, and to at least consider putting arms control measures in the service of detente efforts and, hopefully, over the long run in the service of the cause of German unity. In fact, Bonn put forth its own ideas on a European settlement and suggested that such matters be discussed within NATO's so-called Harmel Committee, which was established in 1967 to assess the future tasks of NATO. From the beginning of the Grand Coalition, the possibility of mutual East-West troop reductions had figured prominently in Bonn's detente program (although it was hard to see why the Soviet Union should have made any significant concessions since NATO was making unilateral reductions voluntarily), and in the summer of 1967, Foreign Minister Brandt wrote:

A relaxation of tensions between East and West is useful and desirable, but our policy aims beyond that. We view it as our political task to eliminate the causes of tension . . . and to create a situation that . . . provides no cause for new and dangerous tensions. The period of relaxation toward which we are striving should be used to lay a solid groundwork for European security and to create a lasting peaceful order in Europe—that is, to solve the German question and aim for agreement on urgent questions which go beyond the confines of Europe.[26]

Brandt also speculated about two possible European security models—one based on cooperation between NATO and the Warsaw Pact (the two-alliance model), the other envisaging their gradual dissolution and replacement with a new arrangement (the end-of-alliance model). There was a clear implication that a connection existed among the two-alliance model, conflict control, and a military security pact; with a similar relationship existing among the end-of-alliance model, conflict resolution, and a European peaceful order. Brandt was careful, however, to reiterate Bonn's continuing reliance on NATO (for security purposes as well as for coordination of Western detente efforts) because, he said, "NATO will have fulfilled its military task only when we have solved our political task."

The invasion of Czechoslovakia invalidated many of the hopeful assumptions underlying such calculations because it demonstrated unequivocally that the Soviet Union was determined to maintain control over central Europe (that is, it was determined to oppose a resolution of conflict on terms acceptable to Bonn), thus diminishing Bonn's major long-range incentive for acceding to European arms control measures. It should be stressed, however, that the Western powers' incentives for conflict control remained unimpaired after Czechoslovakia, because they stemmed from abiding national interests in military stabilization and detente in central Europe. For Bonn's allies, conflict control was and is much more relevant than conflict resolution, since they have no major political demands to make on the Soviet Union and Eastern Europe. This lack of congruence between the interests of West Germany and the interests of her allies is of course one of long standing, but it was reemphasized by the Soviet invasion which had a much more damaging effect on the prospects of conflict resolution than on the prospects of conflict control.

This was clearly reflected in the rather innocuous Western response to the invasion. There were three major reasons for the mildness of the response. In the first place, budget-minded parliaments and voters in NATO countries were unwilling to finance a conventional force contingent that would match the capabilities of the Soviet bloc, and NATO's nuclear deterrent obviously could not be expected to apply in a situation involving the Soviet Union and one of its client countries within the Soviet sphere of influence. Second, after the initial shock and consternation had worn off, the West began to view the Soviet action as a harsh but not entirely erratic measure to maintain the status quo in central Europe, rather than as the first in a series of intemperate adventures to overthrow it.[27] Third, and most important, the United States and the Soviet Union were anxious to resume their bilateral negotiations on arms control, which had been interrupted by the invasion.

Indeed, arms control was one of the most sensitive aspects of German-American relations in the late 1960s. Perhaps the most complex and controversial aspect of the proposed Soviet-American arms control scheme was the issue of a ballistic missile defense (BMD), or, as it is more popularly called, an anti-ballistic missile (ABM) system. In addition to arousing a good deal of domestic opposition, the Nixon Administration's decision to go ahead with the development and deployment of a watered-down version of an ABM system was not received enthusiastically by the European allies. The prospect of both the United States and the Soviet Union deploying ABM systems had caused apprehension in Europe as early as 1967, because the Europeans feared that deployment of even a limited ABM system would induce the United States to develop an isolationist "fortress America" strategy. Secretary McNamara sought to allay such fears during the Ankara meeting of NATO's Nuclear Planning Group in September 1967. Nonetheless, European members considered the possibility of developing an ABM system for Europe, although there seemed to be general agreement that this would not make much technological or economic sense.

Like many Americans, many Europeans feared that deployment of an ABM system could upset the relative stability of the Soviet-American nuclear balance through creating uncertainties about the system's effectiveness, which in turn would lead to the development of new weapons systems in an attempt to maintain or restore deterrence. An American commentator, Franklin Long, noted in December 1968 that "the added uncertainties which will confront the United States and the USSR as a consequence of extensive BMD deployment will have their impact on the European countries also. The principal stresses will probably enter in strategic and political spheres and long-range planning." In the long run, and in the context of a continuing arms race, Long continued:

> The pressures toward a political restructuring of European alliances and toward the development of some kinds of independent nuclear forces will probably be irresistible. It appears almost inevitable that a continued U.S.-USSR arms race, with its clear implication that the two superpowers are giving an overriding priority to their own security, will cause a drastic weakening of the current NATO and Warsaw Pact alliance structure.[28]

Some European commentators, as well as some United States Senators, also perceived a contradiction between the "vertical proliferation" that might result from an ABM-inspired Soviet-American arms race and the prohibition against horizontal proliferation embodied in the nonproliferation treaty. (Article VI of the treaty, included at the insistence of non-nuclear powers, obliges the nuclear powers to pursue in good faith negotiations to curb the nuclear arms race, and clearly was intended to impose some parity of obligations on the nuclear haves and the nuclear have-nots). Yet at the same time as European NATO allies were expressing concern about the possibility of a renewed arms race—especially about the production of multi-warhead nuclear missiles (MIRVs)—the Bonn government feared that the long-projected Soviet-American strategic arms limitation talks might damage

German interests. During the summer of 1969, when both superpowers were preparing to negotiate some kind of agreement on slowing down the strategic weapons race, the joint communiqué issued by President Nixon and Chancellor Kiesinger after their Washington meeting in August said they believed that progress in the arms limitation talks "is interrelated with a climate favorable for dealing with long-existing European problems." But it was obvious that the ambiguous term "interrelated" was a compromise and did not fully satisfy Kiesinger, who wanted to specifically link the resolution of outstanding European problems (such as the division of Germany) with a Soviet-American arms control scheme. It was also clear that Kiesinger intended to further postpone West Germany's accession to the nonproliferation treaty in order to retain some bargaining leverage while awaiting the specific outcomes of the projected arms limitation talks.

The conflicting American and European (especially German) attitudes on arms control measures reflect an important reality of East-West relations in the middle and late 1960s: the likelihood of war in Europe has diminished substantially during the last decade. Europeans no longer fear a major conflagration in Europe, and Washington's priorities have shifted from the Cold War policy of region-by-region, "forward" containment to an attempt to reach an essentially bilateral accommodation with the Soviet Union on matters of overriding mutual interest, such as a stabilization of the global strategic balance of power. As a consequence, as Pierre Hassner observed in 1968, "Today, the search for a European security system has nothing to do with any direct search for security . . . and can be based only on political objectives."[29] Although this is something of an overstatement, especially with respect to Germany, all major participants in the East-West dialogue on arms control have used "security policy" to articulate and advance political objectives. This has led to a situation not only where technical military matters are subject to legitimate political guidance but where the solution of political problems is sought in military arrangements. The trend toward translating political concerns into military-strategic rhetoric poses special problems for Bonn because in this area the Germans must speak softly indeed. Bonn's implied threats to carry a big stick through joint nuclear control, or to obstruct progress on a detente by opposing the nonproliferation treaty, have met with considerable opposition from her allies as well as from her opponents; and the more cautious attitude of the Grand Coalition on this question stemmed from a realistic reappraisal of the limits and opportunities of German policy.

The need for restraint on the sensitive question of nuclear bargaining is only the symptom of much more confining limits imposed on Bonn's security policy. Throughout the twenty-year history of the alliance, NATO's military policy, which was largely formulated in Washington, was adjusted not only to technological changes affecting the East-West balance of power but also to political shifts in East-West and intra-alliance relations. Both political and strategic considerations led to periodic and more or less drastic alterations of military policy—alterations to which the Federal Republic was especially sensitive and responsive because her military command structure was fully integrated in NATO. For example, in the period from 1956 to 1958 when the Bonn government was seeking to implement its NATO commitments by establishing a conventional army, the Radford Plan was announced in Washington and the German government, in the face of strong domestic opposition, had to shift its planning from conventional defense to tactical-nuclear defense; during 1958-1961, when the Federal Republic gradually adjusted to the new NATO strategy, there was a good deal of international as well as domestic opposition to equipping the Bundeswehr with the weapons systems (primarily tactical nuclear carrier weapons) which this strategy required; from 1961 to 1963, when the Bundeswehr had already been partially equipped with these weapons, the Kennedy Administration introduced the conventional force option and applied pressure on the European allies to raise conventional troop levels. This situation improved somewhat in the following years with more extensive consultations among the allies, but the 1967 NATO decision to make "flexible defense" official NATO policy was not entirely out of character.*

These shifts in Washington, coupled with the inevitable time-lag that delayed the strategic rethinking required in Bonn and at SHAPE, led to serious discontinuities—as when Bonn embraced the concept of massive retaliation at a time when it was already under serious attack in the United States. There were other discontinuities as well. As Uwe Nerlich has pointed out,

> Despite the fact that the differences of opinion on strategy questions between Washington and Bonn reached a peak in the years 1961 and 1962, there was a good deal of complementarity during that phase with respect to the development of armed forces. Under the impact of the 1961 Berlin crisis, the Federal Republic extended military service time from 12 to 18 months and agreed to raise troop levels from 350,000 to 500,000 men, while the United States raised its nuclear strength in Europe by 60 per cent. . . . It is a remarkable paradox that the strategic conceptions of Bonn and Washington became extremely opposed in 1961-62 when their defense policies became more complementary while there was a good deal of correspondence between Bonn and Paris on strategic conceptions when their defense policies had more and more ceased to serve common interests.[30]

The necessity for Bonn to adhere to the political as well as the military aspects of the strategic guidelines promulgated by Washington was of course precisely what the Western powers had intended when Germany became a member of NATO. But this

---

* In 1965, Franz-Josef Strauss argued that European doubts about whether the United States could be relied upon "to incinerate themselves in a nuclear holocaust for the sake of Europe's freedom" were enhanced by "the frequent changes in American strategic doctrines. . . . We have had the Radford Doctrine, which was a modified John Foster Dulles Doctrine. We have witnessed the introduction of nuclear weapons into the alliance by giving the Allies the means of delivery for tactical nuclear weapons and retaining control and custody in American hands. Then came the McNamara Doctrine, from counter-city strategy to counter-force strategy, the theory of a pause on the threshold, and now an increased trend back to massive retaliation, not automatic as at the time of the Radford Doctrine, but in the case of extended military operations or to halt an aggressor when he has reached a certain line." (*The Grand Design*, p. 50.)

adherence became highly problematical for Bonn in the early 1960's, because NATO's political and military purposes were much less compatible than they had been during the 1950s when Washington's political and military containment policies were mutually reinforcing and when the alliance was not split by Franco-American disagreements. Moreover, the more NATO's preoccupations shifted from military to political matters, and the more the alliance suffered from centrifugal tensions—with both changes propelled by the East-West nuclear standoff and by the apparent lessening of the Soviet military threat—the more difficult became the position of the Federal Republic, because it was precisely on the political level that German influence within the alliance was most precarious. The international system's shift from Cold War to coexistence reduced Germany's leverage within the alliance, and Bonn could never have hoped (even if it desired) to emulate de Gaulle's independent political and military course. Instead, the German government was forced to make painful choices between Paris and Washington—without being able to exploit this pivotal position, owing to contractual, political, and psychological restraints. Unwilling and unable to loosen her indispensable security ties to the United States, West Germany incurred the opposition of France as well as of the Soviet Union —the countries that held the keys to the two German foreign policy goals that (unlike the goal of security) the United States could not significantly advance by itself. Those goals—Germany's recovery in the context of Europe, and reunification—will concern us in the following chapters.

CHAPTER TWO/ POLITICAL AND ECONOMIC RECOVERY

The new German state that was established by the three Western occupation powers in 1949 under the Occupation Statute was endowed with only a limited and revocable measure of sovereignty. The Allied High Commission, which succeeded the military governors of the occupation regime, for all practical purposes controlled the Federal Republic's political and economic relations with other countries, and was invested with the power to regulate, or at least to supervise, domestic political and economic developments. In particular, the High Commissioners were charged with preventing the recartelization of German industry, and with ensuring that the new state would develop along democratic lines.

For Konrad Adenauer and his supporters, the goal of political recovery meant, in its widest implications, the right to have a foreign policy and the return of a democratic Germany to the society of Western nations. More specifically, Adenauer aimed to include Germany as an equal and respected partner in a Western European community; and he wanted Germany securely tied to the cultural, religious, and political traditions of Western Europe in order to forestall the recurrence of a Nazi, or any other, dictatorial regime. The content and direction of Germany's sociopolitical order were to be shaped by a close and permanent attachment to the cultural values of the Western democracies. These aims necessarily required a fundamental and lasting rapprochement with France and the United States, and the restoration of legal independence, so that Germany could participate as an equal with freely given consent in a European integrative venture. The sovereignty that Adenauer sought for the West German state was thus of a rather special kind: he was willing to relinquish some of its elements, once they were gained, to contractual arrangements that would bind Germany to the West in integrative international structures. As a consequence, the Bonn government could advance its demands for political and legal equality in the name of European integration and the Western alliance, rather than in the name of a discredited German nationalism.

Considering the growing importance of the planned German military contribution to the Western alliance in the early 1950s, it is not surprising that Bonn's leverage increased rapidly. The successful pursuit of political recovery was directly connected with the rearmament of Germany. From the beginning, the link between German rearmament and the restoration of sovereignty was so clearly acknowledged in treaty provisions that it was obvious the Federal Republic "was to pay for its sovereignty by being irrevocably bound to the western military alliance through the European Defense Community on which the validity of the whole arrangement rested."[1] In the fall of 1951, the Western powers agreed that in return for Germany's rearmament, the Occupation Statute would be replaced by a treaty restoring sovereignty, and that West Germany would be admitted to the European Coal and Steel Community (ECSC) on the basis of equality. Since these so-called Bonn Conventions were to take effect at the same time as the treaty for the European Defense Community (EDC), Germany's progress toward political recovery seemed to come to an abrupt halt when the French National Assembly voted down the EDC treaty in August 1954. In fact, however, the Allies anticipated many of the provisions of the Conventions, and already acted in accordance with them as much as possible in their dealings with the Bonn government.

In any case, NATO and the enlarged Brussels Treaty Organization quickly supplied an alternative contractual framework with which to restore German sovereignty. The Paris Agreements of October 1954 included essentially the same provisions as the Bonn Conventions of 1952. In addition to the restrictions placed on German armaments (mentioned in Chapter One), the three Western powers retained their rights regarding German reunification, a final German peace treaty, and Berlin. The political connections that had throughout linked a number of foreign policy issues were most poignantly reflected in the legal interlocking of the components of the Paris Agreements. The following were signed in conjunction on October 23, 1954: the protocol for terminating the occupation regime, the declaration that officially invited Germany to join NATO and the Brussels Pact, the Saar Agreement, and the Status of Forces Convention, (the last of which retained certain rights for the Western Allies). On the day the Paris Agreements took effect, May 5, 1955, the Federal Republic became a sovereign state.

The Western powers were not interested only in West Germany's military potential. A German military contingent could perhaps have been established by conscripting West Germans under the command of Allied occupation authorities. But this would not have permanently integrated West Germany in the Western alliance. Merely "deputizing" a German army under Western command—as France had suggested when the rearmament debate was beginning—would have placed a West German military contribution in a sociopolitical and economic void. The Western powers wanted to integrate the Federal Republic in the Western alliance through more fundamental and penetrating elements of support: commitment to a Western system of values, interdependence of economies, political consultation and perhaps supervision, domestic consensus and political stability, and so forth. This point cannot be stressed too strongly because in the quest for political recovery these larger considerations gave Bonn much greater and more effective bargaining power than did rearmament alone.

As the Federal Republic turned more and more toward the West, the restoration of sovereignty became a less critical concession for the Allies, especially since many functions of sovereignty that were being restored were immediately "frozen" in the international organizations Germany joined. When Bonn made such deals—as it did when Germany joined NATO, the Western European Union, the European Coal and Steel Community, etc.—the primary payoff came in equality rather than in independence. This met with no objection from the Bonn government. For

Adenauer and other "Europeanists" in Bonn, political recovery meant the integration of West Germany in a tightly knit Western European community—hence it was not difficult for them to renounce some freedom of action, so long as the agreements they signed brought greater equality. The creation of international and supranational organizations had a positive and perhaps decisive influence on this process: by providing mechanisms for controlling German sovereignty as soon as it was granted, these organizations made the restoration of sovereignty less risky and less painful for the Western powers, especially France. In turn, Bonn's continued agitation for political and economic concessions prompted the Allies to quickly set up integrative structures that could supervise the Federal Republic. Thus, Adenauer's Europe-oriented policy was an essential precondition for Germany's political and economic recovery. It eased the way for political recovery because its integrative features, tirelessly stressed by Adenauer, demonstrated Germany's willingness to tie herself to the West, rather than pursuing a "seesaw-balancing" policy between East and West. Furthermore, because of French fears that West Germany's political and economic recovery would proceed along national lines, international arrangements seemed imperative. At least they would help control German resurgence, and at best they might enlist for French purposes Germany's political and economic potential, thus buttressing the French position vis-à-vis the Anglo-American powers. At the same time, France consistently sought to curtail West German influence in international arrangements—while the United States was constantly pushing for a solution that would be acceptable to the Bonn government and thus would bring West Germany into the Western military alliance as soon as possible.

Disagreements between the United States and France were not the only pressures on Bonn's goal of political recovery. Conflicts arose from the dual nature of the goal itself. Political recovery had two distinct aspects: the essentially *legal* aspect entailed in the restoration of sovereignty, and the more substantive *political* aspect, which, for Adenauer, meant the inclusion of Germany in a Western European union. These two aspects took on a special meaning after 1955—when the legal goal had essentially been accomplished, although the political element was still a point of contention on both the international and domestic political scenes. But even before 1955, the tensions between the legal and political dimensions of recovery posed serious problems for Bonn. The Western powers had enough interest in German rearmament and in European integrative measures to allow the Federal Republic to pursue its recovery policy—in a European context—forcefully and effectively. In fact, the similarity of the French, Italian, Dutch, Belgian, and West German concepts of European integration immeasurably aided Bonn's pursuit of a viable Europe policy. But because of France's persistent attempts to curtail Germany's influence and relegate the Federal Republic to a secondary place in the alliance, the legal aspects of recovery—that is, legal equality and the restoration of full sovereignty—generally had to be pursued with only the support of the United States. At the same time, Adenauer's long-range political goals—a European union and reconciliation with France—required France's sympathetic cooperation. This situation was at times awkward for Bonn, but it was still manageable as long as the Western alliance was fairly cohesive and Bonn could advance its interests in the name of an integrated Western alliance. But the pre-1955 tensions between the legal and political dimensions of recovery foreshadowed the much more serious dilemma that German leaders had to face in later years, when they saw that taking sides with either the United States or France tended to widen the developing fissures in the Atlantic alliance.

The international developments that had such a profound effect on West Germany's political recovery were equally important for economic recovery.[2] In the late 1940s and early 1950s, there were four major problems for economic reconstruction. First, a large quantity of industrial equipment had been destroyed or dismantled, and production in key industries was curtailed by Allied controls; second, a severe balance-of-payments deficit hampered foreign trade; third, insufficient investment slowed down economic growth; and last, unemployment had risen to 10 per cent of the labor force. The economic philosophy and program of the Bonn government—the "social market economy"—assigned in theory and practice a considerable role to government, but it also relied heavily on individual incentive and the free play of market forces. Both elements would have been undercut severely by inflation. In the currency reform of 1948, the monetary system had sustained a most drastic cure and inflationary trends following on its heels would have had disastrous psychological and economic effects. Furthermore, inflation would have made it difficult for the government to fulfill its commitment to the liberalization of internal and external trade, and exports would have suffered so that the balance-of-payments problem could not have been remedied.

This situation seemed to call for a tight monetary and fiscal policy and whenever possible a balanced budget. In view of the high level of unemployment, such a conservative policy was at times hard to adhere to and hard to defend. But it had very beneficial effects on German exports, which became highly competitive as a result of uninflated price levels and the domestic underconsumption caused by unemployment. Producers were forced to concentrate on export markets; and growing exports allowed a gradual liberalization of import restrictions. Liberalization of external trade complemented what the Bonn government was trying to achieve by relaxing controls on domestic markets.

The Cold War had a profound, though at times somewhat general and indirect, impact on the course of Germany's economic revival. In the first place, the economic reconstruction program advanced by the American and British occupation authorities prior to 1949 guided the West German economy in a direction that, although not irreversible, would have proven costly and disruptive if redirected fundamentally. In addition to initiating the currency reform and channeling counterpart funds into critical sectors of the economy, Allied economic policy made its most important and lasting impact on the economy by stressing the need for free markets and liberalized trade. Initially, these policies were conceived of as complementing the Allied program for decartelization and the decentralization of the German economy; they received an added and decisive impetus from the Marshall Plan, which was intended by Washington to bring about European recovery not only through the massive injection of American aid but also through the long-range liberalization of European trade-and-payments policies.* To the extent that these developments were an outgrowth of the tensions between the Soviet Union and the Western powers, the Cold War had left an imprint on the West German economy even prior to the establishment of the Federal Republic. After 1949, East-West tensions continued to provide an incentive for the Western powers, and especially the United States, to assist West Germany in the quest for economic recovery—if only to lay the economic and social foundations for the political and military integration of Germany in the Western alliance.

Following the outbreak of the Korean War and the decision to rearm Germany, the Western powers gradually lifted their controls over production in key industries; and in 1955 the Agreement on Industrial Controls, an adjunct to the treaty structure that restored West German sovereignty, officially abolished the remaining economic controls. The step-by-step removal of Allied controls in the early 1950s was highly important, because it opened up production bottlenecks that had impeded economic recovery since the late 1940s. At the same time, Allied controls over production also had produced some beneficial effects. Curtailment

---

* This was the primary American purpose in establishing the Organization for European Economic Cooperation (OEEC), which served as the coordinating agency through which Marshall Plan funds were channeled. In 1960, the OEEC was superseded by the Organization for Economic Cooperation and Development (OECD), of which the United States and Canada became members, and through which the United States sought to induce the now affluent European countries to share the burden of aid to underdeveloped countries.

The Bonn government's determination in the early 1950s to liberalize domestic and international trade was in the long run advantageous politically as well as economically, since it underlined Bonn's commitment to political "internationalism"—a commitment that met with a sympathetic and appreciative response in Western capitals, especially in Washington.

of production, coupled with the conservative economic policy followed by Ludwig Erhard, the Minister of Economics, created an actual and potential excess capacity in the German economy that helped check inflationary trends and made German exports highly competitive in international markets. Between 1952 and 1954, exports and the gross national product continued to rise rapidly, and by the end of 1954 the gold and foreign-exchange reserves of the Federal Republic amounted to more than $2.5 billion.

The establishment of the European Coal and Steel Community (ECSC) is especially significant and illustrative in this context.[3] In May 1950, the French Foreign Minister, Robert Schuman, proposed a common market for coal and steel that would include France, West Germany, the Benelux countries, and Italy. This proposal can be attributed to two aspects of the Cold War. In the first place, the rearmament of West Germany seemed inevitable, and France was determined to create at least a rudimentary international body for supervising it before agreeing to it; international arrangements for regulating the production and marketing of coal and steel looked like an effective check on the war potential of Germany. Second, France was acutely conscious that German influence within the Western alliance was increasing, because the Western defense system needed the Federal Republic. The Ruhr industrial complex was still under the control of the International Ruhr Authority, which had been created by the occupation powers, but French policy makers were afraid that the growing influence of Germany might lead to the scrapping of Allied restraints. To preclude exclusive German control over the industry of the Ruhr basin, France proposed the ECSC.

For West Germany, the establishment of the ECSC meant the abolition of the International Ruhr Authority, and represented a significant advance toward the restoration of German sovereignty: the ECSC replaced an Allied instrument of control with an international organization in which the Federal Republic would participate as an equal member. This promised gains both for the legal aspect of political recovery and for Adenauer's larger aspiration—a fundamental reconciliation with France in the context of a Western European community.

The establishment of the ECSC exemplifies the kind of mixed legal-political-economic advances the Bonn government made through its policy of reconciliation and cooperation with the West. Bonn did not gain traditional forms of sovereignty—such as unrestrained freedom of action and political mobility—but rather gained equal legal status in an international structure to which the Federal Republic was bound both contractually and politically. West Germany won economic benefits as well. The Schuman Plan removed the steel-production bottlenecks that had hampered economic reconstruction, and its provisions indicated that coordination of coal and steel management, which had been outlawed by the Allies and from which German industrialists expected great benefits, would be reinstated. The lifting of Allied coal and steel controls was crucial also because it freed basic raw materials at a time when their shortage seriously retarded economic reconstruction.

Throughout the early and middle 1950s, economic recovery was skillfully aided by the government's policy on political recovery—and by extension, by its policy on security and rearmament, on which the whole construct rested. In such mixed political-economic ventures as the ECSC, political and economic gains went hand in hand, and were achieved through a calculated, coordinated strategy that encompassed both dimensions and advanced German demands in the name of European and Atlantic unity.

The complementarity of the political and economic aspects of Bonn's recovery goal was further exemplified by the European Economic Community (EEC), which was established in 1957 through the Treaty of Rome. After two years of negotiations, the six countries already joined in the ECSC—West Germany, France, Italy, and the Benelux countries—agreed to create in three successive four-year stages a common market for industrial and agricultural products by eliminating customs barriers and import quotas among the Six, and by establishing a common external tariff. They also agreed to coordinate social policy, and to create a European Atomic Community (Euratom), with the understanding that there would ultimately be a single administrative body for the ECSC, Euratom, and the EEC. French and Belgian overseas territories gained an associated status, and a joint development fund was established to help finance investments in these territories.

The political aspirations reflected in the Treaty of Rome, which specifically acknowledged that its signatories intended the Common Market to be the next phase in building a united Europe, gave rise to the hope among "Europeanists" that crucial and perhaps painful economic measures would be assessed by the participants in light of the larger promise of political union. After attempts to unite Europe militarily had failed with the EDC, economic integration was to pave the way to political union, and Adenauer's goal of a united Western Europe seemed to have proceeded one step further. Although Adenauer himself assessed the value of the Common Market primarily in political terms, the long-range economic benefits for Germany were substantial. By 1957, the West German "economic miracle" was well under way (indeed, it would be inappropriate to continue talking about the goal of economic "recovery"), and on the whole the West German economy was well equipped to operate within economies-of-scale such as the EEC, especially in trading industrial products. The major trouble spot was agriculture, having been traditionally shielded from foreign competition through direct and indirect subsidies. Nonetheless, German industrialists and economists believed that Germany could well hold her own in international markets, integrated or not. Also, as F. Roy Willis notes,

> German industrialists were extremely worried that the common external tariff, based solely on the mathematical average of national tariffs irrespective of the extent of a nation's trade in a given product, would force Germany to raise its tariffs and discourage trade with countries outside EEC. German manufacturers of machinery and transportation equipment, chemicals, and manufactured goods, which constituted 88 per cent of German exports, were especially sensitive to this threat to their European markets, since they exported more of their production to countries outside EEC than to the Six. Over a quarter of all German exports went to the non-EEC states of Europe, mainly Switzerland, Austria, the United Kingdom, and Scandinavia. For this reason, German

industry pressed for the conclusion of a free trade area agreement with the European countries unwilling to join the Common Market itself, in direct opposition to most French industrial and agricultural groups, which saw a guarantee of prosperity in a protected market restricted to the Six.[4]

These economic misgivings, which were forcefully articulated within the Bonn government by Ludwig Erhard, were coupled with equally sensitive political considerations. The Bonn government had insisted throughout that it favored a broader EEC membership and would especially welcome the inclusion of Britain. However, Britain's own misgivings, both political and economic, made her accession unlikely in the foreseeable future, and de Gaulle, who had returned to power in 1958, was known to be highly critical and suspicious of British (and American) influence in the realm of the Six, since he aspired to the leader's role for France. Although Adenauer continued to stress that Bonn did not oppose extending an open-ended invitation to European countries, new developments soon threw grave doubt on his determination to enlarge the Common Market.

Great Britain, having failed in its attempts to organize a seventeen-nation free trade area—an issue that divided the Six for a long time—had agreed with Norway, Sweden, Denmark, Austria, Switzerland, and Portugal to form the European Free Trade Association (EFTA), which would become effective in May 1960. During the fall and winter of 1958, there were intricate negotiations on whether to allow an expansion of the Common Market to accommodate the proposed free trade area, and if so, under what conditions. Although Adenauer and de Gaulle had quickly established a remarkable rapport, Franco-German tensions were already developing—tensions that foreshadowed the dilemma that confronted Bonn in 1963, when de Gaulle vetoed British accession to the EEC. During 1958, Adenauer, and especially Erhard, made repeated attempts to mediate between London's proposal for a free trade area (which Erhard favored himself) and de Gaulle's insistence that the EEC be kept pure by the exclusion of Britain, a country with dubious "European" credentials that might water down EEC provisions right from the beginning by seeking to maintain her close economic ties with the Commonwealth. Although important industrial and commercial circles in West Germany were becoming uneasy about the impending economic split of non-Communist Europe, and despite the fact that there was a good deal of opposition in Bonn to Adenauer's pro-Gaullist orientation, the chancellor's overriding concern with Franco-German reconciliation and a Western European union finally led him to throw his support behind de Gaulle. Soon thereafter, de Gaulle reciprocated by endorsing Adenauer's determined stand on the developing Berlin crisis of November 1958, during which the Anglo-American powers showed a much more conciliatory attitude and a greater willingness to negotiate than did Bonn and Paris.

Britain's hopes of inducing the EEC to consent to a wider European economic community had clearly faded by 1961. Early in the year, Britain began to show interest in forming a commercial link with the Six, and proposed a "harmonized" common tariff between the Six and Britain, with the proviso that Britain would not be required to apply the common tariff to its six EFTA partners and to the Commonwealth states. Agricultural products were to be excluded from the arrangement entirely. By mid-year, however, London applied for full membership, realizing that de Gaulle would probably veto an association limited to industrial goods and that Britain would have little to fear from the political evolution of the community in light of de Gaulle's rather contemptuous attitude toward supranational institutions. Apparently Britain decided to apply for membership because she hoped it would help her deal more successfully with her serious economic problems, and because the Kennedy Administration strongly urged it. (The United States had all along advised Britain against the establishment of EFTA because it would create additional problems for the already precarious American balance-of-payments situation. However, Washington continued to support the Common Market, which created the same problems, because of its important political functions, such as fostering a Franco-German reconciliation.)

The American and British expectations that the EEC could be turned from a "little Europe" into a less exclusive organization reinforced de Gaulle's already substantial and deep-seated misgivings. The Labour Party's swing against the Common Market, the bracing pro-de Gaulle plebiscite in France, and the increasingly tense negotiations at the Common Market headquarters in Brussels may have contributed to the stiffening of the French position on British accession. Most important, perhaps, were the scrapping of the Skybolt missile program and the signing of the Nassau Agreement by President Kennedy and Prime Minister Macmillan (discussed in Chapter One).

The timing of this important event was almost unbelievably maladroit. De Gaulle suspected that a decision with such fundamental ramifications must have been considered by both sides for a considerable time—which suggested that Macmillan had been less than candid in his recent conferences with de Gaulle. The Nassau Agreement also meant that the British nuclear deterrent was now specifically dependent upon the United States—at a time when Britain was expected to cast her lot wholeheartedly with the European cause. The dowry of nuclear capabilities and secrets that Britain might have presented to her future Common Market partners now was indefinitely committed to Washington and NATO, and British political inclinations still seemed primarily "Atlantic-oriented" rather than "pro-Continent."

Whatever de Gaulle's primary reason for excluding Britain from the EEC may have been, it is clear that the conflicts which developed between the Anglo-American powers and France during the late 1950s and early 1960s immensely complicated Adenauer's task of integrating Germany in a Western European community. Though Germany could hardly afford to weaken her military and political ties with the United States, de Gaulle, the indispensable partner for Adenauer's Europe policy, was determined to shut out Anglo-American influence in Europe (and especially in the realm of the Six), and he consistently sought to enlist Bonn's support in this effort. Moreover, it was becoming obvious that de Gaulle's concept of Europe was significantly at odds with that of Adenauer. Although both de Gaulle and Adenauer preferred a "little Europe" solution, de Gaulle opposed genuinely integrative measures that would curtail the national independence of member states, and he apparently expected his European partners to help buttress France's position in world politics by providing economic and political support.

Matters were further complicated by the fact that West Germany's goal of political recovery had taken on a new character after Bonn had successfully gained legal equality. Even before the restoration of sovereignty in 1955, there had existed considerable tensions between the legal and political aspects of recovery, because the legal aspect—equality—generally had to be pursued with the support of the United States and Great Britain and in the face of French opposition, while the political aspect—German membership in a Western European community—clearly required France's sympathetic understanding. By and large, however, these tensions posed no insuperable obstacles to Bonn: the Atlantic alliance was still cohesive, and Bonn had the leverage provided by the issue of German rearmament. The situation was quite different in the late 1950s and early 1960s. Once the legal aspect of the recovery goal had been largely resolved with the restoration of sovereignty, the remaining political aspect was subjected to severe cross-pressures because the disagreements between the United States and France were splitting the Western alliance. Moreover, Bonn's Atlantic-oriented security policy no longer complemented its recovery policy, since the latter necessarily became focused on France—in part because France held the key to the Western European community, and in part because the United States had run out of sovereignty payoffs for Bonn. In addition, Adenauer was obliged to turn to Paris for support of Bonn's Eastern policy, since the United States and Britain appeared eager to reach an accommodation with the Soviet Union, perhaps on the basis of the status quo in Germany.

By early 1963, the choices confronting Adenauer allowed little equivocation in the developing tug-of-war between France and the Anglo-American powers. In the fall of 1962, de Gaulle and Adenauer had drafted a Franco-German friendship treaty which provided for regular meetings between French and German officials (twice yearly between heads of state and government, every three months between the ministers of foreign affairs, defense, and education, and every two months between the chiefs of staff and the ministers responsible for youth affairs), and which established an interministerial commission in each country to coordinate the action of the ministries involved and report to the governments on the state of Franco-German cooperation. The treaty also required that the two governments consult each other on all important questions of foreign policy prior to any decision, and envisaged cooperative efforts in defense matters, agricultural policy, industrial development, and cultural exchange programs.

Although it contained no explicit provisions of great importance, this treaty must have looked to Adenauer like the capstone of his policy of reconciliation with France. A few days before Adenauer was to arrive in Paris for the official signing of the treaty, de Gaulle held his famous press conference of January 14, 1963, and announced the French decision to exclude Britain from the EEC. Most likely, not even Adenauer's intervention on behalf of Britain could have induced de Gaulle to reconsider. In any case, a determined stand by the Bonn government on the question of British accession would have meant that the friendship treaty, the most dramatic symbol of Franco-German reconciliation, might fall by the wayside or become meaningless.

For de Gaulle, proper timing was crucial. Adenauer was a lame-duck chancellor and his successor could not be expected to show equal understanding toward de Gaulle's ambitions in Western Europe. In fact, because of his unswervingly pro-French policy, Adenauer had become increasingly isolated both at home and abroad. His relations with the Kennedy Administration were much less cordial than his relations with the Eisenhower Administration had been, largely because of disagreements over United States policy toward the Soviet Union. Furthermore, his relations with London had been strained for some time because of his support of French interests and because of his suspicions that the British were willing to negotiate a Cold War detente with the Soviet Union on the basis of partial disengagement in central Europe. At home, Adenauer's foreign policy and his increasingly authoritarian manipulations had split his own party and Cabinet and were drawing sharp criticism from many quarters. By that time there were in effect two German foreign policies, not one. The first was Adenauer's, which resulted in the Franco-German friendship treaty and which allowed de Gaulle to blackball Britain's membership in the EEC with Germany's implicit acquiescence. The second was that preferred by Economics Minister Erhard and Foreign Minister Schröder, who advocated a more flexible course, and who tended to support the Anglo-American position not only on matters pertaining to the Common Market and the Atlantic alliance but also on a more imaginative Eastern policy.

When Ludwig Erhard succeeded Konrad Adenauer in the fall of 1963, the policy differences between France and Germany were leading to a major confrontation, if not a crisis. Since the Algerian cease-fire in the spring of 1962, de Gaulle had considerably solidified his domestic and international position, and he was beginning to implement his overall policy program more forcefully. Yet practically every item on this agenda opposed German foreign policy, at a time when the new chancellor in Bonn was much less sympathetic to French projects than Adenauer had been. This was not merely a question of personalities. Toward the end of the Adenauer Administration, Bonn and Paris already had serious disagreements, which stemmed primarily from Adenauer's Atlantic-oriented military-strategic policy. These disagreements were generally balanced, however, by Adenauer's support of de Gaulle on other issues, such as his Europe policy, with which Adenauer could at least partially identify on intrinsic grounds. Since Erhard and the other "Atlanticists" in Bonn did not share de Gaulle's (or for that matter, Adenauer's) concept of a European order, the balance between agreements and disagreements all but disappeared from Franco-German relations during the Erhard Administration. F. Roy Willis says,

Faced with French indifference to their interests, the German leaders, to Adenauer's distress, responded by paralyzing the implementation of the Franco-German treaty, opposing de Gaulle's aims within the European Community, and turning ever more closely to the United States. During the last eight months of Adenauer's Chancellorship and the three years of Erhard's, relations between the two governments were at best correct and at worst vituperative. De Gaulle found that the systematic flouting of his partner's wishes was an insecure foundation for an alliance.[5]

A major difficulty with Franco-German relations during the 1960s was that each side, but especially France, had such a tightly structured and fully enunciated foreign policy program, with all components logically and politically interlocked, that compromise on a single component became difficult because it threatened, either in reality or in perception, the construct as a whole. For example, Franco-German disagreements over NATO and over the size and nature of the EEC, which developed into major issues during the Erhard Administration, were closely related to both sides' overall foreign policy conceptions. De Gaulle had all along opposed an enlargement of the Market's membership, and especially the inclusion of Britain, because it would undermine the cultural, political, and geographic cohesion of the Six, and because it would presumably allow the United States to perpetuate and extend its influence in Europe by proxy through London. (It is likely that de Gaulle also intended to create an EEC-based defense system and force a change in the structure of NATO.) This policy was in direct conflict with the preferences of the "Atlanticists" in the Bonn government, who wanted a larger membership for precisely the reasons that de Gaulle objected to it. For years, Erhard and Schröder had favored a larger framework for European cooperation than that provided by the Six—for economic and military as well as political and cultural reasons—and they had consistently argued that this larger European enterprise could, and should, be part of an Atlantic partnership with the United States. Thus, while de Gaulle was opposing practically every facet of American foreign policy—NATO, the MLF, the Nassau agreement, the test ban treaty, Vietnam—Erhard was aligning Bonn with Washington's positions. Paris and Bonn pursued policies which were based on fundamentally different conceptions of a desirable European order; and the more de Gaulle widened the gap between American and French foreign policy, the more he forced Erhard to declare himself in favor of Washington.

The dilemma that these circumstances posed for Bonn's policy became glaringly apparent during the "NATO crisis" of 1966. Bonn and Paris had for some years disagreed about the desirable future of the Western alliance, and Franco-German disagreements over NATO and the Atlantic alliance reached a critical point when de Gaulle announced early in 1966 that France would withdraw from NATO's command structure. De Gaulle declared that French troops (including those stationed in Germany) would no longer remain under NATO control, and that NATO bases and the NATO command would have to be removed from French territory. This step posed a threat to German security, and raised the touchy political and legal question of how French troops could remain in Germany (as the Bonn government hoped they would, for reasons of deterrence) once they were withdrawn from NATO control and returned to a national French control. This question was finally resolved in the early days of the Grand Coalition, when the Germans consented to the continuing presence of French troops in Germany on French terms. But the entire episode highlighted the serious conflict between French and German foreign policy conceptions: Bonn, convinced of the continuing need for a unified Atlantic alliance defense posture in Europe, consistently sought to strengthen NATO and the American presence in Europe, which meant aligning Bonn with Washington against Paris on a matter which de Gaulle regarded as crucially important.

The second major source of tensions between Bonn and Paris was the future of the Common Market and, in a larger context, the political future of Europe.[6] France and Germany disagreed about the optimal size of the EEC, because their fundamentally different world views and foreign policy conceptions gave them different ideas of what the EEC ought to be. From the beginning of the European integration movement, it was intended that the economic integrative structures of the Coal and Steel Community, the Common Market, and Euratom would pave the way for political integration, and that the executive authorities of these organizations would be transformed into genuinely supranational governing bodies, responsive to policies made in a strengthened European Parliament rather than to those promulgated by the national representatives in the Council of Ministers. Although de Gaulle was of course opposed to any development that would undermine national sovereignty, there were no serious disagreements among the Six about the future of the Market's institutions so long as each member had a veto in the Council. Beginning with the third stage of the Treaty of Rome in 1966, however, majority voting in the Council of Ministers was to be adopted, and there was great hope among proponents of political integration that this would begin the transformation of the Common Market into a supranational political union. The most that de Gaulle was willing to concede, however, was institutionalized, regular consultations among the governments of the Six, similar to the bilateral consultations arranged for in the Franco-German cooperation treaty.

This attitude contrasted sharply with that of Erhard, who called for the establishment of an EEC political authority, with limited but specific powers, and who proposed that specific legislative powers should be delegated to the European parliament and that the Common Market should have its own financial resources. Erhard's attitude was something of a surprise, since he had been notably unenthusiastic during the 1950s about a political and economic integrative structure limited to the Six. He changed his mind partly because he wished to avoid narrowing Germany's Europe policy to a bilateral arrangement between Bonn and Paris. As the chances for British membership in the EEC diminished, and as it became clear that de Gaulle viewed West Germany primarily as an object of his foreign policy rather than as his partner, Erhard must have felt that German interests would be best served by strengthening the political and economic cohesion as well as the future integrative potential of the Six, rather than by holding out for the uncertain prospect of an enlarged community. (This attitude was not fully shared by Italy and the Benelux countries, all of which strongly favored British membership before proceeding toward supranational political arrangements.)

De Gaulle's attempts to use the Franco-German cooperation treaty to further his own aims were bound to be unproductive as long as Bonn perceived serious incompatibilities between French and German foreign policy programs. In this connection, Bonn was hardly reassured by de Gaulle's disruptive NATO policy and by his increasingly conciliatory relations with the Soviet Union. Two crucial policy areas were at stake for Bonn, and in both French policy seemed designed to frustrate German aims. (For example, in 1964 de Gaulle warmly celebrated the twentieth anniversary of the Franco-Soviet alliance pact, extended seven-year credits to the Soviet Union through a new trade agreement, and generally exhibited great cordiality toward the Soviet Union and Eastern European countries. In his February 4, 1965 press conference, de Gaulle stressed that reunification was a European problem which would have to be settled largely by Germany's neighbors, implying that Germany as well as the United States would play a secondary role in a settlement.)

Not surprisingly, when Franco-German disagreements about political fundamentals were further aggravated by disagreements about economic specifics, a major crisis hit the Common Market. After protracted negotiations, the EEC partners had reached preliminary agreement on a common policy for beef and dairy products in 1963. During 1964, the EEC's major concern was to reach a conclusive agreement on agriculture, and especially on a common cereal price, in order to match in the agricultural sector the internal tariff reductions already achieved in the industrial goods sector. This required Franco-German agreement on a compromise formula which would balance German concessions on agriculture, which were strongly opposed by agricultural interest groups in the Federal Republic, against French concessions on a common external tariff for EEC, which were of great importance to German industrial interests. This issue was finally settled by a compromise: Germany accepted a uniform EEC cereal price (which involved paying heavy subsidies to German farmers), and France agreed to a considerably shortened "exception list" of products that would not be affected by the common, across-the-board EEC tariff cuts to be negotiated in the Kennedy Round.*

It was the very resolution of this issue, however, that led indirectly to the Common Market crisis of the summer of 1965. Throughout the deliberations on agricultural questions, Bonn had argued for lower external tariffs on agricultural products because this was expected to help German industrial exports to the United States and the EFTA countries. This lowering of protective barriers required extensive subsidies for EEC agricultural products. The Six had made provisional arrangements in 1962 for the operation and funding of an agricultural fund (Fonds Européen d'Orientation et de Garantie Agricoles, or FEOGA) to subsidize exports; this would help EEC agricultural goods compete on the lower-priced world market and would compensate EEC farm interests for their loss of intra-EEC markets. The fund would pay one-sixth of the total subsidies during the first year, one-third during the second year, and one-half during the third

* The "Kennedy Round" of tariff negotiations had its origin in the Trade Expansion Act of 1962, which authorized the President to negotiate, within the context of the General Agreement on Tariffs and Trade (GATT), reciprocal tariff cuts on a wide range of commodity categories rather than on a commodity-to-commodity basis as under the preceding Reciprocal Trade Agreements program. The Trade Expansion Act was a direct response to the establishment of the Common Market, since the anticipated common external tariff of the Six made it seem desirable to achieve across-the-board reductions of tariffs in the United States as well as in Europe. West Germany was especially anxious to see the Kennedy Round brought to a successful conclusion because of the benefits that would accrue to German industrial interests, and the Bonn government was willing to make considerable sacrifices to France on agricultural issues within the Common Market in order to gain French approval for significant tariff cuts during the GATT negotiations. After complex and at times acrimonious bargaining, the 53 members of GATT agreed in 1967 to reduce tariffs over a five-year period by an average of 37-38 per cent (the goal had been 50 per cent), primarily on industrial items. See Hinshaw, *European Community;* and Feld, "Common Market."

year. The income of the fund during this three-year period was to derive from national budgets (100 per cent in the first year, 90 per cent in the second, 80 per cent in the third) and from levies on agricultural imports from non-EEC countries (10 per cent in the second year, 20 per cent in the third). France, Germany, and Italy agreed to contribute equal shares—an arrangement highly advantageous to France, since French farm interests expected a lion's share of the subsidies. With the common cereal price issue out of the way, in the spring of 1965 the Common Market Commission drew up a set of proposals for the fund's operation that would have, in effect, endowed EEC with supranational authority by giving the Commission a large income independent of the members' national control. This was to be accomplished in three interlocking steps. First, anticipating the final stage of a single agricultural and industrial market, FEOGA would, by 1966-67, pay five-sixths of the cost of subsidies. Second, to finance these expenditures, which would greatly exceed the income from import levies, all income from tariffs on industrial goods would be paid directly to EEC. Third, since this would leave a surplus after FEOGA's agricultural expenditures, the European Parliament should be allowed to dispose of the surplus, thus transforming it from an ineffectual debating forum into a legislature with genuine fiscal powers.

As expected, de Gaulle's reaction was wholly negative. The French government not only was opposed to the substantive provisions of the proposal, but was deeply annoyed because it had been publicized in the European Parliament without prior submission to the national governments. As F. Roy Willis writes:

Long struggles in the Commission itself preceded the decision to issue this outright challenge to de Gaulle, but [Commission president Walter] Hallstein undoubtedly felt that France's urgent desire for an agricultural Common Market, which would so greatly benefit the French farmer (and so strengthen de Gaulle's hand in the forthcoming presidential elections) constituted the main hope for realizing the supranational union that had been the ultimate goal of the Treaty of Rome. Hallstein, however, had underestimated the opponent. In the struggle with de Gaulle, he was to lose not only the battle for supranationalism but his job, too.*

Moreover, the Germans, who were expected to pay over a third of the anticipated revenue, and the Belgians were not enthusiastic about transferring industrial tariff revenues to the EEC, and hence were not totally opposed to the French, who wanted only agricultural levies turned over to the Common Market. (This is not to say that Bonn wanted to treat the issue of agricultural financing in isolation. On the contrary, the Germans hoped to link agricultural policy with commercial and monetary policy and tax harmonization.)

As it turned out, the issue of agricultural financing alone led to a major confrontation between the Common Market partners, which resulted in a decisive setback for the supranational potential of EEC. In June 1965, Germany and France agreed to an advanced effective date for a common agricultural policy, with the understanding that industrial tariffs would also be conclusively abolished at that time. Even so, the French felt with some justification that Italy and Germany were seeking to postpone a final agreement on a common agricultural market as long as possible, and that both were still opposed to the principle established in January 1962 which penalized EEC members for pur-

---

* Willis, *France, Germany, and the New Europe,* p. 343. Professor Walter Hallstein, a devoted advocate of European integration and President of the EEC Commission since its establishment in 1958, had frequently incurred de Gaulle's displeasure for attempting to enlarge the functions of the Common Market (and the Brussels Commission) beyond economic integrative measures toward a coordinated program for common social, commercial, and fiscal policy, and, ultimately, toward a supranational political union. When the French finally agreed on a fixed time for the fusion of the executive bodies of the Common Market, the Coal and Steel Community, and Euratom in 1967 (the merger treaty had been signed as early as April 1965 and was ratified by the six parliaments by October 1966) one of their conditions was that Hallstein would not become the head of the integrated Commission. Hallstein's successor, Belgium's Jean Rey, was not much more to de Gaulle's liking, however, since Rey was also fully committed to the cause of European economic and political integration.

chasing food from non-EEC countries. (In 1962, Italy had agreed to contribute as much as France and Germany toward the FEOGA budget, and to subsidize her agricultural exports by taxing non-EEC food imports. Because of Italy's rapid industrialization, however, her overall economic policy was moving closer to the German than the French position on agricultural matters. Moreover, the Italians, fearful that they had taken on excessive obligations by agreeing to contribute as much as France and Germany, opposed a definitive agreement on FEOGA financing and wanted any agreement limited to two years—even though the French were willing to assume part of Italy's FEOGA expenditures.) Although France, Germany, and Belgium finally reached agreement on a simultaneous effective date for the abolition of industrial tariffs and the establishment of a common agricultural market, the Italians, supported by the Dutch, insisted that any agreement be limited to a two-year period. After lengthy and fruitless discussions, the French staged a walkout in early July 1965: they recalled their representatives to the Communities and the Council of Ministers, and French experts in Brussels were instructed to participate only in routine technical matters.

The consequences of the French boycott were far-reaching. After the EEC Commission presented a compromise formula on the agricultural issue during the late summer, it soon became apparent that de Gaulle's main objection was not agricultural policy but supranationalism. Although the issue of agricultural financing was resolved in May 1966, almost a year after the walkout, in the interim de Gaulle had reexamined the supranational potential of the Treaty of Rome. As a result, he set up three conditions for continued French participation in EEC: that the EEC members would agree on agricultural financing, that they would renounce the Commission's supranational political-economic ambitions; and that the majority-voting provisions in the Treaty of Rome would be deleted. In January 1966, the foreign ministers of the Six met in Luxembourg and reached a compromise on de Gaulle's conditions: they agreed to retain the principle of majority voting, but the French also made it clear that they would reserve a veto power when important French interests were threatened; the Commission's formal powers of initiative remained essentially intact, but its independence was significantly curtailed through the stipulation that the Commission consult with the member governments prior to making important policy proposals.

Bonn's reaction to these economic and political developments was mixed. There was relief that the Common Market was once again operative (although German farmers felt that their interests had been slighted), and that the EEC had agreed to stand united during the Kennedy Round. But the Common Market crisis also demonstrated that the members were deeply divided on the political future of the Community; and the Luxembourg meetings had led to a direct and abrasive confrontation between France and Germany. Miriam Camps notes that:

> Two features of [the first Luxembourg] meeting of the Five and the French were significant. First, the fact that the solid front of the Five had held, thanks in part to French obduracy on majority voting; and second, the fact that Dr. Schröder, the German Foreign Minister, had taken a very firm position in opposition to the French and had been turned to by the rest of the Five as their natural leader. Heretofore the Germans had been reluctant to assume the role as leader of the Five in opposition to the French, and the others had been ambivalent about having the Germans assert their leadership. Now they welcomed Dr. Schröder's firmness.[7]

Paradoxically, though de Gaulle's tenacious insistence on a final settlement of agricultural issues had advanced the economic cause of EEC by ensuring that there would be a common market for industry and agriculture by July 1968, his inflexible opposition to supranational principles had dealt the political and psychological cause of the European Community a decisive setback. De Gaulle's timing was no coincidence. By 1965 the focus of the Common Market was shifting from the removal of trade barriers within a customs union to the more ambitious project of adopting common commercial and monetary policies in an economic union—functions traditionally reserved for national governments. If this tentative "spill-over" effect had been allowed to go unchecked, the freedom of national governments to manipulate their economic, monetary, and social programs would have been curtailed, with far-reaching repercussions in the two decision-making areas where de Gaulle wanted maximum flexibility—foreign policy and defense. This was the real issue underlying the Common Market crisis.

> By 1965 it was completely clear that the Five, and particularly the Germans, would not accept French views on defense. . . . The real lesson of the cereals prices 'victory' at the end of 1964 was not that the Germans yielded to the French on this point or had put loyalty to the Community above the interests of the German farmer, but that they had stuck to the MLF and were conceding on what they considered to be a far less important issue. The steam may have gone out of the MLF by the spring of 1965, but presumably one of the reasons why the United States felt that it could let the steam out was that it had, by then, few doubts as to where German loyalties lay if they were ever forced to choose between the United States and France. Nor had General de Gaulle.[8]

Although Bonn may have been forced into making a choice between the United States and France, its reluctance to do so was again demonstrated in November 1966, when the CDU party caucus nominated Kurt Georg Kiesinger to succeed Ludwig Erhard as chancellor. Kiesinger was acceptable to the party's Atlanticists (though they would have preferred Foreign Minister Schröder) as well as to its Gaullists (who were divided between Franz-Josef Strauss, Eugen Gerstenmeier, and Rainer Barzel), so he was a natural compromise candidate: he was a known francophile, he had consistently supported European integration, and his tenure as minister-president of Baden-Württemberg since 1958 had allowed him to refrain from taking controversial positions on foreign policy questions. Bonn's attempt to maintain a balance between Atlanticists and Gaullists was also reflected in the makeup of the Grand Coalition cabinet which Kiesinger put together with the Socialists: Strauss became Minister of Finance, and Schröder was shifted from Foreign Affairs (where he had consistently opposed de Gaulle) to Defense to make room for the

SPD's Willy Brandt, who was known to favor a more positive and imaginative policy toward France.

With Kiesinger as chancellor and with Brandt in the Foreign Ministry, it was not surprising that the style of Franco-German relations initially took a turn for the better. Both men were determined to restore a more harmonious political climate—Kiesinger spoke of "an absolute reanimation" of the 1963 Franco-German treaty—and during the first half of 1967 there was a marked improvement in Franco-German relations, sustained primarily by Bonn's evident desire for accommodation and cooperation. Kiesinger postponed his first visit to Washington until he had had a second conference with de Gaulle, he refused to intervene on Britain's behalf when London renewed its application for EEC membership,* and perhaps most significantly, he relented in the face of insistent French pressure and agreed to the removal of Walter Hallstein as head of the EEC Commission.

In spite of these German concessions, however, the substantive disagreements between France and Germany proved to be as pronounced and intractable as they had been during the Erhard Administration. Although the two countries managed to arrive at an agreement on the continued stationing of French troops in Germany—a legal-political issue stemming from the French decision in 1966 to withdraw from NATO—other issues large and small remained unresolved. Bonn continued to support the Atlantic alliance (even though the Grand Coalition was more assertive vis-à-vis Washington than Erhard had been), to favor the

---

* "The German economic interest clearly lay in British Common Market membership. Yet [Prime Minister] Wilson found the Germans reluctant to press Britain's case at the risk of jeopardizing the 'special relationship' with France which the Kiesinger Government had striven to restore. . . . For another reason, however, the Germans had reservations about British EEC entry. With her accession to the Rome Treaty, Britain might replace Germany as the principal French ally in Western Europe. Collaboration in the development of advanced technology, the possibility of creating an Anglo-French nuclear force, and the prospect of agreement on major political issues might lead to a new Franco-British entente, isolating Germany." (Pfaltzgraff, "Britain and European Community," p. 107.)

admission of Britain and the Scandinavian countries to the Common Market, and to resist French efforts to make Bonn renounce access to nuclear weapons control.

Most important perhaps, Bonn continued to be deeply disturbed by the fundamental shift of French policy toward the Soviet Union. This shift toward a Franco-Soviet accommodation, which actually took place during the Erhard Administration, had a profound impact on Franco-German relations and became especially pertinent for Bonn's Grand Coalition, since Kiesinger and Brandt were themselves committed to a more dynamic and flexible Eastern policy. De Gaulle's new course not only called into question a long-standing and fundamental premise of Bonn's reunification policy, but also served notice to Bonn that de Gaulle intended to fully exploit the new circumstances of the international system, at Germany's expense if necessary.

After de Gaulle's return to power in 1958, Adenauer and de Gaulle had developed a special understanding that Bonn would, as much as possible, support France's Atlantic and European policy if France would support Bonn's Eastern policies. France sometimes ignored this understanding (as when de Gaulle recognized the Oder-Neisse line in 1959), but it seemed solidly based on the mutual assumption that France and Germany were equal partners in a common European enterprise, an assumption that was also reflected in the provisions of the Franco-German friendship treaty of 1963.*

* Alfred Grosser says, "without being able to prove it in any way, I believe that as early as September 14, 1958, there was a sort of gentlemen's agreement between the General and the Chancellor—non-explicit, unsigned, undrafted, based on reciprocity: the Federal Republic would aid France in her Atlantic and European ambitions, and France would give firm support to the Eastern policies of the Federal Republic. On reunification and Berlin, France was never to take any initiatives that did not first emanate from Bonn. Since no initiatives ever emanated from Bonn in this domain, likewise none emanated from Paris. This theory was confirmed on December 31, 1963 at 8:30 p.m. in a single phrase spoken by General de Gaulle during his New Year's address. Indeed, in naming Pankow among the capitals of totalitarian states —totalitarian, but states—he was serving notice to Chancellor Erhard: 'If you don't respect your promise of support in Atlantic policy, I can change my

Undoubtedly, Ludwig Erhard was remiss in failing to nurture this special relationship with more devotion and circumspection. But the larger reasons why de Gaulle allowed the understanding to lapse were essentially beyond Bonn's control because they stemmed from fundamental shifts of power and alignment in the international system. After World War II, the developing polarization of power and tensions between the Soviet Union and the United States became a major obstacle to French interests because France was forced to join the Western alliance to avoid diplomatic isolation, and thus could not play the flexible and mediatory role she would have preferred. Moreover, the influence pattern that emerged within the Western alliance—constantly fed by Cold War calculations—tended to favor a renascent Germany whose location and power potential made it an indispensable partner for Washington's containment policy. The Cold War thus seriously inhibited French maneuverability vis-à-vis the two superpowers, and put France, compared with Germany, at a distinct disadvantage within the Western alliance.

All this began to change in the late 1950s and early 1960s when the two Cold War blocs loosened up and American and Soviet leaders began to explore the possibilities of peaceful coexistence. Germany, which had played a crucial role during the Cold War phase of the postwar international system, not only lost some influence in Western councils during the coexistence phase, but was at times viewed (especially during the Kennedy Administration) as an irritating obstacle to a more flexible American global policy. France, on the other hand, gained considerable leverage from the fragmentation of bipolarity because the new international system provided Paris with a wide range of opportunities to restore flexibility and dynamism to French foreign policy. Alfred Grosser said in 1963:

If every French Government since 1947 has lived in hope of a Summit Conference it is because a relaxation of tension has seemed to be in

---

terms concerning the German problem.' In my view, these simple words provided a sort of confirmation of the Adeneuer-de Gaulle 'deal' dating back to 1958." (*French Foreign Policy*, pp. 60–61.)

France's interest. Why? Because whenever there has been tension between East and West, the attractions of the Federal German Republic have increased in the eyes of the United States while dissension has grown in France, where, as the Pentagon knew, a quarter of the electors voted Communist. On the other hand, when tensions relaxed, Federal Germany relapsed into the role of a pawn on the international chessboard while France again became one of the Big Four discussing the German problem.*

It was de Gaulle's genius to exploit and accelerate the trend toward polycentrism and the general relaxation of East-West tensions with a foreign policy style that was eminently suited to the circumstances and that demonstrated how a secondary power could stake out an area of maneuver between the superpowers. For a variety of political, strategic, and psychological reasons, the Germans could hardly emulate the example set by de Gaulle. As a consequence, an important change took place in Franco-German power relationships—a change that was largely favorable to France and greatly increased her determination as well as her maneuverability.

An essential element of de Gaulle's reorientation of French policy was a loosening of ties with the Western alliance (especially the United States) and a corresponding establishment of closer contacts with the Soviet Union and Eastern Europe. Both dimensions—which were highlighted by de Gaulle's decision to withdraw from NATO and by his state visits to the Soviet Union in 1966 and to Poland in 1967—raised some awkward problems for Bonn. To be sure, de Gaulle's argument that the division

* Grosser, "Foreign Policy of the Fifth Republic," p. 206. Perhaps this explains why, "in contrast to France, two-thirds of the West German leaders continue to see the world as a bipolar power system, dominated by the United States and the Soviet Union, and they believe it will remain so. Among the French leaders, on the contrary, nearly three-quarters see an increasingly multipolar world around them." (Deutsch, Edinger, Macridis, and Merritt, *France, Germany, and the Western Alliance,* p. 265.) Of course the West Germans, confronting hard-line East Germany, also had less reason to perceive a softening of the Soviet bloc.

of Germany could be overcome only through the reconciliation of Eastern and Western Europe was also being voiced in Bonn and was reflected in the more flexible Eastern policy of the Erhard and Kiesinger Administrations (to be discussed in Chapter Three). But the French and German approaches were not coordinated, nor were their underlying purposes altogether complementary. The principles of "detente, entente, cooperation," which de Gaulle held out to the Soviet Union and the East bloc (except East Germany) clearly implied the exclusion of the United States from a European settlement—a situation which was unacceptable to Bonn; and the lack of policy coordination added a competitive edge to French and German efforts to revitalize relations with the Soviet Union and Eastern Europe.

In this competition Germany was at a distinct disadvantage. Bonn's flexibility was curtailed by close alignment with the United States; the Germans were seriously handicapped in seeking a rapprochement by the burdens of the past as well as by the ineptness of their previous policies; and the hostile relations between Bonn and Moscow deprived Bonn from effective access to the center of Soviet power in the Kremlin. With respect to Eastern Europe, Pierre Hassner noted in 1966:

> Four relatively lasting elements besides the person of de Gaulle and his general policies on the international scene give France a political advantage over Germany, despite the latter's superior population and resources: the sympathy it enjoys in Eastern Europe, the fear and hostility still evoked by Germany in several countries (above all in Poland and Czechoslovakia), the possession by France of a nuclear force which is forbidden to Germany, finally the division of Germany. Of the four, it is the last which seems most important.[9]

With each new Gaullist success in Eastern Europe, there was an increasing suspicion in Bonn that de Gaulle intended to place German reunification policy under French tutelage (with France acting as a broker rather than as Bonn's partner)—or even worse—that de Gaulle was toying with the idea of returning to his postwar plan for a Franco-Soviet understanding. Zbigniew Brzezinski wrote in 1965:

De Gaulle's preoccupation with East Europe reveals the strong element of 'sacro egoismo' and deception in his policy. Since his concept of Europe is one led by France, it follows that the two alternatives for France are (1) Europe divided on the Elbe, in which a divided Germany depends on France for eventual reunification, or (2) a united Europe including not only a 70-million-strong Germany but also East Europe (and even Russia), for the latter combined with France would more than balance Germany. He therefore could not welcome a reunification of Germany while East Europe remained in the hands of a hostile and perhaps fearful Russia.[10]

Since American and British support on the German question had flagged considerably over the years, de Gaulle's new Eastern policy put Bonn's reunification policy on an even more precarious footing, threatening Bonn with diplomatic isolation.

The end of the Franco-German understanding on Eastern policy affected all other aspects of Franco-German relations (which were already strained because of other issues) and disagreements became even more pronounced after the Soviet invasion of Czechoslovakia in August 1968. This event, which collapsed some major assumptions underlying both French and German policy toward Eastern Europe, reportedly gave rise to serious recriminations between de Gaulle and Kiesinger, with de Gaulle echoing the Soviet argument that West Germany was to blame for the invasion because its aggressive economic policy and great economic power would have exerted an irresistible drawing power on an independent Czechoslovakia, and with Kiesinger remonstrating that de Gaulle's encouragement of centrifugal tendencies in the Soviet bloc had caused more trouble than any German policies.[11] Soon afterward, Franco-German relations reached a low point as a result of the French monetary crisis of October 1968.

The crisis of the franc had a particularly damaging effect on Franco-German relations, because it followed in the wake of a series of corrosive disagreements over almost every important aspect of German and French foreign policy, and because it pitted French interests directly against German interests in a contest of wills that aroused strong emotions on both sides. Like all monetary crises, the crisis of the franc had its origin in a deficit in the balance of payments. For a number of years the French economy had suffered from moderate inflationary pressures (and moderate stagnation), which increased greatly during the summer of 1968 after the French government arranged for generous settlements with the labor unions in order to end a series of crippling strikes.[12] These wage increases, averaging 13 per cent, coupled with an expansionist monetary policy designed to facilitate recovery and stimulate economic growth, substantially increased the amount of money in circulation and led to a rise in industrial costs and the cost of living. Inflation, in turn, raised the price of exports and increased the volume of imports to meet consumer demand. The resulting outflow of gold and hard currencies created a crisis of confidence in the franc, a crisis that was further aggravated as speculators sold francs for marks: between June and November, France lost more than $4.5 billion in reserves, and during the month of November alone West Germany acquired $2 billion in such speculative funds, with a sizable portion coming from France.

The fact that speculators sold francs for marks (rather than for dollars, for example) was an indication of why the crisis of the franc became a crisis in Franco-German relations. While the position of the franc deteriorated rapidly (being propped up largely by internationally negotiated fixed exchange rates), that of the mark further solidified. During 1968, the German economy was recovering from a recession caused by stringent anti-inflationary measures, and the German wage and price level had been restabilized as a result of the reduced demand for goods and services. As a consequence, German export prices were highly competitive, leading to a massive trade surplus (approximately $4 billion during 1968), which, together with the inflow of capital funds and a low inflation rate, made the mark one of the strongest currencies in the foreign exchange markets. All these factors raised the expectation that West Germany, which already held a huge surplus of foreign currency reserves, might make an upward revaluation of the mark similar to that made in 1961. This expectation encouraged speculators to sell francs for marks, thus further depressing the market value of the franc and increasing the value of the mark. In short, the weak franc and the strong mark were feeding on each other.*

When the finance ministers of the ten leading non-Communist financial powers met in Bonn in November for a three-day session to resolve the monetary crisis, it was not surprising that the French and German positions were diametrically opposed. De Gaulle, who had characterized the possibility of devaluing the franc as "the worst of absurdities," instructed his finance minister, François-Xavier Ortoli, to push for an upward revaluation of the mark, a position which was supported by the United States and Britain. The Germans were adamantly opposed, arguing that revaluation would raise their export prices and could lead to loss of foreign markets and a domestic recession; and Kiesinger had already committed himself on nationwide television not to permit revaluation of the mark during his tenure as chancellor. Both sides viewed the immediate economic issue as inextricably tied to fundamental political questions. De Gaulle clearly intended to impose his will on Bonn once again and to extract concessions that would leave French prestige and political-economic maneuverability unimpaired. The Germans felt that their prosperity was well earned—they were industrious, they exercised self-discipline in resisting inflationary trends, and they had made outlays for modern and efficient capital equipment (while France and Britain

---

* This was possible because the present monetary system is unable to adjust to international differences in price levels and economic activity, except within the relatively narrow "trading bands" of currency exchange rate fluctuations. When the market price of a currency moves above or below the trading bands —which are the limits set by the International Monetary Fund (IMF) for day-to-day fluctuations of currency values—a country's central bank is required to sell or buy sufficient quantities of its currency until the currency price reverts to the parity level on currency exchange markets. Dissatisfaction with this system was strengthened during the crisis of the franc and led to new pressure for basic reforms such as readjustment of major currency parities or greater flexibility of exchange rates (One reform measure taken in 1968 provided for the establishment of two gold markets—an official one where central banks buy and sell gold at $35 an ounce, and a free market, where the price is allowed to fluctuate according to supply and demand.)

were offering few incentives for their industries to modernize). And they felt that they were being asked to pay the price for the inflation in France, caused in part by the exorbitant costs of such Gaullist trimmings of power as the force de frappe, which, in turn, were being used by de Gaulle to impose his foreign policy conceptions on Bonn.*

Although de Gaulle's manipulations during the gold crisis of November 1967 had gravely endangered the fixed gold-dollar-pound parity, the United States and Britain were highly sympathetic to the French plight one year later, since they also suffered from balance-of-payments difficulties. Also, a French decision not to devalue the franc was expected to work to Britain's advantage, at least in the short run, because it would keep French products from gaining a competitive edge over British exports and avert immediate danger to the pound. (Indeed, at one point during the Bonn conference, the French finance minister threatened to devalue the franc as much as 15 per cent, which would have endangered the pound and most of the Commonwealth currencies.) Washington had long favored a moderate upward revaluation of the mark, and it was American pressure which had

---

* The Germans had complained about what they called "imported inflation" as early as 1964. Karl Blessing, president of the German central bank (*Bundesbank*), explained that a favorable balance of trade with inflation-prone countries was not an unmixed blessing: "Our balance of trade surplus has grown and feeds us foreign currencies. These currencies—transformed into German marks in Germany—contribute to the heating-up of our economy and draw our costs and prices into the inflationary suction from the outside." *Der Spiegel*, 27/1964, p. 28. *Der Spiegel* went on to say that "through the loss of value incurred by exchanging sound marks into consumptive lire and francs, West Germany involuntarily finances Italy's development program in Southern Italy and Sicily as well as de Gaulle's expensive dream to become the world's fourth atomic mushroom." No doubt, de Gaulle's military expenditures (especially the costly force de frappe program) and his reorientation of economic planning toward measures which would complement French foreign policy, contributed to inflationary trends in France and exacerbated the sociopolitical problems which erupted during the spring 1968 general strike. (See Duboff, "Decline of Economic Planning"; Albrecht, "Die Reservewährungen"; and Prybyla, "French Economy.")

forced the Germans to revalue (4.75 per cent) in 1961. Italy, Holland, and Belgium, on the other hand, leaned toward the German position because the existing parities among the mark, lira, guilder, and Belgian franc were relatively realistic, and because these countries would have suffered from an upward revaluation of the mark.

After a series of acrimonious sessions, the German viewpoint prevailed on the major question of revaluation. The mark would not be revalued upward, but the German government would make selective tax changes to lower the price of imports and raise the price of German exports, with an effect equivalent to a 4 per cent revaluation. The finance ministers also agreed to make available to France $2 billion in credits. (Germany was reported to have offered France a unilateral loan of $1 billion even before the Bonn conference, which was apparently turned down because Germany refused to revalue and demanded that additional anti-inflationary measures be imposed on the French economy. Of the $2 billion loan made to France in November, Germany contributed $600 million, the United States $500 million, Italy $200 million; the balance, in smaller amounts, came from the other conference participants.)[13] These agreements were not contingent on French devaluation, but it was widely assumed that the French had little choice but to devalue the franc between 10 and 15 per cent. It came as a surprise, therefore, when de Gaulle made a terse announcement that the franc would not be devalued, which was soon followed by another announcement spelling out a tough domestic deflationary program to help correct domestic economic difficulties and to keep the franc afloat.

Most likely, de Gaulle's decision was influenced by the humiliating circumstances in which the devaluation would have been carried out, and by his resentment of the way the strength of the German economy was translated into political power at the Bonn meetings. The irritations that had been building up on both sides during years of controversy clearly made the outcome of the currency confrontation a question of national prestige, and lent the crisis a psychological significance that was at least equal to its economic and political significance. The political ramifications can hardly be exaggerated. Aside from incurring intangible political costs, de Gaulle's decision required postponement of some of his most cherished ambitions, such as the development of intercontinental ballistic missiles, the equipment of the French army with tactical nuclear weapons, and the completion of the H-bomb testing program in the Pacific.[14] Moreover, the domestic austerity measures initiated by the French government—price and wage freezes, spending cuts, increased "value-added" tax to reduce the volume of imports, currency exchange controls, and several others —were politically controversial and posed a threat to France's precarious domestic tranquility, which had just recently been restored. These factors may well have contributed to the retirement of de Gaulle in April 1969.

The Germans also paid a heavy political price for their "victory" at Bonn. Their demonstration of economic power caused a good deal of resentment, and created a community of interest among France, Britain, and the United States, since all three countries suffered from balance-of-payments difficulties that would have been ameliorated by the revaluation of the mark, and since de Gaulle's decision not to devalue the franc provided a welcome breathing spell for the ailing pound and dollar. Thus Bonn found itself in the uncomfortable and unusual position of being opposed by its three major allies simultaneously, a position that was even more awkward than having to choose sides between Washington and Paris. Most damaging in the long run, of course, was the blow dealt to the remnants of Franco-German amity. In taking uncompromising and psychologically charged stands on the revaluation issue, both sides showed a lack of imagination and circumspection. The Germans, deeply aware of and frustrated by the disparity between their economic power and their political influence, found in the currency crisis an irresistible opportunity to demonstrate to their allies (and to themselves) the continuing importance of Bonn in Western councils. De Gaulle, who had consistently nourished German frustrations by brusquely treating Bonn as, at best, the junior partner of the Franco-German entente, approached the crisis with his usual arrogance, taking it as a matter of course that rules of reciprocity were suspended in favor of France.

The Germans also paid an economic price. There was by no

means unanimous agreement in West Germany that the government's refusal to revalue the mark was based on sound economic reasoning. Since the taxation of exports and the subsidy for imports applied only to manufactured goods (it excluded services, agricultural products, and capital transactions), the burden of the government's decision was placed primarily on export-sensitive sectors of the economy without much benefit accruing to the German consumer, and the government was accused of sacrificing the interests of German export industries for the purposes of German foreign policy. It was also argued that the across-the-board adjustments which accompany revaluation would have been more efficient as well as more equitable, because they would not have required the services of the bureaucracy's fiscal apparatus. As it was, most monetary experts viewed the taxation of exports as at best a stopgap measure, which, by leaving open other options for the future, was intended to strengthen the government's hand during negotiations on more fundamental reforms of the international monetary system.

Given the system of inflexible exchange rates, Germany in effect had only two major remedies for the persistent balance-of-payments surplus: revaluation or inflation. (Even flexible exchange rates would pose problems. Wider trading bands, for example, could have a fragmentary effect on the Common Market's agricultural financing system since the program is not tied to a common fiscal and monetary policy.)[15] Inflation—that is, fiscal and monetary manipulations by the government designed to heat up the economy and push up demand for goods and services with a correspondingly higher price and wage level—was in fact implicitly recommended to the German government in an OECD study of 1967, which urged Bonn to relax governmental control over economic expansion and take other inflationary measures to equilibrate the balance-of-payments surplus.[16] After experiencing two disastrous inflations in 1923 and 1948, the Germans were understandably reluctant to engage in such inflationist adventures, especially since they felt that they were being asked to emulate what they regarded as undisciplined monetary practices by other governments.

France and Germany were not the only losers in the currency

confrontation. Inasmuch as the crisis reflected and dramatized the basic inadequacies of the international monetary system, perhaps its most damaging aspect was the bad (and possibly tempting) example set by the two major antagonists. Instead of overcoming the disparity between the franc and the mark by a compromise adjustment of rates of exchange, both sides resorted to fiscal manipulations, with France imposing currency outflow restrictions and other controls as well. By employing fiscal surrogates for parity adjustments, the French and German governments raised the specter that the relative liberalization of currency and capital transactions achieved since World War II would be reversed, with disastrous consequences for world trade and finance. Moreover, French measures to boost exports and curb imports violated the spirit if not the letter of Common Market regulations and placed an added strain on intracommunity relations.

The resignation of General de Gaulle in the spring of 1969 quite naturally led to speculations about the future of Franco-German relations. The official response in Bonn was cautiously optimistic, but both the German government (which faced an election in September) and the new French government under Georges Pompidou (which was preoccupied with the tasks of transition) clearly preferred to postpone major initiatives until the fall. The major exception to this was the surprise announcement in early August that the French government had decided to devalue the franc by 12.5 per cent.

The French decision followed in the wake of a new "crisis of the franc" in early May which was the direct result of de Gaulle's resignation and which followed roughly the same pattern as the crisis of November 1968. During the May 1969 crisis the Bonn government renewed its pledge not to revalue the mark—a decision which a government spokesman called "final, unequivocal, and for eternity"—but in contrast to November 1968, there was relatively little international agitation and acrimony, and the repercussions of Bonn's stubborn determination were largely felt in domestic politics.

The French devaluation move, however, once again raised

intricate issues between Paris and Bonn, largely in the context of the Common Market's farm pricing system. The major problem—which was the subject of intense discussions in Brussels among the finance and agricultural ministers of the Six—was how to adjust the Common Market's uniform support levels for farm prices to the devaluation of the franc. Since EEC farm prices are based on a unit of account equal to one American dollar (with payments converted into national currencies, however), French farmers would have gained by the amount of the franc's devaluation, with the result that overall price increases would have diminished the anti-inflationary effects of the devaluation. Three major options were available to the Common Market negotiators. First, stand pat and allow rising French farm prices to push EEC farm surpluses, already high because of price supports, to even higher levels—a solution detrimental to the purposes the French government sought to further with devaluation, and unacceptable to France's EEC partners because of the increasing financial burdens of the surplus subsidies. Second, devalue the unit of account—which is what French negotiators pushed for initially, but which was also unacceptable to the Five because it would have hurt their farmers by automatically reducing their subsidized earnings. And third—the solution finally accepted—suspend uniform support levels for farm products and "isolate" the French agricultural market (for 28 months), which, together with fiscal manipulations, would raise French farm prices only gradually.*

The sealing-off of the French farm market agreed on in Brussels had several important implications. In the first place, it required Pompidou to reverse de Gaulle's policy of insisting on

---

* Actually, there was a fourth alternative, unsuccessfully advocated by the Dutch in the face of strong French opposition: imposition of purely internal French tax measures. This alternative was partially incorporated in the compromise reached over whether France or the EEC would control the apparatus for isolating the French market. The agreement provided that the French government would tax farm exports and subsidize farm imports; and that by January 1, 1971 prices for 200 French agricultural products would be allowed to rise by half the franc devaluation amount, with the other half being allowed to rise by January 1, 1972.

a common agricultural policy among the Six, with the result that painfully forged agreements were being watered down and that the cohesion of the Market was suffering. Second, it set a precedent that could work to Britain's advantage in seeking Common Market membership: once exceptions were being made on the sensitive issue of farm products for France—a country that had all along insisted on the speedy establishment of a common market for agricultural products—exceptions might also be made for Britain—a country whose major economic reservations about joining EEC were centered precisely on the agricultural obligations resulting from membership, because they would raise food prices in Britain. Moreover, President Pompidou had previously demanded that prior to a reopening of negotiations on British membership, the Common Market members would have to agree on final farm financing regulations, a condition which could no longer be met now that the common farm program was suspended. Finally, the August negotiations in Brussels again demonstrated that some of the issues dividing Germany and France could not be attributed solely to the personal idiosyncracies of the decision-makers in Bonn and Paris but stemmed primarily from genuine economic and political conflicts of interest.

These conflicts of interest, especially within the context of the Common Market's agricultural financing system, were again demonstrated in the wake of the Grand Coalition's last major decision (it was in fact made the day after the September 28 elections that provided the basis for the new SPD-FDP coalition), which effected a de facto upward revaluation of the mark. In order to forestall a new monetary crisis, the caretaker Bonn Cabinet instructed the German central bank to cease its buying-and-selling operations on the foreign currency exchange market, which had maintained the parity of the mark within the one per cent parity fluctuations allowed by the International Monetary Fund, thus detaching the mark from its internationally agreed "pegs" and letting the rate "float" upward. In short, the Bonn government allowed supply-and-demand factors to determine temporarily a new parity level. Over the next four weeks, the central bank guided the mark on a steady upward course by feeding out dollars, and on October 24, the new Bonn government under Chancellor Willy Brandt and Vice Chancellor and Foreign Minister Walter Scheel officially revalued the mark by over 9 per cent, thus returning the German currency to the fixed-parity system. While these steps were strongly welcomed by Bonn's trading partners, the revaluation of the mark automatically reduced the income of German farmers because of the Common Market's farm financing rules; and West Germany's EEC partners were extremely reluctant to aid the Bonn government in compensating German farmers for an estimated $425 million annual loss, thus setting the stage for a new Common Market crisis.

Another potential conflict area between the Pompidou government and the Brandt government lay in the implications of the projected Soviet-American arms limitation talks. There was wide speculation in Europe in the summer of 1969 that these talks might lead to the limitation and control of nuclear arms within NATO and the Warsaw Pact as well as to military disengagement measures that might significantly reduce American conventional forces in Germany. In such circumstances, a reported British proposal for nuclear sharing within an enlarged European community, which would provide an independent European deterrent based on British and French nuclear forces, would presumably prove attractive to Britain's future EEC partners.[17] With France notably unenthusiastic about German access to nuclear decision-making, however, an intricate bargaining relationship was expected to develop between London, Paris, and Bonn, in which Britain's accession to the Common Market would be a crucial element.

CHAPTER THREE/ REUNIFICATION

Of all German foreign policy goals, the goal of reunification has proved to be the most difficult to attain, because the division of Germany was a direct consequence (as well as an important cause) of the deep and abiding disagreements that developed between the victorious Allies soon after World War II. The division of Germany had its origin in the conflicts among the four occupying powers that controlled Germany in the postwar years, and the division was institutionalized with the establishment of the Federal Republic of Germany (FRG) in Bonn and the German Democratic Republic (GDR) in Pankow in 1949. Both the Bonn and the Pankow regimes owed their very existence to the tensions which divided the Soviet Union and the Western powers; owing to Cold War tensions, the four occupying powers could not exercise the joint control and administration of Germany they had agreed upon. Finding it impossible to rule Germany together, and determined to deny each other control over all of Germany, the Cold War antagonists established German client states in their zones of occupation and effectively incorporated them in their respective zones of influence. The Iron Curtain, which divided central Europe as well as Germany, became the line of demarcation between the Cold War blocs and the forward line of defense for Washington's policy of containment.

It was clear to the Bonn government from the beginning that in contrast to other West German foreign policy goals—such as security, or political and economic recovery within the framework of the Western alliance—the unification of Germany required at least the acquiescence, if not the direct sponsorship, of both Cold War blocs. Consequently, the Adenauer government's long-range reunification strategy was based on two central tenets: (1) that Washington and Moscow held the key to the German question, and (2) that with the passage of time the balance of power between the Cold War blocs would shift in favor of the West, thus allowing negotiations "on the basis of strength" which would induce the Soviet Union to settle the German question on Western terms. The first of these tenets (which was essentially correct) clearly required, above all else, a solidification of the German position within the Western alliance. Because of West Germany's relative weakness, the most immediate aim of Bonn's unification policy was to enlist the active support of the Western powers, especially the United States, and to ensure that the West would not treat the German question as a secondary issue that could conceivably be traded off in an overall American-Soviet settlement of the Cold War.* These objectives were based on the realization that the Western powers would view the prospect of a unified Germany with some apprehension. Thus, the Bonn government's unification policy was to be implemented by increasing the political leverage of Bonn within the Western alliance in order to solidify on the political plane the legal and moral commitment of the Western powers to support reunification and to regard the Bonn government as the only legitimate spokesman for all of Germany. Bonn, in turn, pledged to faithfully support Germany's treaty obligations, to forswear the use of force in seeking unification, and to develop a united Germany along peaceful and democratic lines.

The complementary aspect of this policy—oriented toward

---

* Bonn's other "reunification" project—the return of the Saar territory to Germany—was brought to a successful conclusion precisely because it could be accomplished within the context of the Western alliance, where Bonn's influence was increasing steadily. After World War II, the Saar territory was placed under international control, but was administered by France, in whose zone of occupation it was located. Although France had by 1948 incorporated the Saar economically, and had attempted to solidify the Franco-Saar economic union politically and contractually, the Adenauer government managed by 1956 to negotiate the return of the Saar to Germany—by skillfully exploiting the opportunities of the Cold War international context, which provided Bonn with considerable leverage vis-à-vis France within the Western alliance. See Freymond, *Saar Conflict;* Fischer, *Die Saar;* and Willis, *French in Germany* and *France, Germany, and the New Europe.*

Moscow—was much more passive and vague, because it was merely an appendage of Bonn's Washington-oriented policy. This was perhaps unavoidable. The Western powers most likely would have viewed German overtures to the Soviet Union with misgivings, and a more active Eastern policy would have jeopardized the entire treaty structure that was to restore sovereignty to the Federal Republic. This would have undermined the power base from which Adenauer expected to deal with the Soviet Union at some future date, not to speak of the risks Bonn would have incurred in dealing with Moscow independently. As a consequence, Bonn's Eastern policy inevitably appeared flaccid and unimaginative, especially in contrast to the political acumen and tenacity displayed by Adenauer in his dealings with the Western powers.

Bonn's Moscow policy was static because it consisted almost entirely of negative elements. For example, the Bonn government refused to recognize the East German government or deal with it on an official basis, arguing that since the latter was not freely elected, the Bonn government had the duty as well as the right of "sole representation" of all Germans, including those in East Germany. (To buttress its claim of sole representation, and in order to isolate the East German regime diplomatically, in 1955 the Bonn government formulated the so-called Hallstein Doctrine on the basis of which the Federal Republic withheld or withdrew diplomatic recognition from governments that recognized the East German regime—except for the Soviet Union.) The negative quality of Bonn's Eastern policy was also reflected in the government's refusal to recognize the Oder-Neisse line as the permanent border between Poland and Germany. After the East German government and all the other East-bloc states recognized Poland's claim on the Oder-Neisse territories and East Prussia, the Bonn government adamantly refused to regard the territorial status quo in that area as anything but provisional and subject to revision. This refusal, which rests on the Potsdam Agreements' provision that no permanent revision of Germany's border could take place before a final all-German peace treaty, was supported consistently, if rather perfunctorily, by the Western powers until de Gaulle recognized the Oder-Neisse line as permanent in 1959.

Even though the Western powers supported Bonn's rigidly legalistic stand vis-à-vis the Soviet bloc, they showed no great enthusiasm or determination in furthering the cause of German unity. Both Cold War camps considered it politic to give at least verbal support to German aspirations for unification, but neither the United States nor the Soviet Union supported the creation of a unified Germany that would be genuinely free to conduct its external affairs. The first choice of either side—to draw a united Germany into its respective orbit under effective supervision—could be successfully vetoed by the other side, given the power pattern prevailing in the international system. On the other hand, securing the allegiance and power potential of the part of Germany that each Cold War camp already controlled promised a substantial increase of strength for both sides in the East-West confrontation. Power calculations allowed neither side to go beyond repeating its respective interpretation of what constituted an equitable solution to the German problem.

This lent an increasingly unreal quality to the verbal exchanges between East and West on the German question. Throughout the 1950s, the Western powers, reasonably certain that a Germany united on the basis of democratic processes would side with the West, kept insisting on free elections in East Germany prior to the formation of an all-German government, and on subsequent freedom of action for that government. The Soviet Union continually advocated the neutralization of a united Germany and the formation of a government in which East and West Germany would be represented equally. On one hand, agreeing to the Western proposals would have meant high risks for the Soviet Union, especially because the loss of East Germany might jeopardize Soviet control over Eastern Europe. Furthermore, by insisting on free elections and subsequent freedom to join alliances, the West held up to the Soviet Union the unacceptable prospect that not only West Germany but a unified Germany would become a member of the Western alliance. On the other hand, Soviet reunification proposals threatened the West. The Soviet proposals (such as the famous Soviet note of March 1952) allegedly aimed at Germany's neutralization but most likely were designed to prevent the rearmament of West Germany and to create political conditions advantageous to the Soviet Union. At a minimum, the Soviet proposals would have deprived the West of the power potential of West Germany, which was becoming more and more indispensable for Western military strategy, and would have led to the de facto recognition of the East German regime. At crucial junctures of Bonn's rearmament policy—which was the Western powers' condition for restoring sovereignty to the Federal Republic—Moscow came forth with proposals holding out the prospect of unification if West Germany would abstain from military, economic, and political ties with the Western powers. But the Soviet Union demanded in effect that the West accept, or help create, a probably unstable power vacuum in the heart of Europe, with many opportunities for Soviet manipulations and interference, at a time when clearly drawn spheres of influence seemed most promising for Washington's policy of containment. The line dividing the two power blocs in Europe, which ran through Germany, was clear-cut and was manned on both sides by the armed forces of the major Cold War antagonists. This "trip-wire" setting, and the opportunities it seemed to offer for effective containment with a "forward" NATO strategy, was precisely what the United States sought to establish on all Cold War fronts. It is easy to see why the United States was not anxious to replace this relatively tolerable and apparently stable status quo with the uncertainties that would have followed implementation of Moscow's unification proposals. For Adenauer, acceptance of the Soviet proposals to neutralize a united Germany would have meant the end of his most fundamental political aim—including Germany in a Western European union and tying the future course of German society to the cultural, religious, and political values of Western Europe. The West, and Adenauer, had to weigh the uncertain and risky prospect of a neutralized Germany against the certainty of a Western increment of power at a crucial stage in the Cold War.

In such circumstances, the military, economic, and political alignment of either West or East Germany with one of the Cold War camps could not possibly have made unification acceptable to *both* superpowers. The inclusion of West Germany in the Western alliance tended to "tighten" bipolarity and consequently exacerbated the conditions that made unification difficult in the first place. Because of the increasingly symmetrical power pattern in Europe, the two Cold War camps were faced with a double-or-nothing situation, where each side had good reason to expect that acceptance of the opponent's proposals would result in a negative outcome. The stakes were high and involved not only the two Germanies but the cohesion of the two alliance blocs and the viability of their military-strategic planning. The very importance of the issue thus precluded a "global deal" between East and West at another front of the Cold War struggle to bring about a solution of the German question, even though this possibility was frequently alluded to in German political circles.

In short, although the first tenet of Adenauer's reunification policy—that Washington and Moscow held the key to the German question and that reunification required the consent of both—was proved to be correct, the German government found it impossible to formulate and advance a solution which would have been acceptable to both superpowers. By the middle 1950s, when West Germany joined NATO and East Germany became a member of the Warsaw Pact, the Western-oriented dimension of Bonn's policy had proved fairly successful. Germany had achieved a remarkable economic revival, Bonn's political leverage within the Western alliance had increased enormously since 1949, and the Western powers were at least paying lip service to the cause of German reunification. But the very success of this policy, through which Germany became the bulwark of Washington's containment policy, had further accentuated the Cold War division of Europe and sealed the division of Germany. Moscow, especially after the Geneva Summit of July 1955, seemed increasingly prepared to accept the status quo in central Europe and consistently sought to solidify the political division of Europe by following a two-Germanies policy and by seeking to gain Western recognition for the Pankow regime. It may well be that

Soviet interest in a reunited Germany, under Russian predominance if not control, was a Stalinist phenomenon to begin with. In any case, with the full incorporation of the Federal Republic into the military, political, and economic structures of the Western alliance, a solution of the German question on terms acceptable to Moscow seemed unobtainable.

None of this is to say that unification, on terms acceptable to the Bonn government, could necessarily have been achieved if West Germany had *not* aligned herself with the West and joined NATO: the Soviet Union could have sabotaged unification at any juncture in the sequence of steps that the Kremlin proposed for bringing about unification. It is to say, however, that circumstances remaining the same, Bonn could not have hoped to improve chances for reunification by pursuing a policy of integration with the West.

The policy-makers of the Federal Republic, and especially Konrad Adenauer, were fully aware of this. In fact, their long-range calculations anticipated a point where circumstances would *not* be the same, and Bonn's unification policies were designed to bring about more propitious circumstances as quickly as possible. This was the crux of the second tenet of Bonn's unification policy: that with the passage of time the balance of power between the Cold War blocs would shift in favor of the West, thus allowing negotiations "on the basis of strength" that would induce the Soviet Union to settle the German question on Western terms. The single most important development that dashed these expectations was the Soviet Union's acquisition of nuclear capabilities. A Western policy of rollback and liberation of Eastern Europe, or even of applying strong pressure on the Kremlin, became inconceivable in light of the retaliatory power the Soviet Union was developing—as was demonstrated by events in Hungary in 1956. Adenauer's "policy of strength" had become illusory because the developing nuclear standoff was reflected in an East-West standoff on the German question: more than ever before either side could effectively deny the other side the control of both Germanies.

The Geneva Summit Conference of July 1955, which produced no agreement on the German issue, marks the end of a five-year period of East-West maneuvering, during which the line of demarcation running through Germany became increasingly solid and uncontested. Moscow's attempts to deny the Western alliance the increase in power expected of a West German military contribution had failed; West Germany was fully committed to a pro-Western course and was becoming an integral part of the economic, military, and political structures of the Western alliance. The failure of Moscow's Germany policy, however, could not be converted into a success for Bonn's Germany policy, primarily because the Western powers had not achieved the superiority of power vis-à-vis the Soviet bloc which was the second central tenet of Adenauer's policy. On the contrary, the absolute and relative strength of the Soviet Union had increased substantially, and the Cold War balance of power was moving toward a deadlock of which the existing state of affairs in central Europe was one manifestation.

Although it is an exaggeration to say that "the Geneva Summit Conference of 1955 in fact marked the end of the Cold War in Germany,"[1] the Soviet Union seemed by that time prepared to accept the status quo in central Europe and, after the Bantung Conference, turned to other Cold War fronts, especially in the Middle East and Asia. Moreover, instead of becoming more conciliatory on the German question with the passing of time, the Russians' attitudes stiffened in exactly the way they themselves had predicted. After it failed to prevent German membership in NATO, the Soviet Union shifted to a "two Germanies" policy, which found its most specific expression in the Kremlin's readiness to establish diplomatic relations with Bonn in 1955.

For Bonn this posed a painful dilemma. Establishing relations with Moscow tended to underline the division of Germany and in fact lent it a certain de jure recognition. But the Bonn government also believed that it could not block diplomatic channels of such importance for the German question, even if this step appeared to support the cogency of the Kremlin's contention that in fact two equal and sovereign German states had come into being.* Moreover, by 1955 Khrushchev and other Soviet leaders began to stress that the unification of such differently developing societies as those of East and West Germany could not possibly take place at the expense of East Germany, and during Adenauer's visit to Moscow late in 1955 Khrushchev said he was no longer interested even in bringing up the question of West Germany's withdrawal from the Western alliance. The Soviet Union was apparently convinced that the status quo was tolerable, and that time was working for the Kremlin, as was reflected in Khrushchev's remark to Adenauer that "the wind is not blowing in our face."

Clearly, Adenauer's hope to deal with the Soviet Union from a position of strength had not materialized by 1955. Equally important, not even the Western-oriented dimension of Bonn's reunification policy had succeeded entirely. To be sure, the growing German influence in Western councils was acknowledged both legally and politically, and with the ratification of the Paris Agreements the Western powers had reaffirmed their pledge to support by all diplomatic means the unification of Germany. But the development of Soviet nuclear capabilities, coupled with a less aggressive Soviet political posture in Europe, led to a serious reappraisal by the West of the potentially volatile political situation in central Europe and to a corresponding inclination to "defuse" the Cold War in general and the German question in particular. In other words, the Western-oriented dimension of Bonn's policy was not immune to erosion, and the gradual shift from the Cold War phase of the postwar period to a coexistence

* The establishment of diplomatic relations between Bonn and Moscow provided the immediate occasion for the formulation of Bonn's so-called Hallstein Doctrine in December 1955. In order to buttress the West German claim to sole representation of all Germans, which appeared weakened by the fact that two German states were now formally accredited in Moscow, Bonn developed a legal-diplomatic formula which provided that the Federal Republic would withhold or withdraw diplomatic recognition from governments that recognized the East German regime—except the Soviet Union. On the basis of this doctrine, Bonn broke diplomatic relations with Yugoslavia in 1957, when Tito formally recognized the Ulbricht regime.

phase generally tended to diminish the influence of Germany within the Western alliance.

These developments, which raised serious apprehensions in Bonn, were underlined after 1955 by Moscow's Germany policy. Following West Germany's accession to NATO, the Soviet Union persistently tried to further solidify the *political* line of division in central Europe (reflecting the Soviet interest in legitimizing the territorial status quo) and to blur, at the same time, the East-West *military* boundary running through Germany (reflecting the Soviet interest in denying the West the military-industrial power of West Germany). Both purposes were advanced by Soviet pressures on Berlin and by Soviet proposals for military disengagement.

In 1958, a decade after the Berlin Blockade and the Allied airlift, West Berlin again became the focal point of the Cold War in Europe.[2] Since 1949, Berlin had been the last vestige of the Four Powers' responsibility for all-German affairs, and the Allied military and West German political presence in the western part of the city had been a constant source of irritation to the East German regime and the Soviet Union. Since the Soviet Union wanted to freeze and legitimize the political status quo in central Europe, the isolated city presented Moscow with tempting opportunities to extract from the West de facto recognition of East Germany. The Soviets hoped to use Berlin to force the Western powers and the West Germans to deal directly with the Pankow regime. Berlin was a logical tool for such purposes because its political and legal status was not beyond challenge and because the access routes from the Federal Republic to West Berlin were the most vulnerable point of the Western defense perimeter. The Soviets enjoyed local superiority of power, and they could apply pressure and engineer provocations with fine gradations.

Late in 1958, after some preliminary harassing of Western transit to Berlin, the Soviet Union called for the end of the Western occupation of West Berlin and the creation of a demilitarized "free city," and threatened to conclude a separate peace treaty with East Germany unless the West would come to terms with

Soviet demands. These Soviet moves posed a serious threat to what the Bonn government perceived to be its vital interests. The establishment of a free city, perhaps under some form of United Nations supervision and independent of both East and West Germany, would have destroyed the last remnant of the Four Powers' responsibility for German unification, and equally important, it would have severed the already tenuous political-constitutional link between West Berlin and West Germany. As reflected in the special provisions made for West Berlin in West Germany's constitution, the Western powers had never been enthusiastic about a too specific and visible integration of West Berlin into the Federal Republic, primarily because they wanted to preserve the legal fiction that West Berlin was under the authority of the occupying powers. Although there was a de jure separation between West Berlin and the Federal Republic, there was a de facto economic, political, and symbolic connection which was at least as strong and visible as that between East Berlin and East Germany, and which Bonn was determined to preserve. The creation of an isolated miniature state of West Berlin would have shut out the Western powers by abolishing the Four Power Agreement, and it would have excluded the political influence of the Federal Republic. A major political ambiguity standing in the way of the Soviet two-Germanies policy would have been clarified and resolved in Moscow's favor.

During the next three years, the Berlin question was bandied back and forth at East-West conferences held in Geneva, Camp David, Paris, and Vienna. The United States and Britain were apparently willing to come to some sort of terms with the Soviets, perhaps on the basis of a "symbolic" reduction of Western forces, but Adenauer and de Gaulle followed a much more intransigent line. The issue came to a head in 1961.[3] In the intervening three years, refugees had poured into West Berlin from East Germany in increasing numbers, drawing needed manpower from the shaky East German economy and posing embarrassing political problems. By July 1961, the number of refugees entering West Berlin had reached ten thousand a week; it was apparently at a meeting of East-bloc leaders in Moscow at the end of the month that the decision was made to stop this flow by erecting the Wall. On August 13, the East Germany People's Police and the National People's Army occupied East Berlin and began to block transit between East and West Berlin. This step not only closed the last door between East and West Germany but also destroyed the last symbol of the unity of Germany and Berlin. The Soviets had in fact achieved a tightening and clarification of the political line running through Germany; and by "delegating" their rights in East Berlin to the Ulbricht regime, they had for all practical purposes concluded the separate peace treaty they had threatened the West with for so long. The division of Germany was complete.*

The proposals for arms control measures and disengagement plans that the Soviets put forth during the middle and late 1950s most likely were also intended to reinforce the division of Germany. These proposals invariably provided that the status quo—that is, the division of Germany—would serve as the basis for an agreement between the superpowers on arms control; and they envisaged the participation of West and East Germany as equal partners. Thus, acceptance of the proposals would have led to a de facto recognition of the Ulbricht regime as well as to a weakening of the West's military presence at the periphery of the Soviet bloc. Moreover, these proposals threatened Bonn's gradually developing interest in gaining a voice in nuclear decision-making—which was undoubtedly one reason why disengagement proposals multiplied rapidly on both sides of the Iron Curtain. Generally, Adenauer viewed the military and political neutralization of Germany as a pseudo-solution without lasting value, and he believed disengagement would create a political no-man's-land that could not maintain itself between two hostile blocs. Disen-

---

* For an intriguing speculation that links the Cuban missile crisis to the German question, see Ulam, *Expansion and Coexistence*, pp. 668–669. Ulam suggests that the Soviets installed missiles in Cuba in order to negotiate a deal, to be announced at the United Nations in November, which would have included a German peace treaty, an absolute prohibition of nuclear arms for Germany, and a nuclear-free zone in the Pacific designed primarily to contain Red China.

gagement would have ended Adenauer's plans for a Western European community, and, by prying Germany from the Western alliance, would have undermined NATO's "forward strategy," which Bonn sought to strengthen in order to make nuclear deterrence more effective.

Bonn's suspicions of Moscow's motives appeared the more justified since the Soviet proposals were never specifically linked with the question of unification but seemed primarily designed to disrupt NATO and to deny the Federal Republic a share in controlling nuclear arms. All Soviet proposals started with the assumption that two German states existed and that they would participate in negotiations as sovereign equals. Acceptance of even the initial stages of the Soviet plans would have implied Western recognition of the Pankow regime, which then could have sabotaged all further progress toward unification. Adenauer also distrusted Western disengagement proposals—such as the so-called Herter Plan, which linked reunification with arms control and a European security system—because he suspected that they stemmed not so much from a desire to see Germany reunified as from the need to diminish East-West tension and to explore all possibilities for arms control. Adenauer considered these proposals unwise even though it was unlikely that the Soviet Union might accept them, because once they were presented as concessions they would become the basis and starting point for further Soviet demands at the next stage of East-West discussions. From Bonn's perspective, presentation of these proposals implied a willingness to water down the Western position—and would lead to a gradual de jure recognition of the German status quo.

Bonn's attitude on disengagement highlighted a fundamental paradox of the unification issue. Bipolarities of interest, tension, and power are not conducive to the goal of unification: that was the lesson of the pre-1955 period. But the developing nuclear standoff between the United States and the Soviet Union, and the simultaneous decrease in the political cohesion of the two Cold War blocs after 1955, seemed no more likely to bring unification. The sobering specter of mutual annihilation created between the Soviet Union and the United States an important if limited common interest, which was forcefully manifested by the Cuban missile crisis and specifically acknowledged in the test ban treaty. Yet any lessening of tensions or intimations of Western flexibility suggested that conciliatory arrangements between the two superpowers might be made bilaterally and at the expense of the German question. This was the fundamental dilemma for Bonn's unification policy: without an abating of East-West tensions neither side could afford to allow unification on the opponent's terms; yet an East-West detente contained the possibility that the German status quo might get not only a tacit but a legal blessing.

The erosion of bipolarity during the late 1950s and early 1960s was hardly more propitious. On the surface it seems that fissures in the two Cold War alliances would have enhanced Bonn's chances to manipulate the international environment toward conditions more conducive to unification. The enforced relaxation of Moscow's control over its Eastern European satellites and the emerging Sino-Soviet disputes seemed to provide openings for Western probing actions, and the conflicts within the Western alliance helped to make West Germany a pivot whose support was solicited by both Washington and Paris. Advisers and critics in Bonn and elsewhere urged Adenauer to adopt a more flexible and imaginative Eastern policy in order to take advantage of the fragmentation of the Soviet monolith, suggesting a more dynamic policy toward East European countries and a less rigid stand on the Hallstein Doctrine and the Oder-Neisse line. Long-range considerations clearly required that the Germans themselves take some initiative on unification, and that Bonn modify its adamant Eastern policy and establish political and diplomatic contacts with the East European countries whose national interests were directly affected by the German question.

In fact, during the last years of Adenauer's Administration, his Foreign Minister, Gerhard Schröder, initiated steps designed to gradually normalize relations with Eastern Europe and to isolate the East German regime. But even though trade missions were established in Eastern Europe, Bonn still remained unwilling to make compromises that would have weakened its position on the Oder-Neisse line or the legal claims of the Hallstein Doctrine, and refused to deal with the East German regime on an official basis. This gave the Soviet Union a convenient rationale for maintaining its hold on Eastern Europe as the guarantor of the territorial status quo. In any event, the East European countries' concern with security made it unlikely that they would aid Bonn in its efforts to isolate East Germany politically and diplomatically, even though they appeared eager to expand trade agreements and willing to normalize diplomatic relations. The unresolved German question helped contain centrifugal pressures in the Soviet bloc, because it symbolized an important common interest. Moreover, Adenauer was apparently convinced that the Soviet Union and its East European allies were not genuinely interested in seeing Germany unified; hence he clung the harder to a strongly legalistic position, which would have been seriously compromised by shelving the Hallstein Doctrine and by extending a measure of legitimacy to the Pankow government. In short, Moscow's strategy to perpetuate the status quo inevitably shaped Bonn's unification policy and contributed to its intellectual stagnation; on the whole, the major unification efforts made by the Bonn government after 1955 were not really directed toward bringing about unification on terms acceptable to Bonn—for that there was little hope—but rather sought to prevent the legitimization of the status quo in central Europe. This tactical change of aim had important implications for Bonn's policy within the Western alliance, since it meant that the primary function of the Western powers on the German question was to deny the Soviet Union and East Germany a legitimization of the German state of affairs.

The effects on the German question of fissures in the Western alliance were also two sided. With frictions developing between Washington and Paris, the West German government was placed in the difficult position of taking sides, explicitly as well as implicitly, in Franco-American disagreements. This posed serious problems for West German foreign policy in general, and held particularly unpleasant implications for Bonn's unification program. Although de Gaulle had recognized the Oder-Neisse line in 1959, Bonn had every reason to ask and anticipate that the French would help deny legitimacy to the status quo and to the East German regime. This was borne out by French support of Adenauer's tough stand on the recurring Berlin crises, during which the United States and Great Britain were much more conciliatory toward the Soviet Union. Furthermore, many decision-makers in Bonn were convinced that in the long run the unity of Europe would be the key to the German question, and that for this reason alone the support of France would be indispensable. On the other hand, there was some doubt about French willingness to work enthusiastically for unification itself and a suspicion that, in Walter Lippmann's words, "the hard line France takes about Berlin and the Soviet Union is founded . . . on a basic French national determination not to have to live with a large united Germany. At bottom the hard policy is directed not against the Russians but against those Germans who want to make an opening to the East."[4] In contrast, although the United States and Britain supported Bonn's rigid Eastern policy less forcefully, they could perhaps be counted on to support unification itself. In any event, Adenauer could not turn his back on the United States, since the United States was the only Western power that could arrange the East-West "deal" which might result in unification. Yet here again, Bonn had to fear that it was precisely a global deal which would usher in, or reflect, an East-West detente at the expense of Germany. Clearly, the tension between the two aspects of the German question—unification itself, and preventing the legitimization of the status quo—were underscored both by the centrifugal tendencies in the Eastern bloc and by the fissures in the Western alliance. Short-run efforts to prevent the legal and political solidification of the status quo appeared to be incompatible with long-range planning for unification.

By 1963, when Ludwig Erhard became chancellor, dissatisfaction with the stagnation, if not paralysis, of the Adenauer government's Eastern policy had become widespread in West Germany. Although the new chancellor had no intention of departing radically from his predecessor's reunification policy, he did make cautious new beginnings, and the rethinking initiated by Gerhard Schröder toward the end of the Adenauer years now received at least half-hearted official blessing.

Erhard's hesitant revision of Bonn's Eastern policy stemmed primarily from the realization that the international scene had changed significantly.[5] De Gaulle's unilateral overtures to the Soviet bloc, and American and British efforts to nurture the post-Cuban detente, made it clear that the Western allies were not following a coordinated and purposeful reunification program. To keep the German question alive within the Western alliance and to take advantage of the polycentric developments in the Soviet bloc, the Bonn government obviously would have to be more determined and innovative.

This task was very much complicated by the fact that during the three years of the Erhard Administration the countries of Eastern and Western Europe were engaged in a general reassessment of national purposes and international alliances—which, as discussed in the previous two chapters, entailed a gradual redefinition of Germany's role within the Western alliance and within the context of the East-West interplay in central Europe. Bonn had to keep in step with events or risk diplomatic isolation for standing in the way of East-West detente efforts. As the East-West confrontation gradually changed from an essentially bipolar Washington-Moscow tension pattern to a more fragmented Western Europe-Eastern Europe detente pattern, Bonn had to address Eastern Europe as well as the Soviet Union in seeking a solution to the German question. Toward this end, Gerhard Schröder, who remained foreign minister in the Erhard cabinet, continued to advocate his "policy of movement," which was designed to make an "opening to the East" by establishing closer economic, political, and diplomatic relations with Eastern Europe; and during Schröder's tenure as foreign minister in the two Administrations trade missions were set up in Warsaw, Budapest, Sofia, and Bucharest. This more flexible approach, which complemented French and American efforts to develop better relations with Eastern Europe and which was coupled with a more pragmatic attitude on the Hallstein Doctrine, was explicitly intended to adjust Bonn's reunification policy to the changes that were taking place in the Eastern bloc. In the spring of 1964, Schröder said:

> I believe that there are indications that in some East European countries there is a growing understanding for the German problem and that their judgment is more independent than it has been in the past. It appears to me that our desire for true relaxation of tensions is meeting with more understanding in those countries than with the Soviet government for the time being. Let us not underrate this trend, for the voice of these states is beginning to carry more weight.[6]

The obstacles to Bonn's "policy of movement" were formidable—no less so because some of them were self-imposed. In the first place, Bonn's new *Ostpolitik* did not move far and fast enough. Bonn's "desire for true relaxation of tensions" was expressed only in reassurances about Bonn's good intentions, and did not extend to a scrapping of the Hallstein Doctrine or to a more accommodating position on the Oder-Neisse frontier issue. The Bonn government seemed insensitive to the fact that mere declarations of good intentions meant little to Eastern Europe when they were coupled with implicit demands for territorial revisions, demands which were backed up by West Germany's increasing economic and military power. Moreover, the East European governments—which after all were amicably disposed toward East Germany and still highly sensitive to the policy guidelines set forth by the Kremlin—could hardly endorse Bonn's attempt to isolate the Ulbricht regime, an attempt that remained an essential part of the Federal Republic's new *Ostpolitik.* The possibility that Bonn's policy could create dissension among the countries of Eastern Europe, or drive a wedge between them and the Soviet Union, was dismissed by Schröder himself, when he suggested that such an attempt would presumably not only fail but place an even heavier burden on German-Soviet relations.[7]

Although Bonn was willing to trade and talk with the countries of Eastern Europe, the Erhard government, constrained as it was by ingrained habits of thought and by conservative elements within the ruling CDU/CSU, could not develop a more positive policy toward East Germany. Through this failure, the Bonn government denied itself the opportunity to pursue its Eastern policy on all three levels: vis-à-vis Moscow, Eastern Europe, and East Berlin. It may well be, of course, that there was no real opportunity to do so. The East Germans were, at best, only interested in "confederation"; and by 1965, the Ulbricht regime had apparently stopped trying to obtain tacit recognition through increased contacts with the Federal Republic, and had imposed considerably more stringent conditions (such as prior recognition) on negotiations with Bonn.[8] This was exemplified in the abortive "speakers exchange program" of 1966, which had been initially suggested by the East Germans to foster a dialogue between prominent SPD and East German SED speakers and to publicly air opposing viewpoints on the German question in both parts of Germany. Although the East Germans had agreed to a preliminary program, they later changed their minds, apparently because they did not want to give effective West German speakers an opportunity to address the East German people.[9]

Even so, the Erhard government might have profitably ceased seeking to isolate the East German regime, if only to put Pankow on the defensive. However, even a partial modification of Bonn's policy appeared risky. Since the Bonn government's diplomacy toward the Soviet bloc held together with logical (although probably self-defeating) legalistic consistency, compromising one part would have compromised the whole, and scrapping one of its essential tenets would have caused the collapse of Bonn's entire legal-political reunification strategy and perhaps required a revision of its other foreign policy programs as well. A dynamic diplomatic offensive in Eastern Europe would have required recognition of the Oder-Neisse line and the scrapping of the Hallstein Doctrine. This would have undermined both Four Power responsibility for all-German affairs (since Bonn argued that Germany's definitive borders could not be settled prior to a final peace conference) and Bonn's claim to sole representation of all Germans. This in turn would have destroyed the rationale for ostracizing the East German regime. In toto, these changes would have signaled a major reversal of Bonn's longstanding Cold War posture, with important repercussions for Bonn's overall foreign policy program. As Pierre Hassner wrote in 1966:

> It is not unreasonable to imagine all over eastern Europe a variety of communist regimes with multiple degrees of liberalization and independence, but all more or less reconciled with their populations on a national basis and attracted by the West through their economic and cultural relations and through the search for a counterweight to the Soviet Union. So far, in East Germany and between the two Germanys, the evolution seems always to stop earlier because it is always in danger of going further. There seems to be little room for evading the stark choice between the maintenance of the political status quo (even though the daily life within it may be made less oppressive) and a qualitative or revolutionary change which would involve diplomatic negotiations and might affect the military balance.[10] *

Neither Erhard's temperament nor his quickly diminishing political fortunes allowed such a drastic reversal to take place. In the spring of 1966, the Bonn government renewed its efforts to reassure Eastern Europe of Germany's constructive attitude by promulgating a "Peace Note," which set forth proposals that were, in effect, compromise versions of proposals initially made by Warsaw Pact countries. Bonn now cautiously endorsed a nuclear-free zone, non-aggression pacts, and the exchange of military observers with Warsaw Treaty members.[11] These proposals did not offer important concessions on military-strategic matters

---

* Hassner also notes "the paradox of the double and, in a way, contradictory discrepancy between the German and the European situation. Today, precisely because of the potential instability of the East German regime, the German partition is the most rigidly stable element of the European picture. It is not the German problem which is again on the move, it is everything else in Europe which seems to be moving, and it is the German partition which, if only by its links with the presence of Soviet and American troops, constitutes not only the exception but also the limit to this movement." This leads to the further paradox "that while the Soviet position in Europe is declining, the Soviet position in Germany is improving."

prior to political solutions, nor did they change Bonn's determination to isolate East Germany diplomatically and deny it legal recognition, and to insist on the provisional nature of Germany's eastern borders. But at least the proposals symbolized Bonn's willingness to discuss arms control and security questions in the absence of prior political arrangements; and they also reflected Bonn's reluctance to continue automatically endorsing the current Western arms control "package," a practice which had become increasingly problematic with Washington's attentions focused on Vietnam rather than on Europe, and with Paris pursuing its independent military and diplomatic detente policy toward the Soviet bloc.

In any case, Erhard's compromise proposals came too late as far as the Soviet Union was concerned. The Kremlin, whose interest in arms control stemmed largely from the desire to cement the European political status quo, had stepped up its demands on the West considerably since Brezhnev and Kosygin had come into power. During the later Khrushchev years, the Soviet Union had initiated a more accommodating approach to Bonn (though it was short-lived)* and had proposed a non-aggression pact be-

---

* Fritz Ermarth (in *Internationalism,* pp. 29–31) characterizes the Kremlin's initiative as follows:

"It rested on the traditional Soviet appreciation of the German problem as the heart of its European security concerns. But rather than employing pressure on the entire Western position to force the United States into an accommodation, it seemed aimed at coaxing Bonn into a more accommodating posture. The whole drift of Soviet policy caused severe anxiety in East Berlin, however, which the signing of a Soviet-East German treaty of friendship, mutual defense, and cooperation in June 1964 did not allay.

"After a period of signaling an interest in a Soviet-West German dialogue, the highlight of which was a visit to the Federal Republic of Khrushchev's son-in-law, Alexei Adzhubei, who returned to Moscow extolling the wisdom of Rapallo, Khrushchev agreed to pay an official visit to Bonn. In early September, in the wake of the announcement that Khrushchev would go to Bonn, the First Secretary consulted in Prague with the foreign ministers of his allies; East Germany was not represented. Then signs began to mount that Khrushchev faced internal opposition to his German demarche, among them a mustard gas attack on a security technician on Bonn's Moscow embassy

tween the NATO and the Warsaw Pact countries, thus implicitly including the United States and Canada in the arrangement for European arms control. By contrast, the Brezhnev-Kosygin detente model of the middle 1960s (as enunciated in the Bucharest declaration of July 1966) made no mention of non-aggression pacts, and envisaged the dissolution of the two alliances and hence exclusion of the American presence from Europe.[12] Faced with conflict within the Warsaw Pact over alliance reform, and pressured by Ulbricht and Gomulka to apply a hard line toward Bonn, the Kremlin reiterated a series of tough demands: no German access to nuclear weapons, no change in the present frontiers in Europe, and recognition of the East German regime.

The Bonn government's revised reunification policy was deficient not only because it was unable to fashion a truly constructive and innovative approach to Eastern Europe and continued to ostracize the East German regime, but also because Erhard and Schröder found it impossible to establish a working relationship with de Gaulle. Adenauer's central assumption about Moscow and Washington holding the key to the German question continued to be valid in the 1960s; but it required some modification, because the loosening of the Western alliance and the Soviet bloc had increased the importance of France (relative to that of the United States) for resolving the German question. Even though Erhard and Schröder did not manage to act on it, there was an increasing realization in Bonn that Germany's reunification could be accomplished only in the context of a larger Euro-

---

staff, and forceful statements by Brezhnev and Suslov carrying implied warnings against a sellout of Pankow.

"Khrushchev's fall put an end to these German adventures. Whether they actually contributed to his fall must remain a matter of speculation. In any case, these events suggested the peculiar sensitivity of Soviet European policies to the influence of Moscow's seemingly most dependent ally, the GDR, an influence that was to be demonstrated repeatedly in the ensuing period." See also Wolfe, *Soviet Power,* pp. 158–171; and Hyland and Shryock, *Fall of Khrushchev,* pp. 158–183.

pean settlement, and that in this context France was at least as important a partner for Germany's "opening to the East" as was the United States. Generally, the fragmentation of the two Cold War blocs had increased the importance for German reunification of the secondary powers in both alliances. Moreover, there was an increasing feeling in Bonn that Washington and London had neither a program for, nor a deep interest in reunification, and that they were geopolitically too detached to provide much long-range assistance for the cause of German unity. This was coupled with the feeling that, in the words of George Liska,

> West Germany has no real substitute for France; only France can legitimize the German interest in reunification and in politically and otherwise unprovocative military rehabilitation in the eyes of the less forgiving smaller nations of Western and Central-Eastern Europe. She has, moreover, no apparent substitute for a strong France. Only such a France can combine diplomatic firmness with diplomatic flexibility in regard to the Soviet Union; the firmness is guaranteed and the flexibility is circumscribed by France's own need for West Germany if she is to have the respect of the Eastern as well as the Western superpower.[13]

This line of argument appeared especially plausible to the "Gaullists" in Bonn in the light of the Johnson Administration's growing involvement in Vietnam, which not only diminished Washington's stature in Eastern Europe but also seemed to reflect a general shift of American preoccupations away from Europe. Yet de Gaulle's determination to exclude the United States from a "Europe from the Atlantic to the Urals" was unacceptable to Bonn not only because of security concerns, but because the Germans suspected that de Gaulle's real interest in a resolution of the German question stemmed precisely from his desire to speed American withdrawal. Karl E. Birnbaum wrote in 1968:

> While paying lip service to German reunification, the French seem to be primarily interested in the amelioration of the German problem in order to eliminate (a) the main legitimation for superpower presence and influence in Europe, and (b) the block to further rapprochement

between Eastern and Western Europe which the unresolved situation in Central Europe constitutes. If these aims could be achieved by measures that would make the continued division of Germany just bearable to the German people the French are likely to be satisfied.[14]

In short, the debilitating problem that had plagued Bonn during the last years of the Adenauer regime—the need to make choices between Washington and Paris on almost every important item on Bonn's foreign policy agenda—became even more pronounced during the Erhard Administration, when the centrifugal tendencies within the Eastern and Western alliance systems increased the leverage of France enormously. In opting for the United States on most issues that divided Washington and Paris, Erhard also opted for a fundamentally static and conservative reunification program, because Washington (as well as Moscow) found the status quo in Europe entirely acceptable, and although not hostile to the causes of German and European unity, was not prepared to run risks for their advancement. France, on the other hand, was fully committed to a dynamic foreign policy that was intended to exploit the changes taking place in Western and Eastern Europe and thus might have led to a political arrangement congenial to German reunification, but de Gaulle could perhaps not be relied upon to support the cause of reunification itself except in the restraining context of a Franco-Soviet security system.

The Grand Coalition government of Christian Democrats and Socialists, which replaced the Erhard government late in 1966, was determined to overcome the impasse of Bonn's reunification policy and to avoid, as much as possible, the damaging consequences of making choices between Washington and Paris.[15] Generally, Chancellor Kiesinger and Foreign Minister Brandt were committed to a more imaginative foreign policy line and to a more assertive stance vis-àvis the United States. Erhard had been forced to resign at least in part because of his irresolute diplomacy, which had been widely criticized for contributing to the deterioration of Franco-German relations and for failing to further the cause of German unity. Moreover, the SPD had for many years pressed for a more open-minded and innovative reunification policy, and had favored contact with East German officials. Their presence in the government clearly meant that they intended to put some of their ideas into practice. Kiesinger and Brandt were determined to move beyond the Erhard government's hesitant foreign policy revisions and to attune German policy to the changing circumstances of the 1960s. By persisting in a hard-line orthodox Cold War stance, West Germany had run the danger of becoming isolated diplomatically on the German question, since her allies were anxious for an East-West detente and increasingly viewed Bonn as the major obstacle to achieving it.* The Grand Coalition's explicit declarations that Bonn would welcome a detente even if it were not preceded by progress on the German question thus constituted a fundamental reversal of policy: this was most specifically reflected in Bonn's willingness to discuss arms control measures and other institutionalized aspects of the East-West detente even if they were not directly linked to the issue of reunification.

The new departure in Bonn's Eastern policy was soon given verbal and symbolic expression. In widely reported speeches, Kiesinger declared the Munich Agreement of 1938 (which gave Germany territory in Czechoslovakia) no longer valid, thus removing an issue which had clouded Bonn's relations with Czechoslovakia;† he expressed Bonn's desire for a fundamental recon-

---

* Some critics of the Erhard Administration not only feared the diplomatic isolation of Bonn's foreign policy program but envisaged the possibility of diplomatic "encirclement." See, for example, the remarks by Konrad Adenauer and the article "Ost-Locarno, ohne uns?" in *Die Zeit*, October 19, 1965.

† Although the Bonn government had officially disavowed any claims to the Czechoslovakian territory that was ceded to Nazi Germany in 1938 and returned to Prague in 1945, it refused (until December 1966) to declare the Munich Agreement legally invalid, because this would turn the Germans expelled from Czechoslovakia after World War II into Czech citizens. Following the public outcry in the summer of 1964 when Hans Seebohm, West German Minister of Transport and a leader of the expellee movement, insisted that the Munich pact was still valid, Chancellor Erhard declared that Germany had "no territorial claims whatsoever with regard to Czechoslovakia and separates itself expressly from any declarations which have given rise to

ciliation with Poland; and he intimated that even though the Bonn government could not relinquish its legal claim to sole representation of the German people, it was prepared to accept the Pankow regime as the de facto East German government and would not object to a European renunciation-of-force agreement which both Germanies would sign. In response to Walter Ulbricht's 1967 New Year's message, in which he spelled out ten necessary preconditions for a confederation of the two German states (among others: normalization of relations, renunciation by Bonn of nuclear control in any form, an agreement that West Berlin would develop into an autonomous territory, recognition of existing borders, mutual reduction of armaments), Bonn made numerous suggestions—including fewer restrictions on travel, expansion of trade and credit arrangements and other economic projects, cultural and news-media exchanges, coordination of communication networks, linkage of energy markets, etc. Although East Berlin's response was largely negative, there followed an unprecedented exchange of letters and other communications between Chancellor Kiesinger and Willi Stoph, head of the East German cabinet, which was notable not so much for its content —both sides reiterated their familiar positions—but for the fact that for the first time intra-German contacts were endowed with a semi-official status. Willy Brandt explained Bonn's willingness to deal directly with the previously ostracized East German regime by saying that "The Soviet Union and a number of other countries are attached to one another by manifold ties of a political, ideological, and economic nature and . . . the other part of Germany, the G.D.R., is tightly held in this 'field of forces.'

---

a different interpretation." It was symptomatic of the Bonn government's legalistic foreign policy conceptions, as well as of its sensitivity to pressure from refugee groups, that even the Grand Coalition did not declare the Munich Agreement invalid *ex tunc* (that is, from the very beginning)—which is what Prague wanted in order to preclude the possibility that a combined German claim of "right to the homeland" and of self-determination would lead to future demands for border revisions. Nor did the Grand Coalition hesitate to seek to extract concessions from the Soviet Union in return for a German *ex tunc* invalidation.

We would be ignoring this if we disregarded East Germany in our policy of detente—if we neglected this important area in which we Germans have a special responsibility and in which something is expected of us."[16] Bonn's readiness to include East Germany in the framework of its Eastern policy was an important step, for, as Theo Sommer wrote in 1968:

Any German policy on Eastern Europe, depending on how things progress, will be directed at any or all of three parties: Moscow, the Communist countries of Eastern and Southeastern Europe, and East Berlin. For a long time, the West German government focused exclusively on Moscow, claiming that the key to reunification was to be found there and there alone. During the last few years, however, Bonn discovered that if the former "satellites" were won over, Moscow could no longer turn a deaf ear to German desires for reunification. Despite this change, the East German state still did not exist on Bonn's political map. The Grand Coalition was the first to realize that a sensible Eastern European policy could not ignore any of the three parties; that Bonn had to act on three levels—the Soviet, East European, *and* East German level; and that it made no sense whatsoever to speculate on, much less work toward, a break-up of the Eastern bloc or the isolation of Communist Germany. Ever since this realization, Bonn's Eastern European policy has been of a single fabric.[17]

Although Bonn's efforts to establish closer relations with Moscow and Pankow were largely failures—the Kremlin persisted in a generally negative attitude,* and in 1968 the East Germans put new pressures on the access routes to West Berlin, imposing even more stringent passport and visa requirements—the initial re-

---

* In late 1967 and early 1968, Bonn and Moscow held discussions on multilateral declarations abdicating the use of force in international relations, but they failed in large part because the Soviet Union insisted on incorporating highly controversial political issues—such as recognition of East Germany and the existing European borders, the permanent nuclear abstention of West Germany, and the Kremlin's claim to have the residual right (as one of the victors of World War II) to check the forces of "militarism and neo-Nazism" in West Germany.

For a discussion of Moscow's response to the Grand Coalition, see Wettig, "Moskau und die Grosse Koalition."

sponses in some East European capitals were more encouraging. The most visible result of the Grand Coalition's initiative in Eastern Europe was the opening of diplomatic relations with Rumania in January 1967 (which had been initiated during the Erhard Administration), the establishment of a trade mission in Prague in August 1967, and the resumption of diplomatic relations with Yugoslavia in early 1968. Although Kiesinger used the occasion of the German-Rumanian agreement to reemphasize Bonn's claim to sole representation of the German people, it was clear that the claim and its diplomatic corollary, the Hallstein Doctrine, were in effect being shelved. It would indeed have been difficult to maintain that the Hallstein Doctrine was in full effect when two German states, each speaking for its territory and population, were fully accredited in Bucharest and Belgrade as well as in Moscow. Even so, the Grand Coalition, put under pressure from conservative elements in the CDU/CSU, sought to maintain the legal shadow if not thc political substance of the Doctrine. In order to exempt the East European countries from its applicability, Bonn now reinterpreted the Hallstein Doctrine, saying that it should not apply to countries that had no free choice in the matter of recognizing the East German regime because of their imposed membership in the Soviet bloc. This so-called "birthmark" theory could not cover Yugoslavia, of course, since Tito had recognized the Ulbricht regime in 1957 on his own volition. Before allowing a dispensation of the birthmark theory for Belgrade, the Bonn government was careful to make sure that this further watering down of a watered-down version of the Hallstein Doctrine would not trigger a mass recognition of East Germany by Third World countries.*

---

* For examples of how Bonn used aid programs to induce Third World countries to adhere to the Hallstein Doctrine, see *Der Spiegel,* 12/1965, pp. 29–33.

The Hallstein Doctrine also had led to a considerable embarrassment for the Erhard Administration in the spring of 1965, when Bonn cancelled economic aid to Egypt because Nasser had nurtured increasingly cordial relations with East Germany, culminating in a state visit to Egypt by Ulbricht. As a consequence of this (half-hearted) application of the Hallstein Doctrine, the

But now that the Bonn government was intent on opening up lines of communications with Eastern Europe, and had formulated an Ostpolitik that threatened to outflank East Germany, it was the Pankow regime that sought contractual formulas to contain Bonn's diplomatic offensive. After Bonn had established diplomatic relations with Rumania, the East Germans formulated, with the strong support of Moscow and Warsaw, a "Hallstein Doctrine" of their own, insisting that no socialist country should open diplomatic relations with the Federal Republic until Bonn was ready to recognize East Germany, to accept the existing borders in Europe, to renounce any nuclear role, and to recognize West Berlin as a separate political unit. (East Germany imposed the same conditions on Bonn for entering into negotiations on such substantive issues as trade agreements, the movement of persons, and the unimpeded exchange of publications).

When the East Germans presented this proposal to the Warsaw Conference of Foreign Ministers in February 1967, it did not gain official endorsement, primarily because of Rumanian objections. But during 1967, the East German formula was at least partially accepted and formalized through a series of bilateral agreements with Poland, Czechoslovakia, Hungary, and Bulgaria, in which these countries called for the normalization of relations between the two German states, a security guarantee among neighboring states, and the defeat of "militarism and neo-Nazism" in West Germany. The signatories also stressed the permanence of present borders and viewed West Berlin as a separate, or even independent, unit. (East Germany had already succeeded in incorporating its demands in the Bucharest declaration of the Warsaw Pact countries in July 1966, but they were not specifically connected with the issue of the recognition of the Federal Republic by East European countries.)[18] These contractual obligations were ideologically buttressed by the Karlovy Vary Conference of European Communist Parties in April 1967,

---

majority of Arab states broke off diplomatic relations with Bonn. See Wagner, "Der Rückschlag," and for the pertinent documents, see *ibid.*, pp. D235–246; see also Morgan, "German Foreign Policy," pp. 100–102.

which generally endorsed the East German demands even though it did not, as some members suggested, formulate an injunction that would have prevented Eastern European states from establishing diplomatic relations with Bonn unless the West German government recognized East Germany as a separate German state. However, the conference issued a communiqué that endorsed Pankow's stand on border questions and nuclear matters, and called on West Germany to drop its claim to sole representation of the German people as a precondition for the normalization of relations with Eastern Europe.[19]

As was the case during the Erhard Administration, West Germany's difficulties in charting a more dynamic approach to Eastern Europe resulted not only from Pankow's countermeasures and the Kremlin's resistance but also from the political and conceptual inhibitions of the Bonn government. Some of these inhibitions were unavoidable. For example, Bonn's Eastern policy could not be as flexible and consistent as France's, because the Grand Coalition could not afford to match de Gaulle's disavowal of NATO or his disdainful attitude toward the United States. Other handicaps were largely self-imposed. Although the new government made every effort to move beyond the entrenched Cold War positions of its predecessors, and although long-established central tenets of Bonn's foreign policy were modified, the Grand Coalition (especially its more conservative members and supporters) did not entirely stop trying, or hoping, to extract concessions from the Soviet bloc in return for a more accommodating West German stand on West Berlin, the nuclear nonproliferation treaty, the recognition of East Germany, or the Oder-Neisse line.

The Oder-Neisse issue is a case in point. On the question of the German-Polish frontier, Bonn's position had been ambivalent and inconsistent all along. In spite of Schröder's efforts to normalize relations with Eastern Europe, the Erhard Administration had persisted in arguing that a final settlement of Germany's eastern borders must be preceded by the establishment of an all-German government; thus Bonn held out to Poland the unacceptable prospect of having to deal with a united Germany on a question of vital importance to Poland. Not surprisingly, therefore, the Polish government (and the Kremlin) pictured East Germany as the indispensable bulwark for maintaining Polish security vis-à-vis West Germany, and castigated Bonn for harboring revanchist designs. East European attitudes on the Oder-Neisse issue (and also on other issues) stem from what these countries and the Soviet Union perceive to be genuine national interests; in fact, they symbolize the convergence of Communist and national interests, which has frequently characterized the foreign policies of East European countries toward the Federal Republic and which was cemented by the intransigent Eastern policy of the Adenauer regime. As long as Bonn's policy was based on "strength" and relied on the assumption that German unity would finally be achieved through a Four Power agreement, there was at least some rationale for denying the de facto East German-Polish border arrangement legality. When this assumption was superseded by the premise that reunification required a fundamental German rapprochement with Eastern Europe, an obstinate West German position on the Oder-Neisse question became even more damaging to the prospects of reunification, and more at odds with the basic strategy for its realization, than was the case during the Adenauer period.

Influential policy-makers in Bonn have long realized that reunification and frontier revision are incompatible goals, especially in the context of Bonn's new Eastern policy. In his inaugural statement, Chancellor Kiesinger made no mention of Bonn's traditional demand for the "borders of 1937," and he implied that Bonn would accept the Oder-Neisse line as the eastern border of a united Germany. The issue of whether to recognize the Oder-Neisse border strained the Grand Coalition from the beginning, and was brought out in the open when Foreign Minister Brandt, speaking not in his official capacity but as the leader of the Socialists, defied the long-time policy of the Christian Democrats and called for "recognition and respect" (until a peace treaty would settle the issue definitively) of the

Oder-Neisse border at the SPD's party convention in the spring of 1968.*

The questionable rationale behind Bonn's attempt to trade juridical concessions for diplomatic-political gains was also exemplified by the Bonn government's equivocations about the nuclear nonproliferation treaty (discussed in Chapter One). It is true of course that Eastern European capitals can hardly be expected to calmly accept a nuclear decision-making role for Bonn: distrust of German intentions runs high, and a West German role in nuclear decision-making would significantly alter the central European balance of power, since a similar role for East European countries within the Soviet bloc is only a remote possibility. It is doubtful, however, whether Bonn's tacit offer to withdraw the implicit threat of gaining a nuclear voice could have succeeded in converting East European apprehensions into the conciliatory attitudes Bonn wished to foster. Considering the burden of Germany's past actions in Eastern Europe, the use of veiled threats was a psychologically inept way to dispel suspicions and to create a climate of opinion favorable to reunification.

---

* Brandt made a more cautious statement on the Oder-Neisse line at almost the same time, in "Policy Toward the East," pp. 484–485. In this article, he suggests that "perhaps the declarations we have offered regarding the renunciation of force can be formulated and safeguarded in such a way that the present borders of Poland can be recognized for the period for which the Federal Republic can commit itself, i.e. until a peace settlement. Thus, in the interest of both nations, the border question would no longer stand in the way of a detente or of a European security system. At the same time, this would prevent this question from being used any longer as a pretext for those who oppose a German-Polish settlement."

In May 1969, Gomulka, in a remarkably dispassionate speech in which he reviewed German-Polish relations, categorically rejected the provisional nature of the recognition formula implied in Brandt's position. Gomulka called for a bilateral Polish-West German treaty recognizing the Oder-Neisse line (a treaty identical with the Polish-East German treaty of Görlitz of 1950), and argued that Brandt's formulation was not fundamentally different from the official government position, since it merely formalized Bonn's de facto acceptance of the Oder-Neisse line but still contained a revisionist element by postponing a final settlement until a peace treaty.

Although the Grand Coalition's (and especially Willy Brandt's) attitude on the nonproliferation treaty was much more realistic than that of the Erhard government, influential decision-makers (including cabinet members) persisted in opposing the nonproliferation treaty in purely power-political terms, making it difficult for the government as a whole to dissociate itself from the implied threat of this position.

Bonn's own inhibitions, Moscow's unabated hostility, and the formation of a hard-line East German and Polish response to the Grand Coalition's diplomatic initiative indicates that the success and future potential of this initiative was very much limited, and that Bonn's "policy of movement" had been largely arrested prior to the Soviet invasion of Czechoslovakia in August 1968. All the same, the Soviet invasion dealt Bonn's policy a blow that was not merely tactical.

In the first place, central assumptions of Bonn's long-range unification strategy were undermined by the failure of the liberal experiment in Czechoslovakia, when it became clear that the Soviet Union and some of its client states were unwilling to allow policy deviations that might weaken the bloc's forward position in central Europe. It became apparent once again that Bonn's fundamental interest in changing, or at least loosening, the political status quo in central and Eastern Europe was in direct conflict with the interests of the Soviet Union—interests which seemed to dictate that the status quo be maintained even if this required the use of brute force. The significance of the invasion thus lay less in its immediate impact on reunification itself—even before August 21, 1968 the prospects for achieving German unity in the foreseeable future were remote—than in the feeling of frustration and resignation it engendered in Germany.[20] What appeared to be a rational, temperate, and at least superficially plausible reunification policy seemed to have been invalidated by international developments, and the tenuous consensus that had been fashioned for it at home over the years met renewed attacks. This is not to say that the Grand Coalition's "opening to the East" was ill-conceived. There is considerable merit, moral as well as political, in Bonn's willingness to pursue a policy of reconciliation toward Eastern Europe in the hope that increased contacts may pave the way for a future solution of the German question—or, at the very least, facilitate the rehabilitation of Germany in Eastern Europe. In any case, it is difficult to conceive of any feasible policy alternatives that would not have condemned the Federal Republic to an increasingly outmoded, static, and intransigent role in the flexible interplay between East and West that characterized the 1960s. Nonetheless, after the invasion, the Bonn government was faced with a significantly different situation. Although the Grand Coalition indicated that it would continue its policy of reconciliation with the Soviet bloc, it is clear that the obstacles to rapprochement were even more formidable than before. There was little reason to expect that meeting Soviet demands would advance the cause of German unity, since it now seemed likely that East European developments favorable to reunification would be met by the Soviets with a physical "veto"—while Bonn's acquiescence in Soviet demands would further undermine the familiar foundations of its Eastern policy and arouse domestic criticism.

Second, there was a subtle but direct and important connection between Bonn's new Ostpolitik and the events of August 1968. Even though Moscow was not adverse to a bilateral Washington-Moscow detente—to arrive at what Yugoslav Foreign Minister Marko Nikezic called "hegemonial coexistence"—the Kremlin was dead set against having its allies pursue dynamic and independent coexistence policies with the Western powers at the periphery of the Soviet bloc, precisely because a polycentric detente might upset the bipolar foundations for a Soviet-American understanding by erasing the clear delineation between the two power centers in central Europe. For strategic as well as political reasons, the Soviet Union was especially sensitive to foreign-policy "deviationism" in the northern tier of the Warsaw Pact, since this would threaten the Pankow-Warsaw-Prague triangle, which was the anchor point of Moscow's "forward" policy in Europe. By making the establishment of closer diplomatic relations with West Germany a divisive issue in the Soviet bloc, the smaller successes of Bonn's Ostpolitik—in Bucharest, Belgrade, and potentially Budapest and Prague—helped start a chain of events that led to a larger failure. Even so, Moscow might have continued to reluctantly tolerate the increasing economic and political contacts between Bonn and Prague if by mid-1968 Czechoslovak liberalization efforts had not posed a threat to the continued control of the Communist Party in Czechoslovakia. Given the new relationships between East European countries and Washington, Paris, and Bonn, a drastic transformation of the Czechoslovakian domestic order most likely would have been followed by an equally disturbing reorientation of Prague's foreign policy, a risk that the Soviet Union clearly was not prepared to take. Since Bonn's Ostpolitik was essential for establishing an international setting within which Prague could have extended the liberalization of its domestic policy to foreign policy, the Kremlin's clamp-down on Czechoslovakia simultaneously dealt Bonn's Eastern policy a decisive blow.[21]

Third, the "freezing" of the East European political arena for Bonn's probing actions reemphasized the importance of the other two arenas—Moscow and East Berlin.* Fritz Ermarth suggested in 1969 that:

After August [1968] it was most difficult to argue that the road toward new East-West relationships in Europe lies through Prague, Budapest, and Bucharest. The keys to Europe lie in Moscow, and Moscow intends to keep them. The impact of this lesson fell most heavily where it was intended to fall—on Bonn. The coalition government of the Federal Republic sensibly resisted the inclination of some West Germans to regard *Ostpolitik* as now a dead letter. But where in the past Bonn saw the most favorable prospects in courting East Europe first, the USSR

---

* There are of course other arenas. As early as the 1950s, some Germans engaged in what the late Otto Kirchheimer called the "Chinese projection game," which consists of speculations about how the Sino-Soviet split could be exploited for the cause of German unity—for example, by an alignment between China and Europe. Perhaps as a result of de Gaulle's recognition of Red China in 1964, the Erhard government sought to nurture economic relations with Peking, but had to drop the plan for a trade agreement in the face of strong objections from Washington.

second, and East Germany third, if at all, after August the USSR emerged clearly as the overwhelmingly dominant bargaining partner and even East Germany gained in stature after a fashion. This meant that if Bonn wishes to maintain some sort of *Ostpolitik* in the teeth of Soviet hostility, it must think more seriously than ever before about what have hitherto been deemed impermissible concessions, on the GDR, on the frontiers, and on nuclear weapons. What decisions will be made cannot be foretold. But the fragility of Bonn's bargaining position has been underscored, and that of West Germany's internal politics possibly increased. This was certainly a gain for the Soviets.[22]

All this greatly complicated Bonn's policy at a time when the three-level approach had just been put into tentative operation with a more conciliatory attitude toward East Berlin. For one thing, West Germany's increasing economic influence, which provided Bonn with considerable leverage in Eastern Europe, is much less effective as an instrument of foreign policy toward East Germany and the Soviet Union.[23] After years of frustration with a static and apparently hopeless reunification program, a more dynamic German policy in Eastern Europe had provided a constructive outlet for West German political energies, especially since Bonn could make use of its economic potential, which it had long sought to convert into a political asset.

In addition to the inherently more troublesome difficulties that Bonn encountered in dealing with Moscow and East Berlin, the "freezing" of the East European arena had even larger implications. The polycentric developments of the early and middle 1960s in the Soviet bloc and in the Western alliance had increased the importance for German reunification not only of the East European countries but also of Germany's western neighbors, notably France. This trend was reversed after August 1968. The diminished prospects for creating de Gaulle's "European Europe," within which a solution to the German question might be achieved, renewed the importance of the Washington-Moscow level—at a time, however, when it was more apparent than ever that both the United States and the Soviet Union had tacitly agreed to respect one another's spheres of influence and thus were not about to redraw them. The "condominium" world system to which both superpowers apparently aspire is fundamentally conservative and hence lends significant support to Moscow's attempts to solidify the political status quo in Eastern and central Europe. Bonn's old fears that an East-West detente would be fashioned on the basis of a divided Germany were thus not entirely unfounded. Even more serious perhaps was the fact that in the rudimentary Soviet-American condominium system of the 1960s the vital interests (as they were perceived by the governing elites) of the Soviet Union and East Germany appeared to be more complementary than those of the United States and West Germany, with the result that there may have developed a significant asymmetry in the relationships between the two German states and their respective superpower partners.

Most important, perhaps, this asymmetry was brought to the fore by the Soviet invasion at a time when contacts between the two German governments appeared to be indispensable if any progress on the German question was to be achieved. But even before the invasion, as Bonn's attitude toward Pankow had softened, Pankow had begun to urge its East European allies to unite against West German overtures—a position that was not altogether different from Adenauer's and Erhard's attempts to line up Bonn's allies for a rigid German Cold War posture. The Soviet invasion, by dramatically underlining the importance of the Pankow regime for West Germany's reunification efforts, also showed that Bonn's hard-line attitude toward East Germany during most of the last two decades had produced serious liabilities. Even though the Grand Coalition wanted a more accommodating relationship with Pankow and sought to live with it in a state of "cooperative division," the burdens of Bonn's past policy toward East Germany lay heavily on the Kiesinger government. During the Adenauer and Erhard Administrations, East Germany appeared to be nothing more than an object of Bonn's policy, especially when Bonn explicitly sought to isolate the Pankow regime from its Communist neighbors and from its own people and to deny the reality of the existing order in East Germany. By denying East Germany formal recognition, Bonn in effect imposed harsher conditions for a normalization of relations on Pankow than it did on the Eastern European capitals; this punitive double standard was in a sense reemphasized by the Grand Coalition's drastic revision of the Hallstein Doctrine because the revision weakened Bonn's claim to sole representation of all Germans but did not lead to a reversal of Bonn's non-recognition policy.*

Moreover, to the extent that the Bonn government justified its hard line toward East Germany by stressing the Four Powers' continuing legal and political responsibility for all-German affairs, Bonn weakened its own case by taking independent initiatives on the German question. For although the Bonn government carefully safeguarded its legal position by continuing to invoke Four Power responsibility and the Western Allies' contractual obligations to aid Bonn in achieving unification, its entire Eastern policy was clearly based on the assumptions that a Four Power settlement is not politically feasible in the foreseeable future and that the Western powers have not pressed Bonn's claim hard enough. Since Pankow's major foreign policy goal was

---

* The Grand Coalition's refusal to officially recognize the Pankow regime was also directed at the Western Powers. James Richardson says (in "Germany's Eastern Policy," p. 380): "The political premise of the non-recognition policy is the judgment that it is a way of keeping the issue of German unity on the diplomatic agenda. This is quite realistic. General acceptance of the legitimacy of the separate State of East Germany would further weaken Western support for German unity, and would make it easier for the Soviets and East Germans to depict Bonn as a troublemaker should it raise the reunification issue."

The self-defeating consequences of the Hallstein Doctrine—and the difficulty of scrapping it entirely—were again demonstrated in the spring of 1969 when Iraq, Cambodia, and the Sudan recognized the East German regime. The Cambodia episode touched off a new controversy within the Bonn government (see Chapter Four), which was finally resolved with a compromise: Bonn did not formally break relations with Cambodia but permanently recalled the German ambassador. Now the West German presence in Cambodia was downgraded while East Germany was fully represented by an embassy—an exact reversal of the situation existing previously. (Less "drastic" action against Cambodia—such as cancellation of foreign aid and development credits—was also considered, but rejected as ineffective because of the relatively insignificant amounts involved.)

all along to obtain formal recognition from Bonn, and since Bonn was equally determined to withhold it, partly on the grounds that it would tend to perpetuate the division of Germany, the two German states have for two decades been engaged in a stubborn contest of wills, of which Pankow's sporadic pressures on West Berlin are only the most dramatic example.

Despite the hostility and suspicion engendered by these confrontations, it has also long been recognized in Bonn that German unity depends on the willingness of both German states to arrive at a mutually acceptable political order for a reunified Germany. This implicitly conciliatory aspect of Bonn's policy, which must necessarily view East Germany as a potential partner of that policy rather than as its object, is enhanced by the widespread desire in West Germany to establish closer contacts with East Germany and to encourage an internal liberalization of its regime. The consequences of internal East German liberalization for German unity are difficult to foresee, however. Liberalization would make the East German regime more palatable, both in East Germany and in the West, but it probably would not lessen Pankow's dependence on the Soviet Union. Furthermore, as Zbigniew Brzezinski writes, "Internal liberalization might encourage new public demands for unification. Eventually the people might become emboldened by the decrease in coercion, with the danger of sudden eruption. Soviet intervention would certainly follow, with disastrous effects for the East Germans. The net effect would be not only a threat to peace, but a setback for German reunification." Brzezinski's prognosis, made in 1965, was clearly borne out by events in Czechoslovakia. On the other hand, as Hassner has pointed out, liberalization may lead to a further stabilization and acceptance of the division of Germany if it allows a greater identification of the people with the Pankow regime.[24]

The contradictions between the punitive and the conciliatory aspects of Bonn's policy can only be superficially reconciled with the argument that the former is directed toward the regime and the latter toward the people of East Germany. The East German regime has not been entirely unsuccessful in gaining support for the sweeping economic, social, and political transformations it has made since 1949. The two German state structures have evolved along very different lines during the past two decades, with a corresponding development toward divergent rudimentary "political cultures,"* and it is by no means assured (in fact, it is highly doubtful) that the people of East Germany, given a free choice, would wish to be simply plugged into the institutional, political, and socioeconomic system of the Federal Republic. Unpopular as the East German regime may be in certain respects, its undeniable economic and social achievements, with which many East Germans can identify, because they have made them possible with their own labors and sacrifices, make it psychologically hazardous for outsiders (especially the affluent West Germans) to denigrate the regime too indiscriminately. In 1968, Alard von Schack, a West German commentator, wrote:

> The more time has passed, and the more the German Democratic Republic has succeeded in consolidating its state structure—succeeded not only in exercising governmental functions but in developing a certain independence from the former occupation power, and in fashioning a greater correspondence with the will of the people and granting them some freedoms and rights—the more the Federal Republic's policy needed to recognize this and modify [previously enunciated doctrines].

In this view, this modification extends even to the hallowed principle that unification must be achieved on the basis of self-determination. In the past, self-determination seemed to mean that West Germans and East Germans would together decide their future system of government through nationwide elections. Now, Schack continues, "there is growing recognition in the Federal Republic that when it comes to the question of German unity,

---

* It is true, as Brzezinski has pointed out, that "it is impossible to create a nation artificially in 20 or 30 or even 40 years, particularly through foreign intervention," and that "Soviet presence seems to be a prerequisite for the further maintenance of East Germany." ("Toward a Community of the Developed Nations," in *Department of State Bulletin,* 13 March 1967, p. 418). Even so, the lifting of Soviet control would not necessarily lead to an automatic or frictionless reintegration of the two Germanies.

the people of the German Democratic Republic, after living for such a long time as a separate political unit, must have their own [i.e., separate] self-determination; they cannot [simply] be subjected to majority decision." In applying this federalist principle, Schack says, West Germany should recognize that East Germany is "at least partially a subject of international law—as much, for example, as is the member of a loosely organized federal state that also owes obligations to the federal system."[25]

It is the recognition of these developments, as much as the desire for a more flexible reunification policy, which led the Grand Coalition to reexamine Bonn's policy toward East Germany. But aside from the opposing interest calculations of the Pankow regime, and the overall restraint mechanisms of the Soviet bloc that bear on the German question, Bonn most likely added to its difficulties with Pankow by conducting its reunification policy over the years in a style that could not help but grate the political sensitivities of East German decision-makers. There is a special psychological edge to the enmity between "brothers," and even the Grand Coalition's principle of "acceptance without recognition" was not sufficiently positive to cut through the long-accumulated layers of ill will.[26] Bonn's softened attitudes at no time seemed to stem from a fundamental rethinking of the German question, but rather seemed to stem from an externally imposed, and grudgingly accepted, need to adjust to changing circumstances.

CHAPTER FOUR/ FOREIGN POLICY AND THE DOMESTIC POLITICAL SYSTEM

1949–1955

In a striking way, the East-West polarization of power during the 1950s gave rise to a similarly polarized conflict on the West German domestic political scene. This was not because the government and opposition were divided along pro-Western or pro-Soviet lines, but because the international environment made some of West Germany's foreign policy goals mutually incompatible. This was especially true during the formative years of West German foreign policy—from 1949 to approximately the middle 1950s. As it became increasingly clear that the government's wholehearted alignment with the Western powers aided security and political and economic recovery but failed to advance reunification, the question of foreign policy priorities became crucial. Formulated as abstract goals, the major foreign policy projects of security, political and economic recovery, and unification were not subject to contention; but the apparent incompatibility between pursuing a pro-Western security and recovery policy and simultaneously advancing the cause of German unity led to sharp and sustained domestic conflicts over the implementation, the proper order of priority, and the content of West German foreign policy goals. So long as the opposition perceived acceptable alternatives to the government's foreign policy line, consensus was impossible.

It may well be that no acceptable alternatives were available to begin with. The West was determined to enlist the Federal Republic in the Cold War struggle, and although the Adenauer government managed to extract from the former occupying powers a large number of political and economic concessions, it was not really free to pursue a flexible and dynamic foreign policy—because the diplomatic-political, economic, and military instruments of that policy were effectively integrated in the Western alliance structure. This was not a case of crude control. Although the Socialist opposition at one point referred to Konrad Adenauer as the "Allies' chancellor," the Western powers imposed no specific day-by-day, or even month-by-month, directives on the German government. Rather, the containment policy followed by Washington established an interlocking diplomatic, military, and economic structure that set the framework for the foreign policy projects not only of West Germany but of France, Britain, and other NATO countries as well. (To be sure, the establishment of a moderately influential German state a few years after the end of World War II was viewed with some disquiet and resentment by the West, notably by France; and the special restrictions on West German armaments imposed by the Western European Union clearly showed that although West Germany was gaining legal equality within the Western alliance system, political and psychological equality could be achieved only over the years by following a policy that would rehabilitate Germany in the eyes of her new allies.)

Nor did the strictures on Bonn's foreign policy stem solely from the restraining institutions of the Western alliance system and the policy guidelines set by the United States. Most likely, the opportunities for a more dynamic reunification policy that the Soviet overtures seemed to present were not real to begin with. The Kremlin's proposals were fraught with risks—which inhibited the Western powers and the Bonn government from exploring them more fully—and they were invariably designed to prevent German rearmament, thus striking at the base from which Adenauer expected to gain legal sovereignty and economic recovery. The apparent need to make a choice between security and recovery on the one hand and reunification on the other hand was largely imposed by the power and interest configuration of the Cold War international system; and Germany's weakness and dependence on the Western powers did not leave the Adenauer government much room for maneuver, even if Bonn had been prepared to accommodate the Soviet Union and thus run the risks of failing in its security and recovery policy as well as in its reunification policy.

As it was, even the severely limited choices open to the German government were attractive to Adenauer because they allowed him to pursue a foreign policy line that corresponded with his own preferences. For Adenauer and his supporters in the CDU/CSU, West German foreign policy goals derived their meaning and purpose from an attempt to establish a European political order that would irrevocably tie the direction and structure of German society to the cultural and political forces of Western Europe. This was to be achieved by making Germany an equal and respected partner of the Western powers and by forging a fundamental reconciliation between France and Germany. In the larger context of world politics, and especially for the purpose of meeting the Communist challenge, a united Western Europe was to be anchored to the power of the United States in the framework of an Atlantic alliance.

No doubt Adenauer would have preferred to lead a reunified Germany in the same direction, and was concerned about the apparent incompatibility of pursuing these objectives and simultaneously paving the way for unification: it was a question of putting first things first. Adenauer's overall vision of a desirable political order could be realized even though Bonn had little room for maneuver on the international scene—if only for West Germany. In fact, its realization was accelerated by Cold War tensions, which made the allegiance of Germany a coveted prize. It was the political genius of Adenauer—above all, his supreme sense of the possible—to exploit these circumstances to the utmost and transform necessity into virtue. From Adenauer's perspective, what was possible was in large part desirable, since it allowed him to lay the foundations, through his foreign policy, of a domestic political order that he favored intrinsically.

Chancellor Adenauer, who served also as foreign minister during the early years of the Federal Republic and who was in effective control of his party, soon emerged as the towering influence over the making of Bonn's foreign policy. Even so, not all elements of the heterogeneous CDU/CSU shared in equal measure Adenauer's overriding commitment to a Catholic-oriented, essentially conservative Western European condominium.* Nor did the Free Democratic Party (FDP) and the German Party (DP), both of which joined the CDU/CSU in the coalition governments

---

* The Christian Democratic Union was founded after the war by lay leaders of the Roman Catholic and Protestant churches, with the support of businessmen and trade-union leaders. From the beginning, the CDU and its Bavarian branch, the CSU, aimed to attract a wide and heterogeneous group of supporters, and eschewed any specific ideological orientation except an adherence to general "Christian principles." Although the party soon became rather conservative on economic issues, in that it grew distinctly oriented toward small business, agriculture, and industry, it was also committed to labor-management codetermination and other policies favored by its trade-union wing.

The coalition between Catholic and Protestant elements in the CDU/CSU was at times an uneasy one, and had to be shielded from disruptive influences. This was particularly true regarding some aspects of Adenauer's policy for an integrated Europe. No major figure in the Christian Democratic Union was opposed to European integration or to rapprochement with France. But the Catholic overtones of the gradually emerging Europe of the Six could not be expected to meet with the enthusiastic support of the Protestant elements in the CDU/CSU. The tension within the major party, which was also notable on domestic issues, did not prevent the CDU/CSU from uniting behind the government on such major issues as German rearmament; but the central motivation of Adenauer's foreign policy program, the integration of Germany in a Western European union, was not shared equally by all elements of the CDU/CSU. (Even on the issue of rearmament, the Christian Democrats did not always line up enthusiastically behind Adenauer. For example, Dr. Gustav Heinemann—then CDU Minister of the Interior, subsequently SPD cabinet member in the Grand Coalition, and now President of the Federal Republic—resigned over the issue of rearmament and helped organize protest meetings throughout West Germany.)

established after the 1949 and 1953 elections.* The Free Democrats—whose support came largely from business interests that favored laissez-faire economic liberalism and from anticlerical middle-class voters who resented the Catholic tinge of the CDU/CSU—would have liked Germany to play a more independent role than Adenauer's integrative, pro-Western program would allow, and they were not nearly as committed to his "little Europe" policy as were many of the Christian Democrats. The FDP favored a wider framework of European cooperation, which would include at least Great Britain; the party toyed with the idea of a "third force" in both international and domestic politics; and party spokesmen generally pressed more vigorously for unification than the CDU/CSU. But the FDP's emphasis on national interest

* The results of the 1949 and 1953 elections were as follows:

	1949		1953	
	PERCENTAGE OF VOTES	BUNDESTAG SEATS	PERCENTAGE OF VOTES	BUNDESTAG SEATS
CDU/CSU	31.0	139	45.2	243
SPD	29.2	131	28.8	151
FDP	11.9	52	9.5	48
DP	4.0	17	3.2	15
BHE	—	—	5.9	27
Bavarian Party	4.2	17	1.7	—
Extreme Right	1.8	5	1.1	—
KPD	5.7	15	2.2	—
Neutralists	—	—	1.1	—
Others	12.2	26	1.3	3
Total	100.0	402	100.0	487
Percentage of electorate voting	78.5		86.0	

The Cabinet formed after the 1949 election consisted of 9 members of the CDU (including the Chancellor), 3 from the FDP, and 2 from the DP; the 1953 Cabinet consisted of 13 members of the CDU/CSU (including the Chancellor), 4 from the FDP, 2 from the DP, and 2 from the BHE-Refugee Party.

and mobility in international affairs, coupled with the nationalistic sentiments of some groups in the party, posed no obstacles to pursuing a "policy of strength" and to supporting Adenauer's rearmament-sovereignty barter with the Western powers.

Neither did Adenauer have any difficulty in enlisting the support of the DP. The DP was even less enthusiastic about European integration than the FDP, but found it equally easy to support German rearmament. The German Party's flirtation with a German *Grossraum* policy in Europe made it generally hostile to a full accommodation with the Western powers; and the role of a predominant balancer, which the DP envisaged for Germany, required independent military strength and political mobility unencumbered by international integrative measures. At the same time, the German Party was fully committed to an activist unification policy: a divided Germany would not be strong enough to play the predominant role envisaged for it by the DP. Other DP ideas—such as an almost mystical stress on *Heimat* soil, and its militant nationalism and organismic view of society—tended to reinforce the party's strong concern with reunification. The same was true for the vociferous Refugee Party, whose strident and emotional demands for the return of the Eastern territories almost automatically entailed a militant preoccupation with reunification and regaining German power. Generally, the governing coalition's right wing—which was unenthusiastic about the prospect of an integrated Western Europe and inclined toward an independent foreign policy—was reluctant to postpone unification and make sacrifices in the cause of European union.

Throughout the 1950s, the Social Democratic Party, led by Kurt Schumacher, was the most important and consistent voice of organized opposition to the Adenauer government's foreign policy program. The Socialists' foreign policy priorities were almost exactly the reverse of Adenauer's: they gave top priority to unification, and although they had no intrinsic objections to Adenauer's policy of reconciliation with the West, they also believed that the commitments resulting from that policy—rearmament and membership in the Western alliance—were detrimental to the cause of German unity.* The SPD's deep commitment to reunification had two major sources. First, although the Socialists echoed the CDU's call for European integration and a rapprochement with France, they were very apprehensive about the prospect of a "Carolingian" Western European community with strongly Catholic and conservative tendencies. Initially at least, the Socialists' blueprint for a new socioeconomic and political order in Germany was Marxist-reformist and had pronounced antibourgeois and anticlerical overtones. They had little hope that the values of economic and political socialism would prevail in the Western European union advocated by such Catholic and essentially conservative Europeanists as Adenauer, French Foreign Minister Robert Schuman, and Italian Prime Minister Alcide de Gasperi. The SPD felt a much closer affinity for the sociopolitical and cultural attributes of Britain and the Scandinavian countries, whose political and socioeconomic life had been significantly shaped by their Socialist parties. Second, the division of Germany had weakened the SPD considerably by cutting the party off from the areas that had been sympathetic to it during the Weimar Republic. Thus, reunification seemed essential not only for establishing the political order the Socialists wished to foster in postwar Germany but also for solidifying and extending the power base of the party. The Socialists as well as the Christian Democrats regarded foreign policy as an instrument to guide West German society in the direction they were committed to. Foreign

* Paradoxically, the Social Democratic Party's view of unification was shared by the right wing of the governing coalitions—elements with whom the SPD disagreed on almost every other conceivable issue. There were of course significant differences. The nationalists on the Right, with their deep-seated hostility toward bolshevism and Marxist socialism advocated an extremely tough line in dealing with the Soviet Union. Their call for a "policy of strength," in contrast to Adenauer's, often did not seem to preclude using force to obtain a settlement of the German question. The Socialists, on the other hand, were much more willing than the right wing of the coalitions, or for that matter than the CDU, to conciliate the Soviet Union in the interest of reunification.

policy projects were consistently evaluated in terms of the domestic aims of the various political parties.

This explains in large part the intensity, and at times the acrimony, that characterized foreign policy debate in Bonn during the 1950s. The Socialists agreed with the Christian Democrats that unification should be pursued only by peaceful means, and that democracy would be the only acceptable political order in a united Germany. But they were much more willing than the government to test Soviet proposals and to assume that the Russians were at least partially acting in good faith; and they frequently accused the government of dragging its feet on unification, of letting opportunities for profitable negotiations pass by, and of lacking initiative, flexibility, and foresight. SPD spokesmen argued constantly that the German question could only be resolved by lifting the two parts of Germany from the grasp of the two Cold War blocs, and that this would require a more accommodating posture vis-à-vis the East bloc and abstention from political, economic, and military association with the Western powers. Since all of the government's foreign policies were inextricably interlocked—as was clearly reflected in the contractual obligations of the 1954 Paris Agreements—the Socialists were led to a sweeping and often indiscriminate condemnation of the entire range of Bonn's pro-Western policies: they fought membership in the European Defense Community, in the Coal and Steel Community, and in NATO; and they acquiesced only reluctantly and with grave reservations in plans for the European Common Market.

Precisely because West Germany's rearmament was the linchpin that held together Adenauer's foreign policy program by giving Bonn the necessary leverage vis-à-vis the Western powers, it also became the focal point for the domestic opposition. The SPD objected to rearmament on four major grounds: it would damage the prospects for reunification by aligning West Germany with one of the Cold War camps; it would increase world tensions and antagonize the Soviet Union without substantially improving the Western defense system; it could prove disruptive to the fledgling German democracy because it would bring to the fore militarist elements and other objectionable remnants of the old order; and it would lead to Germany's integration in a conservative Western European union that could split non-Communist Europe. The Socialists also felt that since the Western powers were occupying Germany, the Western powers had undertaken the responsibility for Germany's defense, and that West Germany should not contribute to the Western defense effort until sovereignty was restored.

This latter point is one reason why the SPD had difficulty gaining widespread and effective support for its adamant opposition to rearmament. For although most West Germans viewed rearmament without enthusiasm and were not eager to join EDC and NATO, they were fully aware that Adenauer's foreign policy program was making progress—especially in the area of economic reconstruction and restoration of sovereignty, and that continued success depended upon German participation in the Western military alliance. The objections to rearmament, although widespread, were more than balanced by practical considerations, and furthermore lacked effective political representation in Bonn. The opposition to rearmament had a dispersed constituency—in the trade unions, churches, and among intellectuals and university students—and it had a difficult time coordinating its demands forcefully. With the exception of the Socialists, whose rigidity prevented them from exerting any great influence on the political process, the elements opposing rearmament were not effectively organized and were subjected to divisive cross-pressures. The practical and immediate requirements of economic reconstruction, the desire for an adequate standard of living after years of deprivation, the gains promised in return for collaborating with the Western powers—in short, the recognition that Adenauer's policy showed a way to stability, recovery, and international "respectability"—made opposition to rearmament an essentially emotional issue that had to face a daily test against expediency and the hope for "normalcy."

In retrospect, it seems that the Socialists were not the most effective champions of unification. Their position on domestic issues was consistently undercut by the government's extensive economic and social programs, and the rapid improvement of living standards took most of the wind out of the Socialists' sails. The Adenauer regime soon began to symbolize political stability; prosperity seemed around the corner; and the CDU strategists had correctly counted on the moderately conservative temper of the electorate. Furthermore, their preoccupation with unification caused the Socialists to take a negative attitude on all other foreign policy questions. This made it difficult for them to share credit for Adenauer's foreign policy successes and made it easy for Adenauer to call them rigidly doctrinaire and naively obstructionist. The SPD was deprived of political leverage in Bonn and found it impossible to gain more than a third of the votes on the single-issue campaign it waged on the national level.

Perhaps the major problem the Socialists faced in converting the general desire for unification into votes for the SPD was the lack of practicality and immediacy that began to characterize the unification issue. This is not saying that the Germans did not want unification: by the early 1950s West Germans began to regard unification as the most important problem that confronted German foreign policy.[1] But in contrast to the prompt economic and political benefits that resulted from the government's pro-Western policies, the question of unification became increasingly abstract and hypothetical. In short, the distant nature of the goal of unification stemmed not only from the obvious risks and obstacles of implementing it diplomatically, but also from the problem of relating it to more immediately relevant and concrete issues of the day. West Germans were constantly asked to choose between unification and the possible loss of democratic freedoms or, on a less exalted plane, between unification and the promise of political and economic "normalcy." Even if a large number of West Germans had been willing to pursue unification with determination, the daily realities of political and economic life militated against this alternative. Aside from the forbidding circumstances of the international system, the cause of unification was undergoing a constant process of attrition on the domestic political scene.

Of all organized interest groups, the trade union movement

was perhaps the only one which sought to lend its political support to the cause of reunification and, by extension, to the Socialist Party. Activist union circles looked toward unification as a way to revitalize the rather flabby German trade union movement, because they were convinced that the political predominance of the CDU/CSU resulted at least in part from the fact that the traditional working-class strongholds in East Germany were excluded from the political processes of the Federal Republic. But the cross-pressures that impinged upon the rank-and-file members because of their economic and social interests, and the divisions in leadership and overall lack of vitality in the movement, prevented the trade unions from becoming an effective interest lobby for reunification. Union leaders and members had too much at stake in the government's political and economic recovery program to try to sabotage the pro-Western policy of Adenauer. Nor were business circles willing to exert influence on behalf of a foreign policy program that would have assigned top priority to unification. To businessmen and industrialists, the ramifications of a determined unification policy seemed far-reaching, although difficult to predict. Aside from the economic and political repercussions that could be expected from a more flexible Eastern policy *prior* to reunification—for example, the possible disintegration of the carefully nurtured alliance with the Western powers—the subsequent tasks would require sweeping economic sacrifices and could be expected to result in profound and unpredictable socioeconomic and political transformations. In addition to posing monetary and fiscal problems, including that of adjusting currencies and tax structures, unification would have required the integration of two economic systems that had evolved in different directions. The uncertainties and risks involved necessarily appeared high to West German entrepreneurs.

The problems Adenauer faced in advancing the goal of reunification in the international scene were thus strikingly reflected in the domestic political system. The Western-oriented dimension of Adenauer's unification policies—to strengthen the Western alliance and to obtain political leverage for Bonn in Western councils through rearmament—gained the support of powerful

German interest groups and a large proportion of the electorate because these policies concurrently yielded important economic and political benefits. The Socialists' strategy for achieving reunification—an accommodation with the Soviet Union on the basis of a neutralized united Germany—could not gain the support of the Western powers and thus could not have yielded payoffs for the Federal Republic in terms of sovereignty and economic reconstruction. The FDP deliberately attempted to bridge these two conflicting strategies for reunification—the Free Democrats were generally "pro-West" but always ready to explore openings to the East which appeared to present opportunities for reunification. But the FDP's attempts to occupy the center were undercut on the domestic political scene both from the Right and from the Left, and most importantly, from the Christian Democrats who appealed to a wide group of supporters with the prospect of political and economic normalcy.

The Germans' desire for normalcy practically assured Adenauer success in gaining widespread support for his pro-Western political and economic recovery program, and it explains in good part the opposition's difficulty in attacking it effectively. Understandably, no political group of any consequence opposed the government's efforts to have sovereignty restored. But the specific content of Adenauer's recovery policies, and their anticipated consequences for other foreign policy goals and for the future development of West German society, were contested consistently by the opposition and disputed by the CDU's coalition partners as well. Especially the implications of linking German political recovery to a Western European community were subject to intense political debate because of possible repercussions on the chances for reunification. While rearmament became a key issue because it provided the government with the political lever needed to advance Adenauer's overall foreign policy preferences in the international system, political recovery was a major substantive issue because it represented the specific values that the contending parties wished to instill in the German body politic. The choice of a route to political recovery was the choice of a direction for German society; the pursuit of political recovery in the international system was regarded as having a long-range effect on the future domestic order.

This created some tensions within the government. The Free Democrats were not strongly committed to the Western European order that Adenauer and the European "Federalists" in the CDU sought to create, and the FDP's call for West German sovereignty was generally nationalist and appealed to the right wing of the party. But the business and industrial circles that were attracted by the FDP's laissez-faire economic programs had a substantial stake in the government's pro-Western policy and acted as an effective check on the party's right wing. The German Party and the spokesmen for refugee interests, however, were not encumbered by such restraints. The DP's wish to see a united Germany as a European balancer of East and West, and the party's strongly nationalist program, called for freedom of action and a tough posture vis-à-vis both East and West. To the DP, the restoration of sovereignty meant the opportunity to engage in power politics, and freedom to play East against West unencumbered by contractual restraints that would bind the Federal Republic to the Western alliance.

The Socialists' overall political program and their preoccupation with reunification inevitably shaped their position on sovereignty and political recovery. Their hostility toward German membership in a Western European community with a conservative bias, its potential repercussions on unification, and the fear that the Socialists could once again be accused of self-abnegating "internationalism" (as had happened after World War I) made the SPD the most outspoken advocate of German self-interest. This posed certain problems for the Socialists however. For although they consistently pushed for full equality and legal sovereignty, they could not really accept the restoration of sovereignty without qualification, because of its possibly detrimental effect on unification. Putting undue stress on West Germany's legal sovereignty, even the kind of stress the SPD envisaged—that is, unencumbered by entanglement with the Western Cold War alliance —appeared politically and psychologically unwise, because it emphasized the division of Germany and tended to shift the responsibility for reunification from the Allied powers to the two German governments.

For all parties, the crux of the matter was always the question of what was to be done with the legal aspects of sovereignty that were being restored to the Federal Republic. Because sovereignty, rearmament, and integrative Western European structures were always tied up legally and politically on the international scene, the gains in sovereignty achieved by the Bonn government were never "disposable" for purposes other than the ones earmarked in the contractual provisions. The interests of the Western powers obviously complemented Adenauer's plans for integrating Germany in a Western European union; they were necessarily adverse to the SPD's call for mobility of action that might lead to reunification, and detrimental to the SPD's long-range plans for Germany's domestic order as well. For Adenauer, necessity was combined with virtue; for the Socialists, the international barter that restored sovereignty in exchange for rearmament was objectionable on most grounds. This was no compromise as far as the Socialists were concerned: many of the restored legal aspects of sovereignty immediately tied the Federal Republic to a budding Western European union that the SPD opposed, and Germany's participation in a military alliance directed against the Soviet Union would jeopardize unification and make Germany a potential battlefield of an East-West war.

The Socialists' dilemma was even more poignantly illustrated in the area of economic reconstruction. As noted in Chapter Two, the Schuman Plan for the European Coal and Steel Community was an important milestone on the way to German economic and political recovery because it provided for German participation on an equal basis and removed raw-material bottlenecks that had hampered the revival of German industry. Although the Socialists' opposition to the Schuman Plan was not directed against integration or Europeanization as such, their objections were sweeping and led to some of the most abrasive political fights in the Bundestag. The Socialists argued that the ECSC represented a conservative regional alliance for the perpetuation of capitalism, and that it was designed to shape the development of Germany's economic and social order by continuing occupation policies; they also attacked French attempts to seek admission of the Saar to the ECSC as an autonomous entity, and generally depicted the Schuman Plan as an international conspiracy to impede German unification and to handicap Germany's ability to compete with French industry on world markets.

It was true, of course, that the Western powers viewed the ECSC as a way of keeping an eye on the renascent industrial potential of Germany. But it was equally true that Germany gained important benefits, among which the economic ones were not necessarily the most important. The Schuman Plan seemed to help resolve the Saar question, and it promised to allay French fears that international control of the Ruhr basin would gradually evaporate. Moreover, the ECSC represented a significant gain for Germany's sovereignty, since it replaced an Allied instrument of control with an international organization in which the Federal Republic would participate as an equal.

Clearly, these political gains fit neatly into the overall policy framework of the Christian Democrats—but they were evaluated much more cautiously by the CDU's coalition partners. The FDP and the DP were reluctant to make sacrifices for the cause of European integration; they feared the Schuman Plan would have adverse effects on the Saar question; and some FDP leaders and the industrial interests close to them objected to the ECSC's stringent rules against cartels. At the same time, the Free Democrats and German business circles were interested in abolishing the Ruhr Statute, the regulatory restrictions imposed on the combined management of coal and steel production, and the Allied control over production levels. On balance, the advantages of the ECSC seemed to outweigh the disadvantages, and in the end the 51 votes of the Free Democrats helped the government carry the ECSC treaty by a vote of 232 to 143.

Not even the close relationship between the SPD and the labor movement helped the Socialists enlist support for their opposition to the ECSC. Labor leaders strongly welcomed the removal of allied controls, and they were very sensitive to the need for labor to check the influence of producer organizations within the ECSC. A large number of union spokesmen felt that labor should not lack representation in the ECSC by default, and the coal-and-steel-workers' unions in particular perceived an opportunity to extend to the international level the domestic "codetermination" through which they had gained a voice in the management of their industries. The unions found support for their wage-and-hours demands in the comparative statistical studies undertaken by the ECSC, and although union circles raised objections to the free movement of coal-and-steel labor among the Six, they wished to take advantage of the Schuman Plan's proposal for a forty-hour week, uniform overtime, and extended vacations. The Schuman Plan also appealed to the social aspirations of the workers. The political doctrine of supranationalism seemed to enhance the labor movement's chances for social equality and respectability—which business circles were less willing to grant the unions domestically.

In 1954 the Socialists decided to get out of the isolated position they had put themselves in by opposing the Schuman Plan, and drastically reversed their position. The SPD program of that year no longer objected to the transfer of economic authority to international agencies, but stressed instead the democratic-parliamentary methods with which the transfer ought to be accomplished. SPD spokesmen now called for extended economic planning, for supranationally coordinated economic analyses, and for counter-cyclical measures and investments. By 1955, the Socialists advocated internationally coordinated investment policies and business-cycle controls, and began criticizing the ECSC for not having gone far enough in this direction.

In part, the SPD's about-face can be explained by the change in the complexion of the Saar issue, which had figured prominently in SPD objections to the Schuman Plan, and was now largely settled after the pro-German plebiscite. In addition, the SPD apparently feared that an entirely negative attitude would give control of the ECSC to industrial interests and freeze out Socialist influence by default. Moreover, after the demise of the EDC in August 1954, "the party was no longer compelled, on grounds of consistency, to oppose all supranationalism because it led to militarism and alliances. Hence, its all-German policy could remain intact and pure while economic integration could be supported as well."[2] Political isolation at home and changes in the international system had led to a significant reversal of the SPD position on a major foreign policy issue.

In spite of the Socialists' turnabout on the Schuman Plan—which was the first of a series of policy reversals that gradually narrowed the gap between government and opposition—by 1955 the domestic contest over foreign policy had polarized to such an extent that, as Arnold Heidenheimer wrote:

> Germany is now presented with two clear foreign policy alternatives—for the first time since the war. The first—Adenauer's—sees a strong two-thirds of the country allied with the free world in the hope that a "policy of strength" will sooner or later force the Russians to pull the Iron Curtain back at least as far as the Oder. The Socialist alternative seeks to achieve immediate unification by offering to trade the scheduled twelve German divisions against twenty million civilians of the East Zone.[3]

But the fundamental split between the government and the SPD on the rearmament-versus-reunification issue was lessened and occasionally obscured by limited agreements and ad hoc coalitions among the major political parties and interest groups. Many groups in the FDP and the DP shared the Socialists' fervent commitment to unification, their aversion to a "miniature" Europe, and their pronounced anticlericalism, although the Socialists profoundly disagreed with these groups on economic issues and abhorred the right-wing chauvinism expressed by some FDP and most DP members. The Free Democrats generally agreed with the Christian Democrats on issues of economic doctrine and shared the apprehensions of the CDU Protestants about clericalism; they were not enthusiastic about Western European integration, which was supported by most CDU members, and they felt that Adenauer was dragging his feet on unification. The Socialists, the Christian Democrats, and the Liberal wing of the FDP shared a fundamental commitment to a democratic political order, even though Adenauer himself was frequently accused of neglecting the spirit of the democratic process and preferring to rule over a "Chancellor-democracy."

It was the polarization of viewpoints on how to achieve unification, combined with the overlapping patterns of preference on related lesser issues, that characterized the domestic scene before 1955. The domestic polarization over rearmament and reunification was essentially imposed by the polarization in the international system, even though its meaning and motivation derived from the conflicting blueprints that the contending parties advanced for the nature of German society. After 1955, the important changes that took place in the international system provided a significantly different backdrop for the domestic dialogue over foreign policy, and produced corresponding shifts and realignments in the domestic patterns of conflict and consensus.

1955–1963

The possibilities for a less polarized domestic conflict over foreign policy, which were already dimly visible in the pre-1955 period, gradually became stronger in the late 1950s and early 1960s; and by the end of the Adenauer era in 1963, the bitter and uncompromising contest over foreign policy had given way to a significant, if limited, measure of consensus.*

---

* It seems useful to divide the discussion of the Adenauer Administration into two time periods, 1949-1955, and 1955-1963. Such a division is necessarily somewhat arbitary. Even so, although the events of 1955 (such as the restoration of German sovereignty and the accession of Germany to NATO) did not mark a specific turning point in the postwar international system—large changes in the international system can rarely be pinpointed so precisely—they did mark the end of a distinct phase in West German foreign policy.

As in the pre-1955 period, it was primarily the international environment, with its shifting restraints and opportunities for Bonn's foreign policy projects, which set the boundaries for the domestic political discourse on foreign affairs and which produced a corresponding shift in domestic political alignments on foreign policy questions. Most important, the priority choice of security, recovery, and democratic freedoms on the one hand, or unification on the other—which had been the keystone of the domestic quarrel over foreign policy—had become largely a moot issue with German membership in NATO, and with the effective integration of Germany's political and economic policies in the Western alliance structure. Moreover, since it was now obvious that there was no longer a reasonable chance for unification on terms other than those of the Soviet Union, its most ardent champions were freed from their preoccupation and could assess other foreign policy issues on their own merits and with more detachment. This development strengthened and enlarged the points of agreement that had existed before 1955 among the major political parties and interest groups; it was further enhanced because the influence of the more flexible elements in both the CDU/CSU and the SPD had increased, and thus more agreement was possible.

The narrowing of the gap between government and opposition required much more strenuous exertions and painful adjustments on the part of the Socialists than on the part of the Christian Democrats. The Socialists' position was based on a more clear-cut ideology than that of the CDU/CSU, so it was harder for the SPD to make policy revisions. Furthermore, the Socialists were initially rather far removed from the mainstream of German politics and from the international forces that provided its external setting. But the Socialists' hesitant attempts to attune their party to domestic and international political realities were strongly reinforced by the changing international system, and they were made somewhat less painful by the fact that other political elements—notably the FDP—were going through a similar period of adjustment.

In the area of rearmament and military-strategic policy, the Socialists did not change their attitude until the late 1950s, when it had become obvious that even the most conciliatory overtures to the Soviet Union, such as those embodied in the SPD's 1959 Germany Plan, would probably not aid unification. However, because of the Adenauer government's policy on atomic weapons and its plan to share in the control of nuclear capabilities, in the late 1950s the Socialists intensified the contest over rearmament that had begun before West Germany's accession to NATO in 1955. With the developing nuclear East-West stalemate in the late 1950s, the Socialists felt vindicated in having argued that Germany's rearmament and membership in NATO would diminish the prospects for German unity while increasing the chances that Germany would become a battlefield in a "hot war." They were sharply critical of the prospect that German contingents would become NATO's foot soldiers, but they were equally opposed to Washington's doctrine of massive retaliation. As in the pre-1955 period, the Socialists found it difficult to arrive at a logically consistent viewpoint on the question of Bonn's military policy: on one hand, they objected to the buildup of German conventional forces, but on the other hand they rejected the only possible alternative—namely, American strategic nuclear deterrence. During 1956, when the recruitment method and the make-up of West German armed forces became the major point of contention, the Socialists argued that conscription would be unnecessary and that a small army of volunteers would fill West Germany's security needs because it mattered little in the nuclear age whether Bonn had twelve divisions or six thousand volunteers under arms.

The most heated arguments, however, took place over the issue of nuclear arms. In May 1957, the Bundestag had its first major debate on the military and political aspects of nuclear testing and the storing of atomic arms on German territory, during which the SPD stridently condemned the arming of German forces with atomic weapons, and called for a comprehensive international control arrangement to ban and eventually abolish nuclear arms. Following the fall 1957 election*—which provided the CDU/CSU with an absolute majority of Bundestag seats and which was widely regarded as a popular endorsement of Adenauer's foreign policies—the Socialists renewed their efforts to stir up popular opposition to nuclear weapons. This effort culminated in the spring of 1958 in a SPD-sponsored "Fight Against Atomic Death" campaign, which enlisted scientists, theologians, publicists, and politicians.

The campaign was also supported by the Free Democrats. The FDP's political fortunes had seriously declined since the "Young Turks" revolt split the party in 1956, and the party had been excluded from the CDU/CSU-DP coalition after the 1957 elections. This allowed the Free Democrats to voice their increasingly critical view of Adenauer's foreign policy, which they considered dangerously inflexible and unimaginative—especially with respect to reunification. They now joined forces with the SPD and declared that the nuclear balance between the superpowers made atomic arms for Germany unnecessary, especially since the other

---

* The results of the 1957 elections were as follows:

	PERCENTAGE OF VOTES	BUNDESTAG SEATS
CDU/CSU	50.2	270
SPD	31.8	169
FDP	7.7	41
DP	3.4	17
BHE	4.6	—
Extreme Right	1.0	—
Others	1.3	—
Total	100.0	497

Percentage of electorate voting 87.8

The Cabinet established consisted of 16 members of the CDU/CSU (including the Chancellor) and 2 members of the German Party.

side offered, in the Rapacki Plan, to renounce nuclear capabilities.

The general public was extremely concerned as well. But even though a large number of West Germans opposed atomic arms on German soil under any kind of control, approximately half the people questioned in opinion polls supported West Germany's membership in NATO. An even higher percentage, which had been increasing since 1951, wanted American troops stationed in Germany. Apparently West Germans, although opposed to atomic arms, were becoming increasingly aware of the complexity of defense requirements and were not prepared to reject German participation in the Western defense effort merely because they found atomic arms distasteful.

Although the Socialists were clearly fighting an uphill struggle in seeking popular support for their militant anti-government stand, it was largely international factors that propelled the SPD to drastically shift its position. Most important, the prospects for unification were becoming increasingly dim. Throughout 1957 and 1958, the Socialists, encouraged by the disengagement proposals put forth on both sides of the Iron Curtain which seemed to lend international support to their position, proposed to further the cause of reunification by moving toward a military detente in central Europe—by withdrawing or thinning out conventional forces, by keeping nuclear weapons off German territory, and by neutralizing a united Germany in the context of a central European collective security system. It was largely for this reason that the SPD opposed having American nuclear weapons on German territory—the SPD felt that this would foreclose opportunities to participate in disengagement schemes.

When nothing came of the various disengagement plans, and when it became clear that the Soviet Union was not only willing to live with the European status quo but anxious to solidify it contractually, the Socialists felt that even greater exertions were necessary. In a final effort to test Soviet intentions, in February 1959 Carlo Schmid and Fritz Erler headed a SPD delegation to

Moscow to sound out Khrushchev and exchange ideas on the German question. These discussions made it clear that the Soviet Union was unwilling to agree to unification on terms acceptable even to the Socialists, not to speak of the Bonn government. One week after the return of their delegation, the Socialists presented once more a detailed Germany Plan, which advocated a step-by-step military disengagement to be coupled with the gradual political and economic integration of the two Germanies. This new Germany Plan offered a concession that not even the Socialists had proposed before—a withdrawal of foreign troops from West and East Germany without prior agreement on unification. The plan also embraced to a large extent the Soviet idea of a "confederated" Germany by proposing the establishment of all-German institutions, in which Bonn and Pankow would be represented equally. The issue of free elections and the unhindered activity of political parties in both parts of Germany was relegated to the final stage of a three-stage integration plan.

With the 1959 Germany Plan the Socialists offered the last concession they felt capable of making: they agreed to deal with the East German regime as an acceptable and equal partner in unification projects. But even this extremely accommodating proposal found no meaningful response in the Soviet bloc, and a year after its inception the Socialists themselves considered it a thing of the past. The Socialists did not immediately scrap their interest in disengagement, but the erection of the Berlin Wall in 1961 finally pushed them toward the resigned and fundamentally pessimistic attitude on unification that the CDU/CSU had held for a number of years. During the 1961 election campaign, the SPD began to endorse most of the CDU's Western alliance policy; and Willy Brandt, mayor of West Berlin and the SPD's candidate for chancellor, admitted that "the task of securing the free part of our country seems to have been forced upon us as topic number one, rather than unification."[4]

With this announcement the great reversal of the SPD's policy priorities, which had been in the offing for a couple of years and which had been eased by shifts in the party's power structure,* was now being specifically acknowledged. After the election, Brandt asked that the German issue not be removed from the political agenda of the West, although it was "at present and for an immeasurable time to come, a hopeless issue," and although he felt that "apart from surrendering our freedom, there is obviously no conceivable price for the reunification of Germany."[5] The SPD's unification program had been reduced from the grand conception of the 1959 Germany Plan to a tactic of "little steps."

The FDP's commitment to unification was subject to the same pressures. During the 1961 campaign, the Free Democrats still called for a more "independent" foreign policy for West Germany and asserted that the Germans themselves, rather than the Four Powers, were ultimately responsible for reunification. As late as the beginning of 1962, the FDP proposed that Bonn should hold bilateral exploratory talks with the Soviet Union on the German and the Berlin questions, and some elements of the

---

* Following the disappointing showing of the SPD in the 1953 and 1957 elections, a "right" wing emerged in the party, made up largely of younger members who hoped to revamp the SPD's orientation and image and change it from a doctrinaire instrument of the "class struggle" into a broad-based party that would appeal to a wider constituency. The changes proposed by these reformists not only affected policy issues—they favored acceptance of the EEC, German membership in NATO, and dropping the demand for the nationalization of basic industries—but also entailed a reshuffling of the party power structure. The contest was essentially between the ideologically oriented party functionaries—who generally supported Kurt Schumacher's successor, Erich Ollenhauer—and the more pragmatically oriented SPD politicians in the Federal and Länder parliaments, people such as Willy Brandt (then mayor of West Berlin), Carlo Schmid, Fritz Erler, Karl Mommer, Waldemar von Knoeringen, Herbert Wehner, and Helmut Schmidt. By 1961, the struggle was resolved in favor of the SPD's "liberals." Although Brandt did not become chairman of the SPD until after Ollenhauer's death in 1964, he was selected as the party's candidate for the office of chancellor, and the major planks in the SPD's 1961 election platform had been strongly shaped by Brandt and his supporters.

party were apparently flirting with the prospect of a second Rapallo. In March, however, shortly before leaving to visit the United States, party chief Erich Mende declared that his party had reconsidered its foreign policy stand and that it was now opposed to Germany's neutrality and to disengagement projects for central Europe. The FDP renounced its previous suggestions for bilateral Moscow-Bonn discussions, and at the FDP's conference in the summer the issue of unification remained largely in the background; instead, the FDP emphasized the need for West Germans to press for a liberalization of the Ulbricht regime so as to better the lot of East Germans. In 1962, the FDP's Thomas Dehler, vice president of the Bundestag, regretfully admitted that "the consciousness of Germans that unity is a historical task set for them has atrophied," and that the covenant to work for national unity set down in the Basic Law was apparently no longer regarded as binding.[6]

The Socialists' utter disappointment with the Soviet reaction to their Germany Plan, and the impossibility of reunification in the foreseeable future, permitted them to review and readjust their entire foreign policy program. At the 1959 party conference, the SPD for the first time expressed a positive attitude toward national defense, and began to support a full-fledged German defense effort within the Western alliance. The entire style of the Socialists' dialogue with the government on defense issues gradually began to change. Harangues gave way to a calm and more sophisticated exchange of opinions on strategic problems, and the SPD began to offer positive suggestions about ways to enhance the deterrence posture of the Western alliance. At the 1960 party convention, which chose Willy Brandt as the SPD candidate for chancellor, the Socialists fully endorsed NATO; even atomic armaments had apparently lost their starkest terror. The Socialists primarily objected to an independent West German nuclear policy, arguing for a "sensible distribution of tasks" within NATO, but they were not averse to increasing German influence over nuclear policy in NATO councils.

After the 1961 elections,* in which the Socialists had made some gains, Brandt declared that "our nation has a natural interest in the fact that decisions concerning the life or death of our nation cannot be made without consulting our own Government," but counseled a "certain reserve" to protect the reputation of the fledgling German democracy; he suggested that the question of furnishing NATO with nuclear weapons should be decided on the basis of "political prudence and military expediency."[7] The real victors in the elections—the Free Democrats—were moving in the same direction. When the FDP joined the CDU/CSU in the uneasy coalition of 1961, it also began to reverse its position on military-strategic matters, and rejected the go-it-alone approach it had toyed with previously. The 1962 FDP Düsseldorf conference fully endorsed NATO and West German defense planning.†

---

* The results of the 1961 elections were as follows:

	PERCENTAGE OF VOTES	BUNDESTAG SEATS
CDU/CSU	45.3	242
SPD	36.2	190
FDP	12.8	67
DP, BHE [a]	2.8	—
Extreme Right	0.8	—
Neutralists	1.9	—
Others	0.2	—
Total	100.0	499

Percentage of electorate voting 87.7

The Cabinet Cabinet established consisted of 16 members of the CDU/CSU (including the Chancellor) and 6 members of the FDP.

[a] The DP and the BHE merged in April 1961 to form the All-German Party (GDP).

† The developing consensus on the major strategic line for Bonn was apparently supported by public opinion. Surveys indicate that by 1962 the public's confidence in NATO as a protective shield against the Soviet Union had significantly increased, and there was evidence that the popular attitude on the

By 1963, the SPD regarded itself as the true champion of NATO. The Socialists urged Adenauer to resist de Gaulle's disruptive NATO policies, and they even expressed sympathetic understanding of the problems Washington faced in trying to retain the credibility of the American nuclear deterrent through a doctrine of flexibility. In fact, the Socialists now argued that an effective Western deterrence system required the strengthening of conventional forces. While the Adenauer government was highly critical of the McNamara doctrine and was beginning to question some of NATO's military planning, the Socialists and the Free Democrats were coming much closer to the American position—not so much because they were fully persuaded by its military-strategic rationale, but because they viewed NATO as a restraint on Bonn and Paris. The Socialists feared that de Gaulle would succeed in persuading Adenauer to place Germany's security under the protection of the French rather than the American nuclear umbrella, and they were deeply disturbed by the go-it-alone approach to which the right wing of the CDU/CSU seemed attracted. It was somewhat ironic that at a time when Adenauer began to entertain serious misgivings about the Kennedy Administration's revamping of American strategic doctrine his most vociferous critics belatedly endorsed his earlier unqualified support of NATO.*

These changes in the Socialists' and Free Democrats' attitude

---

presence of American troops in West Germany was even more positive than it had been in 1958. Half the respondents, however, rejected nuclear arms for the Bundeswehr, and only 28 per cent indicated approval. Nonetheless, the comparable figures five years previously had been 72 per cent and 13 per cent. (*DIVO-Pressedienst,* Frankfurt, Apr. 1 and Aug. 11, 1962.)

* Raymond Aron (in *The Great Debate,* p. 90), suggested that the Socialists apparently understood fully that "the United States was forced to give up the doctrine of massive retaliation," and that:

"European nations acquiring national deterrents—i.e., limited and vulnerable forces—will have to follow suit for identical and even more compelling reasons. . . . The Social Democrats seem inclined towards this view, the practical implementation of which points toward Western reinforcement in conventional arms—that is, parity at all levels."

toward NATO were accompanied by opposition to the government's European policy, which restricted the membership of the Common Market, and by misgivings about the close relationship between Adenauer and de Gaulle. De Gaulle had agreed to support Adenauer's hard line vis-à-vis the Soviet bloc if Adenauer would support de Gaulle's "little Europe" policy. This was distasteful to the SPD, because it opposed the goals of both de Gaulle and Adenauer—the Socialists, still hoping that the polycentric trends within the Soviet bloc might lead to reunification, favored a much more flexible policy toward the Soviet Union and Eastern Europe; and they were also highly critical of de Gaulle's attempts to restrict the membership of the Common Market and gain a position of leadership among the Six.

The anti-de Gaulle dimension of the Socialists' policy was clearly reflected in their attitude toward the Common Market. From the beginning, the SPD's reaction to the EEC had been extremely cautious. The Socialists believed that the EEC was too restricted geographically, and they were concerned that German membership would further deepen the division of Germany. They also criticized the minister of economics, Ludwig Erhard, for objecting to the full equalization of social service payments among EEC members (which would have benefited German recipients), and for obstructing the proposal that the Six should pursue a common economic policy. The SPD's position was a difficult one, and its reaction was equivocal. On one hand, the Socialists had little interest in further strengthening a "little Europe" construct that would give power to the conservative elements in Western Europe and highlight the division of Europe and the split of Germany; on the other hand, it was politically risky to attack the government's proven economic policy, and the SPD entertained hopes that the EEC could be turned into a supranational organization for economic planning. In the end, the Socialists announced that they welcomed extension of the ECSC common market beyond coal and steel, provided (1) that the inclusion of other countries' overseas territories would not saddle the Federal Republic with a colonial policy, (2) that the border between East and West Germany would not become a customs border creating an even deeper division of Germany, (3) that the German tariff level would not be raised excessively, so that German exports and domestic price stability would not be endangered, (4) that membership in the Common Market would be opened to all countries in order to avoid a further division of Europe, and (5) that Euratom would exclusively serve the peaceful uses of atomic energy, and that the whole community would retain property rights to all fissionable material.

Some of the Socialists' misgivings were shared by important German political and commercial circles. The German business community was far from united in assessing the implications of the EEC. One element saw in the EEC great opportunities for exploiting a large "internal" European market, while another group, for whom Ludwig Erhard and the Free Democrats became the spokesmen, feared the loss of markets outside the EEC—which was to be expected because of a higher common external tariff that would primarily benefit France. This group was not impressed with the Europeanists' argument that the Common Market could lead to the political integration of the Six, but rather was afraid that Great Britain and the Scandinavian countries would be excluded indefinitely. The Erhard group also objected to the increase in German social security costs that would result from their standardization among the Six and would add to the contributions that German entrepreneurs were making already. Furthermore, prominent businessmen were suspicious of the Common Market because of its possibilities for economic planning, and some opposed it because it included the loss of tariff protection. Farmers were particularly alarmed by the threat of losing the tariff protection that had traditionally shielded them from foreign competition.

The cross-pressures felt by industrial interests, and the fears of agricultural interests, raised some intricate political questions. For one, Erhard's supporters in the CDU/CSU (who did not share the ardent Europeanism of some Adenauer supporters and who were not overly enthusiastic about the restrictive nature of the EEC) came very close to the FDP on this issue, and the dividing line between the FDP and the CDU's Erhard group became fuzzier. Agricultural interests had a powerful spokesman not only in the Bavarian CSU but also among some elements of the fragmented FDP—and moreover, they were being courted by the Socialists, who were seeking to overcome their traditional handicap in rural areas.

These complex and overlapping interest calculations became even more pronounced after the establishment of the British-led European Free Trade Association. Again, the SPD, the FDP, and the Erhard supporters in the CDU/CSU—a somewhat incongruous "coalition"—pressed for Britain's admission to the Common Market and warned that the reduction of tariffs within EFTA and EEC, coupled with the common external EEC tariff, would lead to tension between the two economic groupings and would, in addition, push up the price level in Germany. All the elements of this grouping were careful, however, not to give the impression that they did not identify with EEC objectives—as long as these objectives did not preclude a union with larger membership.

Clearly, the SPD's international economic policy was by now close not only to the position of the FDP and some elements in the CDU but also to that of the United States: although Washington supported the EEC rather than EFTA for political-strategic reasons, the Kennedy Administration nonetheless favored a less exclusive Common Market (because an economic split of non-Communist Europe would aggravate American balance-of-payments problems and undermine the economic foundations of the Grand Design). Furthermore, the preference for a larger Common Market shared by the Socialists, Free Democrats, and liberal Christian Democrats dovetailed neatly with their support of NATO and their opposition to de Gaulle's design for a Western European construct under French hegemony and under a French-led European nuclear protectorate. Although not intrinsically anti-French, these divergent groups were much less willing than Adenauer to make gracious allowances for de Gaulle's foreign policy, which was disrupting the Western alliance and which they perceived to be contrary to Germany's political, economic, and military-strategic interests. They were all opposed, on political as well as economic and military-strategic grounds, to de Gaulle's design for a European order under French leadership; they called for Britain's membership in the Common Market; they agreed that the cause of German unity required a more flexible and imaginative policy toward the Soviet Union and Eastern Europe; they favored an enlightened and undoctrinaire security policy, based on close cooperation with NATO and the United States; and they all wanted a change of regime in Bonn. It was on this basis that the Socialists, the Free Democrats, and the liberal wing of the CDU established a tenuous, implicit, partial—but nonetheless important—consensus.

Most fundamentally, of course, the impulses for the political realignments in Bonn came from changes in the international system. The blurring of previously polarized positions on political-economic as well as military-strategic issues stemmed in part from the apparent hopelessness of the unification issue and from the gradual fragmentation of the Western alliance, whose concerted actions and harmony of purpose had been the prerequisite for the domestic as well as the international success of Adenauer's foreign policy program. As it gradually became necessary to choose between Washington and Paris, a longstanding incongruence of purpose within the governing coalitions and the CDU could no longer be contained. The disagreements between the United States and France not only created serious problems for Bonn's foreign policy but, because of the sensitivity of the West German political process to external influences, undermined Adenauer's domestic support on foreign policy issues, even within his own party.*

---

* Most likely, Adenauer was saved from becoming politically isolated at an earlier date by the doctrinaire rigidity of the Socialist opposition. For example, at a time when the CDU/CSU was going through a most serious internal crisis as a result of Adenauer's cynical manipulations of the presidential succession, the SPD had separated itself more than ever from the parliamentary majority by proposing, with its 1959 Germany Plan, a unification program that was so accommodating to the Soviet Union it could not even marshal the

By 1962, the most ardent European integrationists—former Foreign Minister Heinrich von Brentano, Walter Hallstein, the group around Adenauer, and several other prominent figures in Bonn—found themselves beleaguered from many quarters, including their own party. (In fact, after the 1961 elections, Brentano had been replaced by Gerhard Schröder as Foreign Minister, because the Free Democrats insisted that the CDU make a pro-Atlantic gesture before agreeing to join in a coalition with it.) From the beginning, the Protestant liberal wing of the heterogeneous CDU/CSU held values different from Adenauer's, and it was not enthusiastically committed to the "little Europe" idea. With the United States and France diverging on military-strategic, political, and economic matters, the choices required of Bonn stirred in the CDU a full-fledged controversy, which was led by a group that had long suffered under Adenauer's authoritarian regime.

In spite of the formidable opposition that had developed against Adenauer's inflexible Cold War stance and his support of de Gaulle, his position was not completely isolated. The conservatives and the devoted Cold Warriors of the CDU/CSU rallied to his cause; and one should not underestimate the strength of highly placed CDU and CSU politicians who sympa-

---

support of all elements in the SPD. At the height of the "succession crisis," Fritz René Allemann said: "The CDU's automatic instinct to support at once the foreign policy arguments of the man who had just dealt it a severe blow —in spite of the party's rebelliousness and disenchantment—seems to be the immediate and necessary consequences of the procrustean policies of the leading opposition party. The more radically the opposition alienates itself from the 'Adenauer state,' the more it relinquishes the opportunity to exploit the fragmentation of the groups that consider this state their own. . . . All thrusts against the chancellor hit a void, as long as there is suspicion that these thrusts are aimed not only at his domestic political regime but also at the core of his foreign policy conception—the insoluble bond between the Federal Republic and the Western alliance." (Allemann, *Stabilität und Krise,* p. 63.)

This phenomenon may also account for the electoral success of the Free Democrats in 1961. Although the Socialists had also gained, it was primarily the FDP that profited from the apparent disenchantment with Adenauer's overall policy program.

thized with de Gaulle—either because they believed de Gaulle held the key to European integration or because they wished to emulate his assertive stance vis-à-vis Washington and Moscow. It was de Gaulle himself, however, who alienated his supporters in Bonn. De Gaulle's hostility toward genuine integrative measures among the Six had put off even the most patient and forbearing Europeanists in Bonn, and his apparent intention of relegating the Federal Republic to a secondary role in European power politics was unacceptable to German Gaullists like Franz-Josef Strauss—who might have been willing to participate in a genuine Franco-German codetermination policy.

The attrition in Bonn of Adenauer's foreign policy support was accelerated by the erosion of his personal authority. In 1959, Adenauer had displayed a good deal of cynicism and lack of respect for the democratic institutions of the West German state when he vacillated about whether he wished to succeed Theodor Heuss to the largely ceremonial office of President of the Republic. Adenauer's power plays during that episode—which were obviously designed to perpetuate his influence on foreign policy in the event of his retirement as chancellor—cost him a good deal of support and prestige not only in political circles but among the people. After the 1961 elections, these developments came to a head. The FDP had made considerable gains (at the expense of the CDU/CSU, since the Socialists had also gained) and now insisted that they would only rejoin the governing coalition if Adenauer agreed to relinquish the chancellorship by 1963. Precarious to begin with, the 1961 coalition collapsed after a year in the wake of the uproar caused by the so-called *Spiegel* Affair. During this unsavory episode, leading staff members of the weekly magazine *Der Spiegel*—long a gadfly to the government and especially to Defense Minister Franz-Josef Strauss—were arrested for publishing allegedly secret evaluations of West Germany's and NATO's military preparedness. The arrests were carried out in a manner reminiscent of Nazi methods, and led to the resignation of Strauss, who had worked behind the scenes to engineer the clamp-down on *Der Spiegel*.

The FDP was finally persuaded to rejoin a reshuffled Cabinet

—after Adenauer had threatened to create a "grand coalition" between the CDU/CSU and the SPD; but although the Free Democrats were restrained for the time being, the internal cohesion of the CDU/CSU had been shaken fundamentally. Adenauer was a lame-duck chancellor, and in 1963 could not even prevent the chancellorship from going to Ludwig Erhard, whom Adenauer had opposed and openly humiliated all along, warning that he was insufficiently astute in international affairs and lacking in political acumen, vision, and experience.

1963–1966

In some significant ways, the partial and tentative consensus that had emerged in Bonn by 1963 on foreign policy matters was symbolized in the person of the new chancellor. Ludwig Erhard was the very embodiment of Germany's successful quest for normalcy. He was the patron saint of the "economic miracle," and his appeal to voters had been an important factor in his selection as the CDU's choice for chancellor. He was obviously less authoritarian than Adenauer, and he had himself suffered from the high-handedness with which his predecessor gradually alienated even his supporters. He represented the pro-Atlantic consensus (manifested in staunch support of NATO and of a wider membership in the Common Market) that reached across Bonn's political spectrum, and he seemed to favor a less doctrinaire and more flexible policy toward the Soviet Union and the countries of Eastern Europe.

On the surface it would seem as if this rudimentary consensus would have provided Bonn with a long-sought opportunity to face foreign policy issues with resolution and on a secure foundation of domestic support. Several factors, however, worked in the opposite direction. First, after more than a decade of high-pitched and abrasive controversy over foreign policy, many West Germans clearly welcomed the more pragmatic and less ideological discourse produced by the partial consensus on foreign policy issues. The abating of the foreign policy contest seemed to offer a chance for turning West Germany's political energies inward, taking them out of the grip of the international system. This seemed especially pertinent since the fiction (embodied even in the Basic Law) that the Federal Republic was only a political-institutional "provisorium," a temporary way-station on the road to a unified German state, clearly had become untenable. Moreover, the two major political issues that went beyond the confines of the Federal Republic and that had commanded intense emotional commitment—reunification and European integration—obviously had to be shelved for the foreseeable future. Replacing Adenauer—for whom economic and purely domestic matters had always been of secondary importance—with a trained economist who had no particular experience or interest in foreign policy poignantly symbolized this attempt to turn away from external affairs.

It soon became apparent, however, that the international environment was as intrusive and compelling as it had been before, and moreover that it continued to evoke divisive responses in Bonn. The biggest obstacle to galvanizing the partial consensus on foreign policy matters into effective policy making was the widening conflict between the United States and France in the middle 1960s. As it became clear that Erhard was inclined (as well as induced by circumstances) to support Washington rather than Paris, the consensus that had been in the making proved insufficiently broad, because it did not fully encompass important elements of the majority party, the CDU/CSU. A new polarization of political viewpoints soon developed, but in contrast to the polarization of the 1950s, it reached within as well as across party lines, since both the "Gaullist" and "Atlanticist" viewpoints were most effectively represented within the CDU/CSU.

This was not really surprising. Ever since 1949, wholehearted support for Adenauer's pro-Western policy had served as an important bond among various CDU/CSU elements that differed significantly on other issues; and this bond had been strengthened by the realization that the CDU/CSU's electoral successes could largely be attributed to this pro-Western orientation, which had proved to be so beneficial for Germany's political and economic rehabilitation. When the premise for Adenauer's policy—a cohesive Atlantic community—collapsed, so did the foundations for the CDU/CSU's internal harmony, with important implications for the political future of the party. As a consequence of the party's internal division, the pro-Atlantic policies pursued by Erhard, Foreign Minister Gerhard Schröder, and Defense Minister Kai-Uwe von Hassel, were backed by a majority of SPD and FDP Bundestag members, but they ran into opposition from within the CDU/CSU. The "Gaullists" of the party—Franz-Josef Strauss (Adenauer's former Defense Minister and head of the powerful CSU), Bundestag Speaker Eugen Gerstenmeier, the CSU's foreign policy expert Karl von Guttenberg, and Adenauer himself (who still acted as party chairman)—held strategic positions of influence, they could count on the support of the Catholic and conservative elements in their party, and their hand was further strengthened by Erhard's inept handling of day-to-day political matters.

At the core of the Gaullists' disagreement with the Atlanticists was a considerable disenchantment with the United States. Especially Adenauer and Strauss prided themselves on their Realpolitik, and they felt that the national interests of Germany had been increasingly slighted by the Kennedy and Johnson Administrations. The Gaullists believed that the globally oriented detente policy of the Kennedy Administration implied Washington's readiness to make deals with the Soviet Union over the heads of Europe and Germany; and that by contrast de Gaulle's foreign policy concept, precisely because it sought to maximize the leverage of Europe in a future multipolar world, held out much greater promise for the resolution of German foreign policy problems. For these reasons, the Gaullists were highly sympathetic to de Gaulle's attempts to fashion a more independent role for Europe in world politics, a role based on close Franco-German cooperation and sustained by the economic and military potential of the Common Market membership. Not surprisingly, they were unenthusiastic about the prospect of British membership in the EEC, and gave only perfunctory support to the government's policies for enlarging the Common Market.

The rapid deterioration of Franco-German relations and Erhard's lack of success in Washington, especially with respect to the MLF (discussed in Chapter One) aggravated these tensions within the CDU/CSU. Moreover, the Gaullists opposed Erhard not only because of what they viewed as his misguided and naive pro-Atlantic policy but also because of the government's more flexible Eastern policy (largely initiated by Schröder), which they regarded as similarly lacking in realism and determination. The Gaullists were much more closely identified, by conviction as well as by past association, with the orthodox Cold War position of the Adenauer years; and the concept of a loose "community" of Eastern and Western European states, which seemed to serve as the basis of their reunification policy, clearly implied a weakening of the Soviet position in Eastern Europe. In particular, they opposed any modifications of the Hallstein Doctrine and the official government position on the Oder-Neisse border issue, and they generally followed a hard-line policy toward the East German regime.

While Erhard and Schröder were attacked by the Gaullists within their own party for making a dangerous "opening to the East," they were chided by their coalition partners, the Free Democrats—led by Erich Mende, Vice-Chancellor, Minister of All-German Affairs, and a longtime opponent of Strauss—for not making the opening wide enough. Going beyond the "small steps" approach favored by Schröder, the FDP's March 1965 party conference coined the slogan "medium steps," and called for the modification of the Hallstein Doctrine to permit the establishment of diplomatic relations with Eastern Europe. Although the Free Democrats were conservative on economic and social issues and in favor of the government's Common Market policy, the FDP's abiding commitment to a dynamic reunification policy led them to attack their coalition partners' hesitant gestures toward Eastern Europe much more stridently than did the Socialist opposition. In fact, the Socialists were stressing "bipartisanship" in foreign affairs. The SPD leadership was determined to completely eradicate in the voters' minds the idea that the party was less security-conscious or pro-NATO than the CDU/CSU, and party spokesmen generally refused to be drawn into the Atlanticist-Gaullist controversy, arguing that Bonn should try not to incur the enmity of either Washington or Paris.

Even so, the SPD remained in the foreground of the increasing debate on the German question that took place in Bonn during the middle 1960s. In the spring and summer of 1966, the SPD participated in an abortive attempt to arrange for an exchange of speakers between East and West Germany; and the Socialists—along with the Free Democrats, a large number of publicists, intellectuals, church groups, and others—continued with their efforts to keep the German question alive in the public's consciousness. Almost all political groups agreed that the changing international circumstances, especially in the Soviet bloc, required new initiatives in Bonn; but they disagreed on how far, and in what direction, Bonn's revised reunification policy should go. In particular, there was a good deal of discussion about the place that East Germany should occupy in Bonn's policy calculations. On the Left, critics of the government's official Eastern policy argued that it would prove ineffective unless Bonn also revised its orthodox position on the Oder-Neisse line and the Munich Pact, and they especially objected to the attempted isolation of East Germany, which seemed to be an essential part of Schröder's "little steps" program for a rapprochement with Eastern Europe. Instead, they favored increased contacts with East Germany, even on an official level, in order to avoid widening the gap and to encourage the liberalization of the East German regime.

The unification proposals made by the different political groups varied considerably, especially with respect to how far Bonn should go to accommodate the demands made by East Germany. Generally, however, critics on the Left realized that their recommended policy, even if it stopped short of recognizing East Germany, could strengthen—at least in the short run—the international and domestic position of the Ulbricht government. But they felt that Bonn's policy toward Pankow should in any case be directed primarily at the younger, up-and-coming party functionaries in East Germany rather than at the entrenched hard-line Ulbricht hierarchy, in the hope that the more pragmatic orientation of this "counter elite" would sooner or later become the dominant voice of East German politics.[8]

Although the dialogue on the Left had no immediately visible impact on government policy, the opposition on the Right was doubly effective because of its leverage in both the Cabinet and the CDU/CSU. As already noted, the Gaullists were determined to restrain the moderately progressive Eastern policy of Erhard and Schröder, and in 1966 they obstructed the establishment of diplomatic relations with Rumania, they resisted opportunities for exploratory talks with Czechoslovakia on the same issue, and they prevailed upon the government to modify the conciliatory language of Erhard's "Peace Note." Frequently, the conservatives expressed their deep suspicion of the Communists by taking recourse to the legalistic certitudes of the Hallstein Doctrine and the Federal Republic's claim to "sole representation," or by resigned realism—for example, Strauss declared in the spring of 1966 that he could not conceive of how a reunited German state could come into being under present or foreseeable circumstances.

Although public opinion seemed open enough on the question of a more flexible German policy, the CDU/CSU remained largely immobilized; and the SPD and FDP were careful to avoid taking a controversial stand on an issue with such doubtful domestic political ramifications. Had it not been for the intermittent voice of more adventurous groups within the SPD and FDP, the leadership of both parties would have been content to discuss Bonn's relations with East Germany outside the context of the political process and remove the issue from the election campaign of 1965. Peter Bender, a commentator who himself favored a conciliatory attitude toward East Germany, caustically remarked in 1966:

> The only way to introduce a new policy in the Federal Republic is to guarantee that it is merely the continuation of an old one. It is true that most politicians think it important not to appear dogmatic. Lately, also, several have made themselves the spokesmen for a revision of Bonn's reunification ideology. Thus Erich Mende, minister of All-German affairs, declared: "We cannot in the year 1966 pursue a reunification policy with the platitudes and clichés of the fifties." And Willy Brandt, Burgomaster of Berlin, said at the SPD conference in June: "Our situation does not permit us to treat sham formulas like sacred cows—as both inviolable and useless." Yet whatever Mende and Brandt

may have meant, expressions such as "platitudes," "clichés," "sham formulas" keep open a secure line of retreat into the safe pastures of orthodoxy. The confusing contradictions between words and deeds in current German politics can be satisfactorily explained only if they are seen as the interplay, the confrontation, and finally the complete confusion between old and new policies.[9]

The lines between the government and the opposition were blurred. The CDU/CSU (and to some extent also the FDP, its coalition partner) not only played the role of the party in power but also acted as the unofficial opposition on some major foreign policy issues, while the official opposition, the SPD, shared several of the government's policy preferences and tried to straddle the fence on the issues that divided the majority party. It may well be that the resulting ambiguity of party images was of considerable help to the CDU/CSU in the lackluster 1965 election campaign, since Erhard proved to be a very formidable vote-getter and since the party almost regained the absolute majority it had lost in 1961.* In 1965, in contrast to previous years, a vote for the CDU/CSU expressed ambivalence about foreign policy and could be interpreted as a refusal to choose either a pro-Atlantic or pro-Gaullist position.

More interesting than the election itself were the negotiations over the formation of a new government that followed it. There

* The results of the 1965 elections were as follows:

	PERCENTAGE OF VOTES	BUNDESTAG SEATS
CDU/CSU	47.6	245
SPD	39.3	202
FDP	9.5	49
NPD	2.0	—
German Peace Union	1.3	—
Others	0.3	—
Total	100.0	496

Percentage of electorate voting 86.8

The Cabinet established consisted of 16 members of the CDU/CSU (including the Chancellor), 5 members of the FDP, and one non-party member.

was of course no question that Erhard would continue as chancellor—at least for the time being. But largely because of the blurring lines between government and opposition, for the first time the possibility of a Grand Coalition between Christian Democrats and the Socialists was seriously considered. Moreover, although the immediate intent was probably tactical, Franz-Josef Strauss's threat to remove the CSU from its long-standing association with the CDU and enlarge it from a regional Bavarian party into a national party did not lack a certain plausibility: it would have supplied the "Gaullist" constituency with a nationwide political instrument and offered the CDU/CSU voters a genuine choice on the major foreign policy issues of the 1960s. Although in the end the traditional CDU/CSU-FDP coalition was reestablished (with Schröder continuing as Foreign Minister, mainly because the FDP strongly opposed Strauss, who wanted to succeed him), this was widely viewed as an interim solution, because Erhard's ineffectiveness as chancellor had already mobilized his rivals within the CDU/CSU in a contest over who would succeed him. Erhard's prestige in Bonn had suffered so much that at the very moment of his party's electoral triumph, to which he contributed substantially, his rivals were making plans to topple him.

The jockeying for position in Bonn led to a curious and paradoxical interplay between domestic and foreign policy considerations. In their determination to ultimately wrest power from Erhard and preclude Schröder from succeeding him, it was the Gaullists (Strauss, Guttenberg, Gerstenmeier, and Adenauer) rather than the Atlanticists who flirted with the prospect of a Grand Coalition with the Socialists—even though the foreign policy conceptions of the SPD were much closer to the Erhard-Schröder line on Atlantic policy and to the FDP line on Eastern policy, and hence in conflict with the preferences of the Gaullists. By contrast, Erhard, Schröder, and von Hassel feared that a Grand Coalition with the Socialists, although relatively acceptable to them from the viewpoint of foreign policy matters, would lead to the absorption of their power in a conglomerate "national front." Nor could the FDP be expected to welcome the prospect of a Grand Coalition—or for that matter, an all-party coalition. The FDP—constantly afraid it would fall below the five per cent of the vote required for representation in the Bundestag, and threatened with exclusion by proposed changes in the electoral law—needed to maintain its "third party" image and leverage in order to survive, even though the major foreign policy lines of a CDU/CSU-SPD Grand Coalition would probably have proven acceptable.

Clearly, all this contrasted with the situation in the 1950s—when the line dividing the government from the opposition was sharp, when foreign policy preferences generally complemented domestic policy preferences and power calculations, and when these various aspects were articulated by specific parties in fairly clear-cut confrontations. Moreover, the intricate patterns of alignment and opposition in the 1960s, and their connections with domestic and foreign policy considerations, were in a sense doubly involuted. The unpleasant necessity of supporting either Washington or Paris led to a polarization of viewpoints that bore some similarities to the polarization of the 1950s. But the very fact that the polarization of the 1960s developed over somewhat different issues—reflecting important transformations of the international system—meant that the constituency of one of the opposing viewpoints, the Atlanticist, was dispersed over a wide political spectrum, and was thus denied the political "institutionalization" it might have gained through being enunciated by one political party. (The location of the Gaullist constituency primarily within one party was no exception to this pattern of noninstitutionalization of viewpoints, since it was compensated for by the fact that the CDU/CSU was also a major spokesman for the Atlanticist orientation.)

This phenomenon had a contradictory influence on the power calculations of various groups and personalities in Bonn. On the one hand, the blurring of the lines between government and opposition made for a greater readiness (as compared to the 1950s) to adjust foreign policy preferences to gain domestic political advantage—a process which was further eased by the pragmatism that had replaced the ideological exertions of the 1950s.

All elements of the political spectrum sought, in an almost promiscuous way, to entice more or less likely bedfellows to join them in small or grand coalitions. On the other hand, the substantive foreign policy disagreements that divided the Atlanticists and the Gaullists in the CDU/CSU were sharpened by the Gaullists' efforts to dislodge the chancellor, forcing both sides to enunciate foreign policy preferences that were based on significant misreadings of the international system. Even though there was a genuine conflict between the United States and France, the positions of the Atlanticists and Gaullists in Bonn were not truly aligned with the positions of Washington and Paris. The domestic alignments on foreign policy issues in Bonn were forming around alternatives that had no real counterparts in the international environment. The apparent foreign policy interests of the Federal Republic—whether interpreted by the Atlanticists or the Gaullists—were no longer fully compatible with those of either the United States or France. As Fritz René Allemann has pointed out:

> The "Gaullists," while eager to move closer to Paris, did not at all see eye to eye with President de Gaulle's Eastern European policies and were rather frightened by his visions of a Greater Europe embracing the Communist East. The "Atlanticists" were lured by the dream of German participation in nuclear defense and of a kind of "special relationship" between the United States and the Federal Republic, even long after it had become clear that Washington had dropped the MLF concept and was as interested as de Gaulle himself in furthering an understanding with the Soviet Union and with Moscow's Eastern European allies. To a large extent, the controversy between these schools of opinion was something like a tragi-comedy of errors: the German clients of France and America still fought out battles which their foreign friends had already abandoned. In reality, however, these battles only masked a fight for power which had little to do with ideological labels.[10]

The complexities of this situation, and the inherent difficulty of dealing with them, would have proven a substantial challenge for any chancellor. Erhard, handicapped by a divided party and coalition as well as by his personal shortcomings, was rapidly losing his grip on the decision-making process in Bonn. His insecure political position severely hampered the government in addressing domestic as well as international problems, and led to a temporizing over decisions to which Erhard was prone in any case.

Throughout 1966, a series of political misfortunes befell Erhard and led inexorably to his forced resignation late in the year. In foreign affairs, where skillful manipulation and a judicious balancing of conflicting courses of action was required, Erhard's diplomacy seemed to consist almost entirely of pro-Atlantic gestures and occasional pro-de Gaulle rhetoric, sustained primarily by good will and personal bonhomie. He had failed to persuade the Johnson Administration to come around to the German viewpoint on the MLF, Franco-German relations were at their lowest point since the establishment of the Federal Republic, and the government's halfhearted overtures to Eastern Europe only annoyed the right wing of the CDU/CSU without particularly impressing the Free Democrats or the Socialists.

On domestic issues, things were not going much better. For the first time since the launching of the economic miracle, a serious recession hit West Germany, causing unemployment and aggravating budgetary and fiscal problems. Increases in tax revenues, which were necessary to continue financing generous social programs, did not materialize; and Erhard alienated many of his supporters through his inept handling of economic and budgetary matters, in which he was supposed to be an expert. The disenchantment with the hapless chancellor among voters as well as among party politicians was powerfully demonstrated in the June 1966 North Rhine-Westphalia state election: Erhard's personal campaigning for the CDU ticket apparently contributed to the Socialists' finishing first with almost 50 per cent of the vote. Since he was selected by the CDU/CSU primarily for his vote-getting abilities, the chancellor's days in office were clearly numbered.

The disquieting electoral gains achieved by the radical rightist National Democratic Party (NPD) in regional elections during 1965 and 1966—which many commentators connected with the attrition of authority in Bonn—and a "management crisis" in the Defense Ministry in the early fall added to Erhard's difficulties. When he returned in the fall of 1966 from his trip to Washington without having gained a reduction or even delay of the German offset payments commitment, the last remnants of the chancellor's prestige evaporated. The immediate occasion for Erhard's demise—the resignation of the FDP ministers over budgetary matters in October 1966—was only the trigger and not the cause of the Erhard Administration's collapse.

1966–1969

In December 1966, the Christian Democrats and the Social Democrats for the first time since the establishment of the Federal Republic joined forces in a national coalition government, which gave them an overwhelming majority—447 out of 496 seats in the Bundestag.

From the beginning, the coalition was an uneasy one. It was, as Willy Brandt put it, neither a love match nor a shotgun wedding, but a marriage of convenience. For the CDU/CSU, it was convenient largely because the party was unable to patch up its differences with the FDP, its long-time coalition partner, and some party leaders were afraid that the centrifugal tendencies already existing within the party might lead to its disintegration in the role of opposition. The Socialists, who had not for 36 years participated in a national German government, were anxious to dispel the electorate's lingering suspicions that the party's Marxist past and the stridency of its opposition in the 1950s rendered it incapable of governing responsibly;* and they viewed the FDP, which suffered from internal divisions, as a somewhat unreliable

---

* Although it is somewhat overstated, there is a good deal of truth in Jürgen Lorenz's assertion that: "In a country one part of which is being oppressed by marxist-type Socialists quite a few people are even suspicious of democratic socialists. Morever, socialism is equated with a planned economy. The man on the street sees a planned economy in terms of the war and immediate post-war years. Communism, planned economy, two inflations—those are the roots of the suspicions entertained by the majority of Germans against 'the Left'." ("Germany after Erhard—An Analysis," *Atlantic Community Quarterly*, 5/1967, pp. 67–68.)

coalition partner, which might cause considerable embarrassment to a Socialist chancellor. Of course, the formation of a SPD/FDP "mini-coalition"—it would have commanded a very slim majority —might have led to a rather pronounced new departure in foreign policy, but it would have suffered from the difference between the Socialists and the Free Democrats over economic and fiscal policy. For essentially domestic political reasons, an authentic alternative to previous foreign policy orientations was thus precluded.

The wisdom of joining the two largest parties in a coalition government was widely questioned within and without both parties. Aside from some political misgivings and ideological considerations, which had to be weighed by the two parties against the anticipated advantages, there was the serious question of how the absence of an effective opposition would affect the democratic process—and in this respect, the Austrian example was not reassuring.[11] But the extensive deliberations and negotiations that preceded the formation of the new government—during which all parties considered the possibility of joining in all possible coalition arrangements—also demonstrated the growing pragmatism and de-ideologization of the West German political process, and the parties' willingness to adjust their policy preferences to political advantage.

This is not to say that substantive political questions—in domestic as well as in foreign affairs—did not figure prominently in the parties' deliberations. In fact, the major justification for the Grand Coalition was that a joint effort by the two major parties could lead to a resolution of major political problems that were confronting Germany: Bonn's foreign policy was in complete disarray; the attrition of governmental authority and the feeling of political drift under Erhard had led to widespread demands for a stronger government; the radical-right National Democratic Party had made significant gains in the Länder election of Hesse and Bavaria (where, for the first time, it gained representation in the state parliaments); there was a serious economic and budgetary crisis; and such crucial issues as amending the Basic Law to guarantee a two-party system and to reform the fiscal relationships between the Federal government and the Länder governments not only called for a measure of bipartisanship and a willingness to accept joint political responsibility but also required, under the constitution, a two-thirds majority in the Bundestag. With respect to issues, as F. R. Allemann put it:

> The CDU facilitated the deal by accepting the main planks in the SPD platform: an economic policy geared to new expansion rather than rigid deflationary restrictions, a foreign policy based on international detente including the renunciation of nuclear ambitions by the Federal Republic and a readiness to accept, in principle, diplomatic relations with all Communist States which did not put up unacceptable preconditions, and a more elastic policy towards East Germany, including Government contacts short of recognition. In addition, it conceded to its new partners nine ministries out of nineteen, among them the Foreign Office, the Ministry for All-German Affairs, and, in the home field, the key Departments of Economics and Justice. The understanding arrived at made clear, moreover, that the Grand Coalition was not meant to be permanent.[12]

The final composition of the new government reflected the precarious balance struck among various party wings, policy orientations, and personalities. Kurt Georg Kiesinger, the CDU/CSU's choice for the chancellorship, was a compromise candidate. His candidacy was helped considerably by the fact that his tenure since 1958 as minister-president of Baden-Württemberg (before that he had been a CDU foreign policy expert in the Bundestag) had allowed him to abstain from the party's national disagreements, especially disagreements over foreign affairs, where he was acceptable to both Gaullists and Atlanticists. He also obtained the important support of Franz-Josef Strauss, head of the powerful Bavarian CSU, who thus secured his own return to the Cabinet, from which he had been excluded since the 1962 *Spiegel* Affair. Although many Socialist parliamentarians and party officials would have preferred a mini-coalition with the FDP, and although the leaders were besieged by vociferous rank-and-file members urging them to reconsider, Willy Brandt's position as party leader was at no time seriously challenged. With Kiesinger becoming chancellor, and with Brandt becoming vice-chancellor and foreign minister, there remained the task of distributing the remaining Cabinet posts among the CDU/CSU and SPD leaders. As John Herz notes,

> Some "strong" personalities of both parties failed to make it. The SPD's military expert, Helmut Schmidt, wanted the defense ministry, but it had been conceded to Schröder of the CDU, because he, in turn, had had to yield the foreign office to Brandt. A CDU minister . . . was left out because he happened to be one Catholic too many; his post [minister of expellee affairs] was given to former Defense Minister von Hassel, who had the merit of being a Protestant; and so it went. The final result was a balance of most forces, wings and types of personalities: ultranationalist von Hassel on one side, former neutralist Gustav Heinemann (Justice) on the other; Atlanticist Schröder and Gaullist Strauss [Finance]; probusiness economic liberal Schmücker and trade unionists Katzer and Leber; "intellectuals" like Carlo Schmid [and his SPD party colleague Karl Schiller as minister of economics] and "technicians of power" like Strauss and Paul Lücke (Interior).[13]

In this intricate conglomerate of political orientations, of diverse personalities and personal ambitions, and of disparate power positions, it appeared in the beginning that the SPD had somewhat greater leverage to move policies (perhaps especially foreign policy). But this initial advantage soon evaporated. Kiesinger managed to look like a circumspect and reassuring guide of the new "dynamism" in Bonn, and the gains of the CDU and the losses of the SPD during several 1968 Länder elections seemed to demonstrate that the Socialists were being skillfully outmaneuvered by the CDU, which took credit for the successes the Grand Coalition chalked up after a few years in office.

The achievements of the Grand Coalition were not spectacular. On domestic issues, the only major success of the government was the neo-Keynesian medium-range fiscal policy (the so-called "Mifrifi") with which the SPD Economics Minister Karl Schiller guided West Germany to a new boom after the recession of 1966. (This was accomplished largely by balancing the budget, lowering the central bank rate, and permitting extensive investment write-offs.)[14] The finance reform, which was to have led to a restructuring of the fiscal relationships between the Federal government and the various Länder, turned out to be a watered-down measure that fell far short of an effective solution; the issue of the statute of limitations on war crimes and genocide was resolved with a compromise; and, perhaps most important, the enactment of a new election law based on the single-member district—which would have assured a two-party system and thus eliminated the need for any future coalition government—was shelved for the foreseeable future.*

With respect to foreign policy, the Grand Coalition's major (and most general) endeavor was to enlarge Germany's room for maneuver and instill a measure of realism. But international and domestic factors combined to make it almost impossible to move toward resolving outstanding foreign policy problems. Even during the Erhard Administration, there had been a clear and widespread

* The reasons for failing to enact this legislation were highly complex. Electoral reform would have worked to the disadvantage of incumbent Bundestag members of both major parties, and the Christian Democrats were expected to sustain losses in urban districts and the Socialists in rural (especially Catholic) districts. It was assumed that, on balance, the CDU/CSU would most likely gain an absolute majority under the proposed new system in the 1969 elections; the SPD therefore sought to postpone the effective date of the reform until 1973.

Also, electoral reform would have eliminated not only the radical-right NPD, but also the Free Democrats, who could not expect to carry any district in a single-member district electoral system. The relationship between the Free Democrats and Socialists had improved considerably, however, when the FDP's votes won the SPD's Gustav Heinemann the Presidency of the Republic in the spring of 1969.

Moreover, Gerhard Lehmbruch (in "Ambiguous Coalition," p. 204), is correct in raising the question whether an electoral reform would actually lead to "an authentic system of alternative government." Lehmbruch writes: "Some authors seem to assume [that it would] on the basis of theoretical reasoning founded on the isolation of some variables of electoral behavior. . . . If one considers the remaining institutional and social conditions as well as the established customs for the management of political conflict, one may expect that many important issues will continue to be settled by negotiations among groups rather than by electoral contest and parliamentary majorities."

sense in the Federal Republic that the general principles which had guided German foreign policy during its formative years under Adenauer—principles formulated in a Cold War setting —were inapplicable in a setting of East-West coexistence. The opportunities for a fundamental (if perhaps agonizing) reappraisal that seemed to emerge from a responsible "national front" government thus raised hopes that the new leaders—all of whom were dissatisfied, in one way or another, with Erhard's foreign policy—could formulate new principles and conduct foreign policy in a more dynamic way.*

Such new departures were in fact charted. However, there was a peculiarly deceptive quality about the new options that the international system of the middle 1960s seemed to offer. Compared with the largely bipolar Cold War setting of the 1950s—which imposed such stark and incompatible alternatives on Bonn's decision-makers—the fragmented and fluid setting of the 1960s seemed to offer much more room for maneuver. (It was for not exploiting this apparent maneuverability that many political elements criticized Erhard's foreign policy.) Yet the clear limitations on Bonn's foreign policy during the 1950s were replaced in

---

* Consider, for example, the glowing hopes expressed by Theo Sommer in *Foreign Affairs* (April 1967, p. 477) shortly after the formation of the Grand Coalition: "The German scene has changed beyond recognition. After years of drift and indecision, a new sense of vigor and purpose permeates Bonn . . . [and] only now is there a government that can face the uncertainties of the future with the comforting feeling that its home base is intact. Probably it took the Grand Coalition to provide a reliable parliamentary majority for any policy of innovation and to produce the new style of leadership: relaxed though determined, self-confident but not arrogant, matter-of-fact but imaginative."

Two years later, his hopes had dimmed somewhat: "Even the election on September 28 [1969] will not change the way the political deck is stacked these days and the way the players have devised their strategy. Presumably Kiesinger will be the next chancellor again, and the next coalition will again hoist the black-red [CDU/CSU-SPD] banner. One should not be fooled, however: this is neither a question of [election] percentages, nor a question of personalities, it is simply a question of lack of will for change. One must note this with regret, because any other coalition would be better for state and society than the present one." (*Die Zeit*, June 27, 1969, p. 1.)

the 1960s by a less visible but equally compelling and even more intricate web of restraints, and Bonn's failure to advance its foreign policy goals very effectively stemmed in large part from the continuing intractability of the international environment. However, it looked as if new opportunities were present, and in its early statements the Grand Coalition promised to exploit them. Hopes were high, and when they were dashed by obstacles abroad, they became serious liabilities at home. Karl Kaiser has aptly described this process with respect to Bonn's Eastern policy:

> A policy of involvement in the East that replaces waiting with activism, and resignation to a temporarily inflexible situation with a belief in real opportunities for progress, is particularly vulnerable to failure. A setback of policy that under earlier circumstances could be seen as the product of an impossible situation now becomes clear defeat.[15]

It was (not surprisingly, perhaps) on the question of sharing political responsibility for either success or failure that the Grand Coalition showed its most serious liabilities. Precisely because different groups in Bonn's policy-making apparatus sought to advance foreign policy goals in different directions and through different means, the proponents of new approaches could blame their failure at least in part on compromises—saying that watered-down, halfway measures cannot be expected to show the same results as clear-cut and forceful initiatives.* Moreover, institutional responsibility for the conduct of foreign affairs was blurred. Kiesinger and Brandt were chairmen of their respective parties; and Kiesinger, as chancellor, had the constitutional right to determine the general direction of policy; however, Brandt, in the

* In retrospect, it appears doubtful whether the more thoroughly revamped Eastern policy that the SPD preferred would have produced better results (in light of the events in Czechoslovakia one could even make the opposite argument), but even an impartial commentator, James Richardson, noted in the fall of 1968 that although a total reversal of the Grand Coalition's foreign policy by its critics seemed out of the question, "it's CDU opponents might be strong enough to affect its *nuances* adversely—and these *nuances* may be decisive in the delicate matter of opening relations with East European governments." ("Eastern Policy," p. 383.)

foreign office, was clearly the innovator in foreign policy-making.

It is unlikely that unadulterated new foreign policy strategies would have yielded different results; but in any case, for the present discussion of the domestic context of foreign policy, it matters little. More important, the foreign policy checks-and-balances that were built into the Grand Coalition led to compromises which not only diluted specific policy measures, but fostered an attrition of governmental accountability. Only rarely did the Grand Coalition speak with one voice—which is not really surprising, considering the conflicting foreign policy conceptions that were "institutionalized" within the government. With respect to the reunification issue and the government's new Ostpolitik, at least two opposing views were effectively represented in the Cabinet. As Karl Kaiser wrote in 1968:

> To the first [view], Bismarck's *kleindeutsche Lösung* ["small-German" solution] of a unitarian German state, a *Reich,* remains a relevant model to guide German policy. Its support is diffuse, but there are identifiable pockets of strength among conservative Protestants, older civil servants (notably diplomats), refugees, and the extreme right. The second conception—partly as a reaction to the first—is groping for a different solution of the German problem, if necessary in the form of a radical departure from the concepts of past decades and of former German regimes. Its contours remain somewhat indistinct, but the common factor is a willingness to accept a political organization of Germany based on separate political entities, linked with each other and neighbouring entities in various forms of association, co-operation, confederation, etc. Its supporters can be found particularly among Catholics, Protestants left of centre, and more frequently in the younger generation than in the older.
>
> The impossibility of immediate unification in one state makes the new *Deutschland*—and *Ostpolitik*—acceptable to the "Neo-Bismarckians" and imperative to the reform-minded "associationists." The truce between them is made possible by implementing a policy based on association between the two German states for the *near* future, while proclaiming a unitarian German state as its eventual goal for the *distant* future.[16]

Even before the Soviet invasion of Czechoslovakia—which seriously discredited the underlying assumptions of both these conceptions—the various political viewpoints on the German question represented in the Grand Coalition were working at cross-purposes, with the more conservative CDU/CSU elements acting as a constant brake on the more innovative SPD elements. Most of the Socialists' initiatives—Herbert Wehner's exchange of views with Ulbricht in the press and his intimation that official contacts with the East German regime would be possible should the situation of East Germany evolve along Austrian or even Yugoslav lines, and Willy Brandt's persistent advocacy of a more active Eastern policy—frequently clashed with the orthodox positions held by CDU/CSU conservatives and enshrined in the claim to sole representation, the Hallstein Doctrine, and the refusal to recognize East Germany and existing borders. Although Chancellor Kiesinger himself contributed to Bonn's new initiatives—for example, by communicating directly and semiofficially with the East German prime minister and by implicitly recognizing the East German regime as the effective government of East Germany—he was intrinsically less venturesome than the SPD, and he was kept in check by the more conservative elements within his own party. By 1968, he came out strongly against recognition of East Germany—criticizing the reformists as an *Anerkennungspartei,* a party of recognition—and he felt obliged to specifically dissociate himself from Willy Brandt's call at the SPD party conference of March 1968 for "recognition and respect" (until a peace treaty would settle the issue definitely) of the Oder-Neisse line.*

---

* It was noteworthy, however, that Brandt's suggestion did not cause much of a public stir. Karl Kaiser (in *German Foreign Policy,* p. 45), summarizes public opinion survey data on this issue as follows:

"Asked whether they would 'recognize' the Oder-Neisse line, 19% of the interviewees of an EMNID poll gave affirmative and 51% negative answers (June 1967); asked whether the Germans should 'resign' themselves to the new frontier, a survey of the Allensbach Institute found out that 35% were for and 43% against it (October 1967). But when asked whether the Oder-Neisse line should be 'recognized if, in return, unity were achieved,' 50% were for and 25% against (Allensbach, 1966); the ratio was 53% for and 33% against 'if recognition were to produce better relations with the East.' (Allensbach, 7 Nov. 1967)."

The situation was somewhat different with respect to Bonn's dealings with

The invasion of Czechoslovakia, from which neither the reformists nor the conservatives could derive any comfort, tended to strengthen the position of the conservatives. The invasion, and the complete imposition of Soviet control in the spring of 1969, seemed to vindicate the conservatives' skeptical attitude toward the Kremlin's "new look" of the 1960s, as well as confirm their argument that the reformists, with no guarantees from the Soviets, were undermining the consistency and legitimacy of the orthodox German viewpoint in the face of an unreconstructed Soviet imperialism.

The conflict between reformists and traditionalists was accentuated during the election year of 1969. Traditionally, the political dialogue in the Federal Republic tended to move toward the Right in national election years; and in 1969 the SPD was hard pressed to defend the more flexible Ostpolitik agreed upon and enunciated in the Grand Coalition's early declarations against the Christian Democrats' increasingly "national-conservative" foreign policy line. The Bundestag's "Germany Debate" in April clearly demonstrated that the invasion of Czechoslovakia and the failure of Bonn's experimental approach toward Moscow and East Berlin had stiffened the conservatives' resolve to limit what they viewed as unrealistic and self-defeating innovations. During the debate, the chancellor himself seemed prone to oversimplifying the complexities of Bonn's Ostpolitik in terms that implicitly supported the traditionalists' misgivings, and even the Socialists felt obliged to use the vocabulary of detente and flexibility more gingerly. The FDP's call for a *Generalvertrag*—an overall treaty to settle the nature of West Germany's relations with East Germany—was not rejected out of hand, but the general tone of the debate in-

---

East Germany. A survey conducted by the Allensbach Institute (reported in *Stern,* March 10, 1968) indicates that 29 per cent of those interviewed were in favor of recognition, and 50 per cent opposed to it—if recognition were necessary for establishing humanitarian contacts with East Germany. In response to a question which omitted reference to humanitarian considerations, 61 per cent were opposed to recognition, 21 per cent were in favor. (Richardson, "Eastern Policy," p. 379, fn. 5.)

dicated that the Christian Democrats might be preparing for a muted version of the "no experiments" campaign that had proved successful on several occasions in the past.*

Even so, the Socialists were unwilling to give too much ground in defending Bonn's new Ostpolitik. At their Bad Godesberg party conference in the spring, the Socialists, prodded by some of their more venturesome Länder organizations for outright recognition of East Germany, decided that the question of formally recognizing East Germany under international law was not really pertinent since East Germany was not a foreign country, but that Bonn should deal with the East Berlin regime "without any discrimination" because the existence of an East German state was undeniable. A similar formula was adopted by the Free Democrats at their party conference, the major difference being that the FDP wished to negotiate with East Germany about normalizing relations as soon as possible, while the SPD, more skeptical about the prospects of success and restrained by their coalition partner, favored postponement until success seemed more likely. The Free Democrats explicitly called for the shelving of the Hallstein Doctrine and Bonn's claim of sole representation, but largely ignored the issue of the Oder-Neisse line.†

The tensions within the coalition over Bonn's Ostpolitik were aired again in public when Iraq, Cambodia, and the Sudan entered

* For example, in May 1969, when Willy Brandt responded encouragingly to a Polish offer to begin negotiations over the recognition of the Oder-Neisse line—an offer that dovetailed with the SPD's 1968 party conference proposal—the right wing of the Christian Democrats (and especially the elements close to organized refugee circles) reacted extremely negatively. See *Der Spiegel*, 22/1969, p. 28.

† The agreement between the SPD and the FDP on how to deal with East Germany, while not surprising, nonetheless was viewed with special interest—since it followed in the wake of the FDP's support of the SPD's nominee for President of the Republic, Gustav Heinemann. The FDP's support resulted in Heinemann's election by the Bundestag in a narrow victory over the CDU/CSU's nominee, Gerhard Schröder. A SPD-FDP mini-coalition after the fall 1969 elections seemed at least conceivable, now that the Free Democrats, under the leadership of Walter Scheel, had proved their party discipline to the Social Democrats.

into diplomatic relations with East Berlin in May 1969. Since Bonn had no diplomatic relations with Iraq and the Sudan (in 1965, when West Germany and Israel entered into diplomatic relations, most Arab states recalled their ambassadors from Bonn), it was the Cambodia episode that set off a new dispute about whether the Hallstein Doctrine should be allowed to lapse further, or whether it should remain operative at least with respect to Third World countries. Foreign Minister Brandt, whose distaste for the Hallstein Doctrine (which he regarded as an outmoded remnant of the Adenauer years) was well known, counseled against breaking off relations with Cambodia—a position shared even by Franz-Josef Strauss. Several CDU leaders, however, including the chancellor, advocated a hard-line approach and called for the application of the Hallstein Doctrine, even though Kiesinger had himself argued within his own party for a special dispensation of the Doctrine for Yugoslavia.

The compromise reached in the Cabinet—a decision not to break off relations but to permanently recall the German ambassador—was a typical example of the self-defeating consequences of the Hallstein Doctrine. Now, having only a "representative mission" in Cambodia, the Federal Republic had downgraded its presence, while East Germany was fully represented by an embassy—a direct reversal of the previous situation. Supporters of the Hallstein Doctrine feared a "chain reaction" among Third World countries—in November 1967 Kiesinger had made an Asian tour to seek reassurances that Bonn's recognition of Yugoslavia would not lead to a mass recognition of East Germany by Asian countries—but now Bonn, by its response to the Cambodia affair, seemed to be passing the initiative in the Third World to East Germany, and there was concern about the precedents being set for the future, when Laos, Burma, or even India might conceivably follow Cambodia's lead. The government stated in effect that in the future the Federal Republic would view the recognition of East Germany by Third World countries as an unfriendly act, and that the Bonn government's "attitudes and measures would depend on its assessment of the interest of all of the German people in given circumstances"—a declaration that prompted one commentator to note caustically, "In other words, there will be a bark in all cases, a bite only in certain circumstances."[17]

Within the Grand Coalition, the disagreements over Bonn's new Ostpolitik were also manifest in conflicting views of Bonn's proper stance on foreign policy in general, and on the question of alliance policy and East-West detente efforts in particular. One of the most striking examples of this conflict was the clash over the nonproliferation treaty. Both sides in the debate claimed, with some justification, that they were being "realistic" by defending their positions. The groups that favored (or at least accepted the prospect of) German participation in the treaty—most of the Social Democrats, Free Democrats, and CDU moderates—realistically assessed the political and psychological liabilities inherent in rejecting a critical element of arms control—an element that promised nuclear stabilization and thus was widely supported by Bonn's allies as well as its enemies.

The opponents of the treaty—most prominently Franz-Josef Strauss (who characterized it as a "Versailles of cosmic proportions") but also ex-chancellor Adenauer (prior to his death in April 1967) and several other CSU and CDU leaders—saw in it a further example of Soviet-American complicity, through which vital German national interests would be fundamentally damaged without compensation, and through which Bonn's present and future mobility would be seriously impaired.[18]

In particular, Strauss maintained that the treaty would damage NATO, the EEC, and Germany's "equal partnership" with the United States, and would deprive Bonn of bargaining leverage on the German question; he threatened in the fall of 1968 to separate the CSU from the CDU and establish it as a nationwide party if the government signed the treaty. (Strauss was also suspected of using the nonproliferation issue to woo potential NPD voters or, even more sinister, to govern with a CSU-NPD coalition in a German-style *apertura a destra.*) Although the treaty's opponents also realistically recognized that Bonn probably could not resist the combined pressures of East and West, they were determined to enunciate (to an international as well as a domestic audience) a foreign policy line that would demonstrate some measure of German independence, especially vis-à-vis the United States; they demanded to see the new assertiveness that the Grand Coalition had promised to instill in Bonn's foreign policy making. This pressure from the right wing of the coalition was not entirely unwelcome to Chancellor Kiesinger, who clearly wished to delay action until after the September elections and who hoped to exploit it in his negotiations with Washington. (And it should be noted that not only CDU/CSU but also SPD ministers in the Cabinet felt that Erhard and Schröder had been too accommodating to the United States.)

The lack of real opportunities to demonstrate this assertiveness on the political-strategic plane vis-à-vis the United States, and the German Gaullists' disenchantment with France's independent foreign policy line (from whose formulation Bonn was excluded even after the Grand Coalition had courted de Gaulle most deferentially), goes a long way toward explaining Bonn's hardheadedness during the "crisis of the franc." During the November 1968 Bonn currency conference, the foreign policy "conservatives"—represented by Finance Minister Franz-Josef Strauss—and the "reformist-liberals"—represented by the SPD Economics Minister Karl Schiller—acted together to hold an inflexible line against revaluation, with the approval of the German public (though some technical experts, including the president of the German central bank, Karl Blessing, were in favor of revaluation). To be sure, Schiller and Strauss had different political-economic motivations. Schiller feared that revaluation would adversely affect his pump-priming economic program, with which he had guided the German economy out of the 1966 recession; Strauss was opposed because revaluation woud have burdened the Federal budget considerably, and more important, because he viewed the currency confrontation as an opportunity to demonstrate the tough "realism" and assertiveness that he felt had been lacking in Bonn's foreign policy for a long time.

In any case, the Schiller-Strauss partnership was short-lived. The possibility, broached in the spring of 1969, of an upward revaluation of the Deutsche Mark proved to be the most explosive issue of the election year, and for all practical purposes split the Grand Coalition.

In part because of the continuing rise in German exports (up 41 per cent in March 1969 over March 1968) and the unreformed international currency exchange rate system, and in part because of de Gaulle's resignation, a new wave of speculative "hot money" rushed into Germany in early May 1969. (This time, in contrast to November 1968, however, very little international pressure was brought to bear on Bonn, and the political consequences were largely felt on the domestic rather than the international scene.) In order to stem the inflow of foreign money, the Cabinet decided early in May, after a stormy session (overriding the German central bank, a majority of academic economists, and most important, Economics Minister Karl Schiller) not to revalue the mark upward, and a government spokesman declared rather theatrically that the decision was "final, unequivocal, and for eternity."

The international and domestic economic ramifications of the entire issue were highly intricate, and not nearly as clear-cut as the two opposing sides portrayed them. The very complexity of the issue encouraged the oversimplification of its projected economic consequences in the public debate—with the Socialists accusing the Christian Democrats of abetting inflation, and the Christian Democrats charging the SPD with manipulation of the mark. The proponents as well as the opponents of the government's decision were very much aware of its political and psychological impact, especially in an election year. The opponents of revaluation—most prominently Finance Minister Strauss, but also, with some hesitation, and after consulting with industrialists and financiers, the chancellor himself—genuinely doubted that a unilateral, nonreciprocal parity adjustment of the mark would resolve the basic inadequacies of the international monetary system, and they were of course aware of the preferences of interest groups that traditionally supported the CDU. CDU/CSU leaders did not wish to alienate the export-sensitive industrial interests, and they feared that revaluation would drive farm voters, who stood to lose by it unless compensated with additional subsidies, into the growing ranks of the extreme-right NPD. (Such a move, by altering the party balance in the Bundestag, would probably have precluded a future CDU/CSU-FDP coalition.) The CDU/CSU leaders also gladly became defenders against "speculators" and wagged their fingers at the countries with allegedly irresponsible fiscal practices.*

The advocates of revaluation—central bank president Karl Blessing, Economics Minister Karl Schiller (who suggested a 6.25 per cent revaluation), his fellow SPD ministers, and many economic experts—felt that the November 1968 stopgap measures

* It is easy but inaccurate to blame sinister "speculators" for the November 1968 and May 1969 revaluation crises. The reality is highly complex. In the first place, a good part of the "hot money" inflow came from large industrial concerns (especially international concerns which increased their investments in their European subsidiaries), commercial banks, and even governmental central banks. All of these concerns sought to put their money reserves in markets that appeared safe as well as profitable. Moreover, many large German industrial firms also borrowed dollars or other foreign currencies and exchanged them, as much as possible, into marks.

Second, much of the inflow was not genuinely "speculative" but reflected an entirely legitimate desire to change terms of payment—for example, purchasers of German export goods insisted on prepayment. Such prepayments can start a whole chain of monetary transactions. The foreign currencies earned by German exporters, after they are turned over to the central bank for conversion into marks, are then "swapped" by the central bank with commercial banks in a rather complex transaction (involving a guaranteed parity rate and foreign currency "futures") which allows the commercial banks to borrow dollars and reconvert them immediately into marks—either to make a profit, or to guard against possible losses, in case of a revaluation. This leads to a "multiplyer" effect. In November 1968 and May 1969, dollars were returned immediately (or even repeatedly) to Germany, thus burdening the central bank with obligations which, in the event of revaluation, are much higher than the "visible" foreign currency reserves held by the central bank: the bank is obliged to buy up its dollar "futures" at the old parity, which can be quite costly. This led the German central bank to quit "swap" transactions in the middle of May.

Third, when "hot money" appeared to be leaving the saturated German money market after the November and May decisions not to revaluate, a good portion of it was in fact reinvested in German stocks, with the result that stock prices rose noticeably, especially since they were undervalued, relative to international levels, to begin with. In a sense, the stock market served as a substitute for immediate revaluation.

had been clearly insufficient to correct the persisting (and growing) trade imbalance, and that the German mark would have to be shielded from the pronounced inflationary trends abroad (France suffered from a 10 per cent inflation rate, Holland's was 7 per cent). Without revaluation, they believed, the inflation elsewhere would ultimately lead to an "imported" inflation in Germany itself, with serious consequences for the German economy. They were concerned that price increases (especially for food and rent) would threaten the stability of the mark.

The line between the two sides in the controversy was finally drawn pretty much along CDU/CSU and SPD party lines, with the FDP castigating both sides for their public squabbling and politicking over a serious economic issue. Both sides not only had their eyes on the September election, but also felt that fundamental goals were being affected. As is the case in most economic controversies, the issue was essentially one of the distribution, or redistribution, of national income—the basic question was: who would pay whom for what? The CDU/CSU conservatives and moderates naturally were sensitive to the interests of their traditional supporters among farmers and small entrepreneurs, and in big business. Schiller, who was not unpopular with the big industrial interests after his economic "revitalization" program helped push up profits an average 17.6 per cent in 1968, nonetheless shared his party's commitment to lower-income groups and small savers; and the Socialists wanted wage earners to share more fully in Germany's prosperity through higher wages without having industrial employers annul these wage gains through higher prices. Stabilizing the mark, and subjecting German industrial and commercial interests to more intense international competition—which was expected to follow from a DM revaluation—would serve that goal as well as helping to slow down the economic boom. When the Grand Coalition decided one day after the September 28, 1969 elections to allow a temporarily "free-floating," upward revaluation (discussed in Chapter Two), this was in some ways a decision forced upon the caretaker Grand Coalition Cabinet: it was taken to forestall a new monetary crisis, and in anticipation of a formal revaluation by the Social Democrats who were expected to become the senior partner in a new coalition government.

In the election year of 1969, the programmatic differences that had all along strained the Grand Coalition intensified, and contributed to an increased stagnation of Bonn's foreign policy line. However, the peculiar interest calculations that had brought the coalition partners together in the first place led most coalition elements both to mute public controversy while simultaneously trying to fashion distinct profiles for their parties and to exploit foreign policy issues for domestic prestige. Neither coalition partner wanted a full and open break before the election. Both the Christian Democrats and the Socialists anticipated that the September election results might force them to continue the coalition, because the Free Democrats might be unwilling to rejoin the CDU/CSU and might be too weak to join a coalition with the SPD.* An open breakup of the coalition also might have impaired Kiesinger's future usefulness, since, as "coalition chancellor," he was integral to the experiment; he would have been placed in the difficult position of having to govern with a minor-

* Indeed, the Free Democrats obtained only 5.8 per cent of the vote in the September 1969 election (as compared to 9.5 per cent in 1965), and the SPD-FDP coalition rested on a slim majority in the Bundestag. The results of the 1969 elections were as follows:

	PERCENTAGE OF VOTES	BUNDESTAG SEATS
CDU/CSU	46.1	242
SPD	42.7	224
FDP	5.8	30
NPD	4.3	—
Others	1.1	—
Total	100.0	496
Percentage of electorate voting	86.7	

The SPD-FDP coalition Cabinet established consisted of 11 members of the SPD (including the Chancellor), 3 members of the FDP, and one non-party member.

ity Cabinet until the fall elections; and the Christian Democrats (excepting perhaps Franz-Josef Strauss who aimed for a pivotal position for his CSU) did not want to foreclose the possibility of establishing another Grand Coalition with the Socialists. A second Grand Coalition would have been hard to justify if the first had ended with an open admission of failure.

The Socialists were motivated by similar calculations. Although the April party conference on the whole reflected the party's new self-confidence (and its intention to stress during the campaign the constructive and rational role the SPD had played in the government), preelection public opinion surveys were not reassuring, and some party leaders (especially Herbert Wehner) felt that the voters still had doubts about the party's respectability. This explains in good part the SPD's reluctance to engage the Christian Democrats in a full-fledged battle over the revaluation issue in May. The SPD's strategists did not wish to break with the Christian Democrats over an issue so ill-understood by the average voter, especially since Schiller, on whose vote-getting power the SPD counted heavily, was so prominently involved. (Strauss was already posing as the "defender of the mark" and, according to a public opinion survey, 87 per cent of the respondents were against revaluation and only 4 per cent agreed with Schiller and Blessing.) In fact, the SPD election strategy mapped out at the April conference seemed to envisage a division of labor: Schiller, who could take credit for having led the German economy from the recession to the heights of a new boom, was an ideal symbol of the party's trustworthiness in domestic (and especially economic) affairs; Willy Brandt was expected to gain support for the party on the basis of the SPD's flexibility and "modernity" in foreign affairs. In short, the SPD hoped to move to the "Right" on economic issues to gain ground among moderates, while moving somewhat to the "Left" on foreign policy issues—thus out-maneuvering the Christian Democrats in both areas.

During 1969, the German public was becoming increasingly uneasy about the impasse of German foreign policy, and apparently willing to at least examine some possible alternatives. Yet it was hard for the political parties to arrive at plausible policy options. There were three major obstacles to effective foreign policy leadership. The first was the "concealment of conflict" among German political parties—which, although it stemmed primarily from power calculations and inter-party accommodations on domestic issues, had a profound effect on the entire political process, including foreign policy making; the second was the nature of the international system of the 1960s; and the third was the attrition of political ideologies in West Germany.

With respect to "concealment of conflict": in Germany, as well as in many other modern democracies, the public's policy preferences and socioeconomic interests are only imprecisely aggregated and articulated in the party system. As a result, German political leaders have tended (especially during the three years of the Grand Coalition) to seek accommodation of opposing viewpoints, using a system of "conflict management" that evaluates policy alternatives not so much on their merits but by finding the lowest common denominator acceptable to the proponents of contending viewpoints. Speaking of Germany, Ralf Dahrendorf says:

> I do not know whether we have reached the end of the party game, but I am quite sure that the present party game, instead of representing the social and political differences of the day, to say nothing of promoting solutions, tends to conceal these differences, and contributes to maintaining an increasingly immobile and therefore increasingly untrustworthy political system.[19]

This phenomenon raises special problems in the making of foreign policy. The muting of conflict in a democratic society, which results when political parties function as flexible interest brokers, undoubtedly has a salutory effect when constituencies are sharply divided, and a willingness to compromise prevents head on, abrasive, and unmitigated conflicts. But in Germany in 1969 the situation was almost exactly the reverse. The leadership of the established political parties was not faced with a groundswell of opposing viewpoints on foreign policy but rather with a general disorientation and malleability. Moreover, in the late 1960s the international system had less impact on the West German domestic system than it had in the formative years of the

Federal Republic. As a result, in 1969 foreign policy decisions had a less tangible effect on the average citizen's daily life than they did in the early 1950s, when Adenauer's pro-Western policies produced direct economic and political benefits. In short, in the late 1960s the public seemed sufficiently interested in, as well as sufficiently detached from, foreign policy issues to support rational alternatives had they been presented.

However, the intractable and complex nature of the international system made it difficult to exercise foreign policy leadership. The all-around intractability of the international system hindered even pragmatic and short-range policy initiatives (which, if successful, might gradually have crystallized into a tentative but coherent program), and at the same time the system's complexity precluded a "grand design" that might have served as a long-range strategy guide and as a device with which to educate public opinion and marshal it behind a convincing foreign policy orientation. Foreign policy leadership invariably requires that political leaders oversimplify a complex reality in a responsible way. The lack of leadership in Bonn came not so much from a lack of will as from a lack of opportunity to abstract from the intricacies of the international environment large alternatives for action. Again, the contrast between the late 1960s and the early 1950s is instructive. The essentially bipolar structure of the international system during the Cold War period lent itself easily (perhaps too easily) to formulating a West German foreign policy line, which, although it probably was denied any realistic alternative, could be promoted by pointing to fairly clear-cut sets of international restraints and opportunities—restraints and opportunities that were clearly and widely perceived. No such plausible abbreviations of reality could be fashioned from the complex and intractable international circumstances of the 1960s.

The domestic and international factors that precluded a coherent foreign policy design were reemphasized by the attrition of political ideologies in the 1960s. From the beginning of the Federal Republic, the CDU/CSU, and also to a lesser extent the FDP, had avoided a precisely defined ideological conception of the public good, because it would only have been a handicap in appealing to a large and heterogeneous group of supporters, and because the demise of the Nazi regime had left most Germans with an ideological hangover. After the scrapping of dogmatic Marxism by the Socialists in the late 1950s, German political parties tended to become primarily functional instruments for the attainment of power rather than spokesmen for political ideologies or consciously structured value systems for political and social action. This process was reflected in and enhanced by the success-oriented pragmatism that began to characterize the political process in the early 1960s, which was facilitated by some important trends in German society. Social barriers and class differences were diminishing in a setting of economic prosperity, and the absence of a recognized ruling elite made for a more flexible and tolerant environment for social and political thought. Affluence brought with it a certain hedonistic utilitarianism that had little use for ideological exertions; the majority of voters seemed to prefer a policy of caution and stability; and the electoral system promoted appeals to the middle-of-the-road majority by penalizing small political parties through weighted representation of parties with larger followings.

In addition to its direct connection with the pragmatic "concealment of conflict" among political parties, this "end of ideology" can be related to the foreign-policy-making process in several other ways. In the first place, the changes that took place in the international system over the previous two decades had a profound, if subtle and indirect, impact on the process of de-ideologization. Since the major parties believed in the 1950s that foreign policy set the limits of domestic policy and ultimately determined the kind of social order that would prevail in Germany, the ideologically-tinged political discourse was necessarily reflected in, and reemphasized by, the contest over foreign policy. During the late 1950s and early 1960s, when the limits of what could be accomplished in the international system became more clearly visible and incontrovertible, the international system forced a more pragmatic and rational assessment of foreign policy projects, and also allowed their protagonists to evaluate domestic issues on their intrinsic merits. The sharp disagreements over foreign policy during the 1950s had frequently been caused by competing value systems; by the end of the Adenauer period in 1963, the breakdown of clearly defined opposing viewpoints among parties, and between the government and the opposition, had contributed substantially to the erosion of the ideological content of the whole political dialogue.

However, neither the Erhard Administration nor the Grand Coalition managed to turn pragmatism into effective foreign policy making or into genuinely innovative domestic reforms. Instead, the absence of effective leadership, the crisis of political imagination, and a certain boredom with political expediency (especially among the young) led to a strong response to the "end of ideology"—to a counter-trend that was reflected in a renewed search for concepts and values with which to make sense of a complex and bewildering reality. This "dialectical" response to the end of ideology—a phenomenon not limited to Germany—resulted to a considerable extent from the frustrations caused by the impasse of German foreign policy. On the Right, the National Democratic Party appealed to the voters with an essentially traditional-conservative nationalism that had neo-Nazi overtones; while the loosely organized extreme Left formed an "extraparliamentary" opposition (the so-called APO), arguing that the SPD's submergence in the German "establishment" had deprived the political process of an opposition party worthy of the name, and that the premises of German foreign policy should be radically reexamined.

More important than the extremists' renewed quest for the certitudes and psychological comforts of a *Weltanschauung* was the political-psychological stance of the middle. Although it is difficult and perhaps hazardous to generalize about such a large and heterogenous group, there seems to have developed a widespread political orientation centering (at least implicitly) around the idea of the "national interest." This orientation reflects not so much a new nationalism—although there are of course political groupings along the wide spectrum of the middle whose attitudes could be characterized that way—but rather a feeling that West German foreign policy should be attuned, more assertively if necessary, to the harsh "realities" of the international environment. This pursuit of the national interest offers a wide and inviting umbrella for political groupings with otherwise divergent attitudes, because it is, at least on the surface, devoid of explicit and divisive ideological commitments, and because it seemingly can provide a guide for short-range pragmatic policies as well as for a psychologically satisfying general view of the workings of world politics. In short, preoccupation with the national interest nicely fits the mood (and self-perception) of a majority of the public: it is "pragmatic" and "realistic," yet offers "meaning" without overt ideological manifestations; it is assertive but not abrasively militant; and it provides a viewpoint that can be sustained even in the absence of specific policy commitments.

Reliance on the "objective" reality of the national interest as a guide to foreign policy making is of limited value to any society, if only for the reason that even if an objective national interest existed, different decision-makers and segments of the public would perceive, articulate, and attempt to manipulate this "objective" reality in subjectively different ways. Its value is even more doubtful in the case of West Germany. The complexities and strictures of the contemporary international system do not in and by themselves "suggest" very clearly what the German national interest might be, and consequently cannot offer any large and plausible guidelines as to the content, and ways of implementation, of West German foreign policy goals. This is strikingly exemplified in the case of the goal of reunification. Not only are the avenues toward implementation strewn with obstacles, but the very nature of the goal—the reunification or association of two states of the same nation—raises the political (and semantic) difficulty of how the "national" interest of one part of Germany, the Federal Republic, can be advanced in the face of the opposing "national" interest of the other part. As Pierre Hassner pointed out (even prior to the invasion of Czechoslovakia):

> The two broad, long-range (perhaps contradictory, perhaps complementary) goals of German policy—the uniting of Europe and the reunification of Germany—have both receded at the same time into an

indefinite and doubtful future. Just as the decline of faith in the first encourages a more national policy, the decline of faith in the second deprives this national policy of its natural goal. The first phenomenon creates a disposition to challenge the status quo; the second demonstrates the likely frustration of this disposition because of the solidness of the status quo. Germany is therefore in danger of having a national policy without national goals, a recipe for instability if ever there was one.[20]

The political-psychological disorientations and frustrations which result from the preoccupation with a national interest that has no achievable natural goal point to one of the most fundamental shifts in the relationship between the international system and the German domestic system during the last two decades. During the formative years of the Federal Republic foreign policy issues were experienced in largely practical terms but often enunciated in ideological-programmatic terms; today the foreign policy discourse tends to stress national-interest-oriented "pragmatism," but foreign policy outcomes have lost their immediate impact on the average citizen in his daily life and are experienced more psychologically. During the late 1940s and early 1950s, the general direction and content of the domestic order were strongly shaped by the international environment, whereas today they seem carried forward much more by an internal momentum, which, although sensitive to impulses from without, is largely self-generated and self-sustaining.

Deprived of a realistic national goal at a time when the idea of a German national interest is on the ascendance, many Germans, including prominent decision-makers in Bonn, have turned toward semi-political and pseudo-political substitutes. This phenomenon is noticeable both in rhetoric and in economic matters: many Germans seem susceptible to a certain "export nationalism,"*

---

* Herbert Giersch, director of the Institute for European Economic Policy in Saarbrücken, said in an interview with *Der Spiegel* (21/1969, p. 52): "Our export offensive, which we subsidize with the undervaluation of the D-Mark, threatens to become a sort of substitute nationalism. When I think of the arguments put forth recently at the NPD party conference, I cannot help but feel that our old political-military nationalism revives as an export nationalism."

which was illustrated in the muscle-flexing during the November 1968 currency confrontation, and which seems to provide satisfactions equalled only by those gained by success at the Olympic Games. It remains to be seen if, and for how long, such palliatives can serve as a substitute for a genuine national sense of purpose.

NOTES

Complete titles, authors' names, and publication data for works cited in short form in the Notes can be found in the Bibliography, pp. 205–215.

CHAPTER ONE

1. Ismay, *NATO,* p. 47.
2. Buchan and Windsor, *Arms and Stability,* p. 38.
3. For full accounts, see Aron and Lerner, *France Defeats the EDC;* and Furniss, *Troubled Ally,* Chapters Two and Three.
4. Speier, *German Rearmament,* p. 210, also pp. 197–212.
5. Richardson, *Germany,* p. 42.
6. Osgood, *NATO,* p. 255.
7. Kissinger, "Unresolved Problems," p. 520 (emphasis in original).
8. Buchan and Windsor, *Arms and Stability,* p. 12.
9. Schlesinger, *A Thousand Days,* p. 790.
10. Buchan and Windsor, *Arms and Stability,* pp. 192–201.
11. Schlesinger, *A Thousand Days,* pp. 780–787.
12. *Ibid.,* p. 780.
13. See Shulman, "Europe Versus 'Detente' "; Gasteyger, *American Dilemma;* and Foster, "New Directions."
14. Brodie, "How not to Lead," p. 23. The statement was made by Under Secretary George Ball on April 10, 1966.
15. *Christian Science Monitor,* March 8, 1966.
16. Sommer, "Bonn Changes Course," p. 486; see also his "Objectives of Germany."
17. Bader, "Nuclear Weapons Sharing," p. 698; for a concise legal exposition, see Willrich, "West Germany's Pledge."
18. See Brandt, *Aussenpolitik,* p. 88; and the interview with Chancellor Kiesinger in *Der Spiegel,* 13/1967, pp. 42–53.
19. *The New York Times,* March 30, 1967, 17:1.
20. Cleveland, "NATO"; Nau, "Militärische Überlegungen"; and Ranger, "NATO's Reaction to Czechoslovakia." The invasion also added to the doubts about the political and military value of the

French force de frappe or a similarly structured European nuclear force. See Delmar, "L'Affair Tchèchoslovaquie."

21. See, among others, the Warsaw Pact proposals of the Prague meeting (October 1969) and the Budapest meeting (March 1969), the "Karlovy Vary Declaration," and the "Bucharest Declaration" of the Warsaw Pact Political Committee. See also, Orlik and Rasmerov, "European Security," pp. 3–8, 14; Sedivy, "European Co-operation"; "Komponenten der europäischen Sicherheit"; Centre d'Études de Politique Étrangère, "Modèles"; Britain's *Statement on Defense Estimates 1967,* p. 4; Gasteyger, *Europe in the Seventies;* and Blumenfeld, "Europäische Friedensordnung." For a post-Czechoslovakia German contribution, see the study sponsored by the German Foreign Policy Association, "Mögliche Entwicklungen."
22. For a full discussion, see Hassner, *Change and Security.*
23. See Bluhm, *Detente;* and Birnbaum, "Das westliche Bündnis."
24. See Wettig, "Europäische Sicherheit"; and Mosely, "East-West Detente."
25. Hassner, *Change and Security,* p. 20.
26. Brandt, *Aussenpolitik,* p. 97; for the summary of a speech with a similar theme by Chancellor Kiesinger, see *Europa-Archiv,* 18/1967, pp. 683–684.
27. Shub, "Lessons of Czechoslovakia."
28. Long, "Strategic Balance and ABM," p. 5; see also Wiesner, "Cold War is Dead"; and Klefisch, "Strategie der siebziger Jahre," and "Brauchen wir Atomwaffen?"
29. Hassner, *Change and Security,* p. 4.
30. Nerlich, "Nukleare Dilemmas," p. 641; see also Richardson, *Germany,* Chapters Three and Four.

CHAPTER TWO

1. McInnis, Hiscocks, and Spencer, *Postwar Germany,* p. 133.
2. See Wallich, *Mainsprings.*
3. For a full account of the ECSC, see Haas, *Uniting of Europe.*
4. Willis, *France, Germany, and the New Europe,* pp. 265–266.
5. *Ibid.,* p. 312.
6. For a full discussion, see Camps, *European Unification.*
7. *Ibid.,* p. 109.
8. *Ibid.,* pp. 117–118.
9. Hassner, "German and European Reunification," pp. 33–34.
10. Brzezinski, *Alternative to Partition,* pp. 108–109.

11. *The New York Times,* Oct. 6, 1968.
12. For a well-balanced description of the French economy during 1967, see *OECD Economic Surveys: France.*
13. *The New York Times,* Nov. 23, 1968, p. 80.
14. For a detailed account of the French cutback on military programs, see *Der Spiegel,* 9/1969, pp. 122–124.
15. See the interview with Bonn's Minister of Economics, Karl Schiller, in *Der Spiegel,* 48/1968, pp. 36–39.
16. *OECD Economic Surveys: Germany,* esp. pp. 24–31; see also the survey on Germany published by OECD in April 1968.
17. *The New York Times,* July 6, 1969.

CHAPTER THREE

1. Watt, "Germany," p. 118.
2. For background discussions, see Smith, *Defense of Berlin;* and Mander, *Berlin.*
3. See Merritt, "Berlin Wall."
4. Lippmann, *Western Unity,* p. 32.
5. For an excellent account of these changes, see Hassner, "German and European Reunification."
6. As quoted by Brzezinski, *Alternative to Partition,* p. 95.
7. Schröder, "Germany Looks at Eastern Europe," p. 21.
8. See *Der Spiegel,* 26/1965, p. 26; 19/1966, pp. 47–48.
9. See *Der Spiegel,* 19/1966, pp. 41–43; 20/1966, pp. 23–34; 23/1966, p. 32; 28/1966, pp. 15–16; and Wettig, "SPD und SED." The East Germans may also have been restrained by the Russians; see Engert, interview with Willy Brandt.
10. Hassner, "German and European Reunification," p. 15. The quotation in the footnote on p. 106 can be found in Hassner, pp. 16–17. See also Schulz, "Moskaus wichtigster Partner"; and Tudyka, "DDR im Kräftefeld," pp. 16–27.
11. For the text of the "Peace Note" of March 25, 1966, and several international responses, see *Europa-Archiv,* 7/1966, pp. 171–175; 18/1966, p. 465.
12. See Wettig, "Moskau und die Grosse Koalition." For an excellent treatment of Soviet policy, which stresses the importance of the German question for Soviet arms control proposals, see Larson, *Disarmament.*
13. Liska, *Europe Ascendant,* p. 80.

14. Birnbaum, "European Security," p. 196; see also Cornides, "German Unification"; and *Der Spiegel,* 19/1965, pp. 27–28.
15. For some concise accounts of the Grand Coalition's Eastern policy prior to the Soviet invasion of Czechoslovakia, see Kaiser, *German Foreign Policy;* Sommer, "Bonn's New Ostpolitik"; and Richardson, "Eastern Policy."
16. Brandt, "Policy Toward the East," p. 481, see also p. 476.
17. Sommer, "Bonn's New Ostpolitik," p. 60, see also pp. 70–78. On the contacts between Bonn and Pankow, see "Bemühungen der Bundesregierung"; and Schwarzkopf, "Gewaltverzicht." For an English translation of the Kiesinger-Stoph exchange of letters, see "Efforts of the Government of the Federal Republic of Germany towards intra-German detente" (Mimeographed, published by the German Federal Foreign Office, Bonn, Federal Republic of Germany).
18. See "Dokumente zu den Beziehungen"; Sommer, "Bonn's New Ostpolitik," esp. pp. 65ff; *Der Spiegel,* 6/1967, pp. 17–18; and "Die Ergebnisse."
19. See Berner, "Karlsbader Aktionsprogramm"; and Birrenbach, "Germany Re-enters."
20. See, for example, the interview with Herbert Wehner, Minister of All-German Affairs, in *Der Spiegel,* 35/1968, pp. 31–32; and the remarks of Willy Brandt quoted in *Die Zeit,* Feb. 18, 1969, p. 7.
21. For a perceptive discussion, see Stehle, "Blockierte Ostpolitik"; see also Griffith, *Eastern Europe,* esp. p. 22.

    For discussions of the relevance of China to West Germany, see Griffith, "European Communism," esp. p. 23; Augstein, "Neue Politik," esp. p. 20; Löwenthal, "Der Einfluss Chinas"; Studnitz, *Bismarck in Bonn,* p. 146; and Smith, "Two Germanies and Two Chinas."
22. Ermarth, *Internationalism,* pp. 121–122.
23. See Görgey, "Emerging Patterns"; Levi, "Les Relations Economiques"; Erler, "Future of Germany," p. 438; *Fortune,* Vol. LXXVI, No. 2 (Aug. 1967), pp. 72–77; *The New York Times,* Feb. 3, 11, and 14, 1967; Pritzel, "Der Interzonenhandel"; and Griffith, *Eastern Europe.*
24. Brzezinski, *Alternative to Partition,* p. 101; Hassner, "German and European Reunification," p. 15.
25. Schack, "Zum nächsten Abschnitt," p. 88. See also Hoesch, "Verfassungsrechtliche Aspekte," esp. pp. 128–130; *Der Spiegel,* 51/

1967, pp. 27–29; and the proposal by Wilhelm Wolfgang Schütz, chairman of the Committee for Indivisible Germany, in *Die Zeit,* Dec. 8, 1967, p. 9.

26. The term "acceptance without recognition" is from Richardson's "Germany's Eastern Policy," p. 379.

CHAPTER FOUR

1. For public opinion survey data, see Neumann and Noelle, *Antworten,* pp. 119–123; and Noelle, *Auskunft über die Parteien,* p. 28.
2. Haas, *Uniting of Europe,* p. 138.
3. Heidenheimer, "Bonn Dispatch," p. 17.
4. *News from Germany,* Vol. XV, No. 7 (July 1961), p. 2.
5. *News from Germany,* Vols. XV-XVI, Nos. 12-1 (Dec. 1961–Jan. 1962), p. 1.
6. Dehler, "Politik für Deutschland," p. 222.
7. *News from Germany,* Vols. XV-XVI, Nos. 12-1 (Dec. 1961–Jan. 1962), p. 2.
8. See Ludz, *Parteielite im Wandel.*
9. Bender, "New Policy," pp. 81–82.
10. Allemann, "Changing Scene," p. 54.
11. For a discussion of the Austrian coalition arrangement, see Engelmann, "Austria"; and Secher, "Interest Groups in Austrian Politics."
12. Allemann, "Changing Scene," p. 58.
13. Herz, "Grand Coalition," p. 227.
14. See Hartwick, "Ein Jahr Grosse Koalition."
15. Kaiser, *German Foreign Policy,* p. 23.
16. *Ibid.,* pp. 125–126.
17. Zundel, "Ende der Doktrin?" p. 6.
18. For a well-argued presentation of this position, see Horner, "Atomsperrvertrag."
19. Dahrendorf, "After Twenty Years," p. 170. See also Loewenberg, *Parliament,* esp. pp. 393–397.
20. Hassner, *Change and Security,* p. 13.

BIBLIOGRAPHY

AILLERET, GÉNÉRAL D'ARMÉE. "Directed Defense," *Survival*, Feb. 1968, pp. 38–43.

ALBRECHT, KARL. "Die Reservewährungen, das Währungssystem und die Politik der EWG," *Europa-Archiv*, 15/1968, pp. 543–556.

ALLEMANN, FRITZ R. "Bonns verschränkte Fronten: Parteiensystem und internationale Politik," *Der Monat*, 35/209 (Feb. 1966), pp. 7–15.

ALLEMANN, FRITZ R. "The Changing Scene in Germany," *The World Today*, Feb. 1967, pp. 49–62.

ALLEMANN, FRITZ R. *Zwischen Stabilität und Krise*. Munich: Piper Verlag, 1963.

ALTMANN, RÜDIGER. *Das deutsche Risiko*. Stuttgart: Seewald, 1962.

AMME, CARL H., JR. *NATO Without France, a Strategic Appraisal*. Stanford, Calif.: Hoover Institution, 1967.

ARON, RAYMOND. *The Great Debate*. Garden City, N.Y.: Doubleday, 1965.

ARON, RAYMOND, and DANIEL LERNER. *France Defeats the EDC*. New York: Praeger, 1957.

AUGSTEIN, RUDOLF. "Wege zu einer neuen Politik," *Der Spiegel*, 39/1965, pp. 18–25.

BADER, W. B. "Nuclear Weapons Sharing and 'The German Problem,'" *Foreign Affairs*, July 1966, pp. 693–700.

BAUDISSIN, WOLF GRAF VON. "NATO-Strategie im Zeichen der Friedenserhaltung: Politische und militärische Überlegungen zur Strategie der 'flexiblen Reaktion,'" *Europa-Archiv*, 17/1968, pp. 627–638.

BEATON, LEONARD. "Kernwaffen-Sperrvertrag und nationale Sicherheit," *Europa-Archiv*, 1/1969, pp. 5–12.

BELL, CORAL. *The Debatable Alliance*. New York: Oxford University Press, 1964.

"Bemühungen der Bundesregierung um innerdeutsche Regelungen," *Europa-Archiv*, 14/1967, pp. D325–330; 20/1967, pp. D472–478.

BENDER, PETER. "In Search of a New Policy," *Survey*, 61, Oct. 1966, pp. 80–92.

BENOIT, EMILE. *Europe at Sixes and Sevens*. New York: Columbia University Press, 1961.

BERNER, WOLFGANG. "Das Karlsbader Aktionsprogramm," *Europa-Archiv,* 11/1967, pp. 393–400.

BESSON, WALDEMAR. *Die grossen Mächte: Strukturfragen der gegenwärtigen Weltpolitik.* Freiburg: Rombach, 1966.

BIRNBAUM, KARL E. "Das westliche Bündnis und die europäische Sicherheit," *Europa-Archiv,* 7/1968, pp. 225–234.

BIRNBAUM, KARL E. "Ways Towards European Security," *Survival,* June 1968, pp. 193–199.

BIRRENBACH, KURT. "Germany Re-enters the Arena," *The Reporter,* May 16, 1968, pp. 9–13.

BLUHM, GEORG R. *Detente and Military Relaxation in Europe,* Adelphi Paper No. 40. London: Institute for Strategic Studies, Sept. 1967.

BLUMENFELD, ERIK. "Wege zu einer europäischen Friedensordnung," *Europa-Archiv,* 3/1967, pp. 95–104.

BRANDT, WILLY. *Aussenpolitik, Deutschlandpolitik, Europapolitik.* Berlin: Berlin Verlag, 1968.

BRANDT, WILLY. "German Policy Toward the East," *Foreign Affairs,* April 1968, pp. 476–486.

BRODIE, BERNARD. "How Not to Lead an Alliance," *The Reporter,* Mar. 9, 1967, pp. 18–24.

BRZEZINSKI, ZBIGNIEW. *Alternative to Partition.* New York: McGraw-Hill, 1965.

BRZEZINSKI, ZBIGNIEW. "Moscow and the MLF: Hostility and Ambivalence," *Foreign Affairs,* Oct. 1964, pp. 126–134.

BRZEZINSKI, ZBIGNIEW. "Toward a Community of the Developed Nations," *Department of State Bulletin,* Mar. 13, 1967, pp. 414–420.

BUCHAN, ALASTAIR, ed. *A World of Nuclear Powers?* Englewood Cliffs, N.J.: Prentice-Hall, 1966.

BUCHAN, ALASTAIR, and PHILIP WINDSOR. *Arms and Stability in Europe.* New York: Praeger, 1963.

CALLEO, DAVID P. *Europe's Future: The Grand Alternatives.* New York: W. W. Norton, 1967.

CAMPS, MIRIAM. *European Unification in the Sixties: From the Veto to the Crisis.* New York: McGraw-Hill, 1966.

CENTRE D'ÉTUDES DE POLITIQUE ÉTRANGÈRE, PARIS. "Modèles de sécurité européenne," *Politique Étrangère,* 6/1967, pp. 519–541.

CHALMERS, DOUGLAS A. *The Social Democratic Party of Germany.* New Haven: Yale University Press, 1964.

CLEVELAND, HARLAN. "NATO After the Invasion," *Foreign Affairs,* Jan. 1969, pp. 251–265.

CORNIDES, WILHELM. "German Unification and the Power Balance," *Survey,* 58, Jan. 1966, pp. 140–148.

CRAIG, GORDON A. *From Bismarck to Adenauer: Aspects of German Statecraft.* Baltimore, Md.: The Johns Hopkins Press, 1958.

CROAN, MELVIN. "Party Politics and the Wall," *Survey,* 61, Oct. 1966, pp. 38–46.

CZEMPIEL, ERNST-OTTO. "Der Primat der Auswärtigen Politik, Kritische Würdigung einer Staatsmaxime," *Politische Vierteljahresschrift,* Sept. 1963, pp. 266–287.

DAHRENDORF, RALF. "Bonn After Twenty Years: Are Germany's Problems nearer Solution?" *The World Today,* Apr. 1969, pp. 158–171.

"Declaration on the Strengthening of Peace and Security in Europe" by the Political Committee of the Warsaw Pact members, Bucharest, July 5, 1966. Bucharest: Agerpress, 1966, pp. 9–10.

DEHLER, THOMAS. "Politik für Deutschland," in Hans-Adolf Jacobsen and Otto Stenzl, eds. *Deutschland und die Welt.* Munich: Deutscher Taschenbuch Verlag, 1964.

DELMAR, CLAUDE. "L'Affair Tchèchoslovaquie et la Logique Nucléaire," *Revue Politique et Parlementaire,* Sept. 1968, pp. 5–8.

DEUTSCH, KARL W., and LEWIS J. EDINGER, *Germany Rejoins the Powers.* Stanford, Calif.: Stanford University Press, 1959.

DEUTSCH, KARL W., LEWIS J. EDINGER, ROY C. MACRIDIS, and RICHARD L. MERRITT. *France, Germany, and the Western Alliance.* New York: Scribner's, 1967.

"Die Ergebnisse der Tagung des Warschauer Pakts in Bukarest," *Europa-Archiv,* 16/1966, pp. D413–424.

DIVO-Pressedienst (Frankfurt), Apr. 1 and Aug. 11, 1962.

"Dokumente zu den Beziehungen zwischen der Bundesrepublik Deutschland und Osteuropa," *Europa-Archiv,* 5/1967, pp. D97–116; 6/1967, pp. D117–135; 8/1967, pp. D187–196; 18/1967, pp. D431–434; 5/1968, pp. D107–108.

DOUGHERTY, JAMES E. "The Nonproliferation Treaty," *The Russian Review,* Vol. XXV, No. 1 (Jan. 1966), pp. 10–23.

DUBOFF, RICHARD B. "The Decline of Economic Planning in France," *Western Political Quarterly,* Mar. 1968, pp. 98–109.

ENGELMANN, FREDERICK C. "Austria: The Pooling of Opposition," in Robert A. Dahl, ed. *Political Opposition in Western Democracies.* New Haven: Yale University Press, 1966.

ENGERT, JÜRGEN. Interview with Willy Brandt, *Christ und Welt,* July 8, 1966.

ERLER, FRITZ. "The Alliance and the Future of Germany," *Foreign Affairs,* Apr. 1965, pp. 436–446.

ERMARTH, FRITZ. "Die Diskussion über die sowjetische Verteidigungspolitik unter Breshnjew und Kossygin," *Europa-Archiv,* 16/1967, pp. 571–584.

ERMARTH, FRITZ. *Internationalism, Security, and Legitimacy: The Challenge to Soviet Interests in East Europe, 1964–1968.* Santa Monica, Calif.: RAND Corp. Memorandum RM-5909-PR, Mar. 1969.

FELD, WERNER. "External Relations of the Common Market and Group Leadership Attitudes in the Member States," *Orbis,* 10, 2/1966, pp. 564–587.

FISCHER, PER. *Die Saar zwischen Deutschland und Frankreich.* Frankfurt a. M.: Metzner, 1959.

FOSTER, WILLIAM C. "New Directions in Arms Control and Disarmament," *Foreign Affairs,* July 1965, pp. 587–601.

FRANK, ISAIAH. *The European Common Market, An Analysis of Commercial Policy.* New York: Praeger, 1964.

FRANK, LEWIS A. "ABM and Nonproliferation: Related Issues," *Orbis,* 11, 1/1967, pp. 67–79.

FREUND, GERALD. *Germany Between Two Worlds.* New York: Harcourt, Brace, 1961.

FREYMOND, JACQUES. *The Saar Conflict, 1945–1955.* New York: Praeger, 1960.

FURNISS, EDGAR S., JR. "De Gaulle's France and NATO: An Interpretation," *International Organization,* 15, 3/1969, pp. 349–365.

FURNISS, EDGAR S., JR. *France, Troubled Ally.* New York: 1960.

GASTEYGER, CURT. *The American Dilemma: Bipolarity or Alliance Cohesion,* Adelphi Paper No. 24. London: Institute for Strategic Studies, Jan. 1966.

GASTEYGER, CURT. *Europe in the Seventies,* Adelphi Paper No. 37. London: Institute for Strategic Studies, June 1967.

GERMAN FOREIGN POLICY ASSOCIATION. "Alternativen für Europa: Modelle möglicher Entwicklungen in den siebziger Jahren," *Europa-Archiv,* 23/1968, pp. 851–864.

GOLAY, JOHN F. *The Founding of the Federal Republic.* Chicago: University of Chicago Press, 1958.

GOODMAN, ELLIOT R. "De Gaulle's NATO Policy in Perspective," *Orbis,* 10, 3/1966, pp. 690–723.

GÖRGEY, LASZLO. "Emerging Patterns in West German-East European Relations," *Orbis,* 10, 3/1966, pp. 911–929.

GRIFFITH, WILLIAM E. *Eastern Europe After the Soviet Invasion of Czechoslovakia*. Santa Monica, Calif.: RAND Paper P3983, October 1968.

GRIFFITH, WILLIAM E. "European Communism, 1965," in William E. Griffith, ed. *Communism in Europe,* Vol. 2. Cambridge, Mass.: M.I.T. Press, 1966.

GROSSER, ALFRED. *The Colossus Again*. New York: Praeger, 1955.

GROSSER, ALFRED. *French Foreign Policy Under De Gaulle*. Boston: Little, Brown, 1965.

GROSSER, ALFRED. "General de Gaulle and the Foreign Policy of the Fifth Republic," *International Affairs,* 39/1963, pp. 198–213.

HAAS, ERNST B. *Beyond the Nation-State*. Stanford, Calif.: Stanford University Press, 1964.

HAAS, ERNST B. *The Uniting of Europe*. Stanford, Calif.: Stanford University Press, 1958.

HAHN, WALTER F., and ALVIN J. COTTRELL, "Ballistic Missile Defense and Soviet Strategy," *Orbis,* 9, 2/1965, pp. 316–337.

HALLETT, GRAHAM. "Britain and the Future of Germany," *The Political Quarterly,* 39, 3/1968, pp. 283–300.

HANRIEDER, WOLFRAM F. "Actor Objectives and International Systems," *Journal of Politics,* Feb. 1965, pp. 109–132.

HANRIEDER, WOLFRAM F. "Compatibility and Consensus: A Proposal for the Conceptual Linkage of External and Internal Dimensions of Foreign Policy," *American Political Science Review,* 61/4, Dec. 1967, pp. 971–982.

HANRIEDER, WOLFRAM F. *"German Reunification,* 1949–1963" in Roy C. Macridis, ed. *Modern European Governments: Cases in Comparative Policy Making*. Englewood Cliffs, N.J.: Prentice-Hall, 1968.

HANRIEDER, WOLFRAM F. "International and Comparative Politics: Toward a Synthesis?" *World Politics,* April 1968, pp. 480–493.

HANRIEDER, WOLFRAM F. "The International System: Bipolar or Multibloc?" *Journal of Conflict Resolution,* 9, 3/1965, pp. 299–308.

HANRIEDER, WOLFRAM F. *West German Foreign Policy, 1949–1963: International Pressure and Domestic Response*. Stanford, Calif.: Stanford University Press, 1967.

HARTWICK, HANS-HERMANN. "Konturen einer neuen Politik, Ein Jahr Grosse Koalition," *Zeitschrift für Politik,* XIV (1967), pp. 428–458.

HASSNER, PIERRE. *Change and Security in Europe, Part I: The Background,* Adelphi Paper No. 45. London: Institute for Strategic Studies, Feb. 1968.

HASSNER, PIERRE. "German and European Reunification: Two Problems or One?" *Survey,* 61, Oct. 1966, pp. 14–37.

HEIDENHEIMER, ARNOLD. "Bonn Dispatch: The German Opposition," *The New Republic,* Oct. 25, 1954, p. 17.

HERZ, JOHN H. "The Formation of the Grand Coalition," in James B. Christoph and Bernard E. Brown, eds. *Cases in Comparative Politics.* Boston: Little, Brown, 1968.

HERZ, JOHN H. *International Politics in the Atomic Age.* New York: Columbia University Press, 1959.

HINSHAW, RANDALL. *The European Community and American Trade.* New York: Praeger, 1964.

HOESCH, JAN. "Verfassungsrechtliche Aspekte der Deutschland-Politik," *Europa-Archiv,* 4/1967, pp. 125–134.

HORNER, FRANZ. "Der Atomsperrvertrag—politischer Idealismus oder Realismus?" *Politische Studien,* 176, Nov./Dec. 1967, pp. 691–704.

HUMPHREY, DON D. *The United States and the Common Market.* New York: Praeger, 1964.

HUNT, KENNETH. *NATO Without France, The Military Implications,* Adelphi Paper No. 32. London: Institute for Strategic Studies. Dec. 1966.

HYLAND, W., and R. W. SHRYOCK. *The Fall of Khrushchev.* New York: Funk and Wagnalls, 1968.

ISMAY, LORD. *NATO, The First Five Years.* Bosch-Utrecht, n.d.

KAISER, KARL. *German Foreign Policy in Transition: Bonn Between East and West.* London: Oxford University Press, 1968.

"Karlovy Vary Declaration." Issued by the Conference of European Communist Parties, Apr. 26, 1967. (Reprinted in *Survival,* July 1967, pp. 208–213.)

KIESINGER, KURT, and WILLI STOPH. "Letters" in "Efforts of the Government of the Federal Republic of Germany towards intra-German detente." Mimeographed. Published by the German Federal Foreign Office, Bonn, Federal Republic of Germany.

KIRCHHEIMER, OTTO. "Germany: The Vanishing Opposition," in Robert A. Dahl, ed. *Political Opposition in Western Democracies.* New Haven: Yale University Press, 1966.

KISSINGER, HENRY A. *The Necessity for Choice.* Garden City, N.Y.: Doubleday, 1962.

KISSINGER, HENRY A. "The Unsolved Problems of European Defense," *Foreign Affairs,* July 1962, pp. 515–541.

KITZINGER, U. W. *The Politics and Economics of European Integration.* New York: Praeger, 1963.

KLEFISCH, JOHANNES WILHELM. "Brauchen wir Atomwaffen?" *Frankfurter Hefte,* 9/1968, pp. 611–620.

KLEFISCH, JOHANNES WILHELM. "Deutschland und die Strategie der siebziger Jahre," *Frankfurter Hefte,* 8/1968, pp. 531–539.

"Komponenten der europäischen Sicherheit: Eine Studie des Polnischen Instituts für Internationale Beziehungen, Warschau," *Europa-Archiv,* 13/1968, pp. 469–477.

KRONECH, FRIEDRICH J. "Politische Aspekte des Aufbaus eines amerikanischen Raketenabwehrsystems," *Europa-Archiv,* 19/1967, pp. 697–702.

KULSKI, W. W. *De Gaulle and the World: The Foreign Policy of the Fifth French Republic.* Syracuse, N.Y.: Syracuse University Press, 1966.

LARSON, THOMAS B. *Disarmament and Soviet Policy, 1964–1968.* Englewood Cliffs, N.J.: Prentice-Hall, 1969.

LEHMBRUCH, GERHARD. "The Ambiguous Coalition in West Germany," *Government and Opposition,* 3, 2/1968, pp. 181–204.

LEVI, MARIO. "Les Relations Economiques entre l'Est et l'Ouest en Europe," *Politique Étrangère,* 32/4–5, 1967, pp. 477–492.

LICHTHEIM, GEORGE. *The New Europe.* New York: Praeger, 1963.

LINDBERG, LEON. *The Political Dynamics of European Economic Integration.* Stanford, Calif.: Stanford University Press, 1963.

LIPPMANN, WALTER. *Western Unity and the Common Market.* Boston: Little, Brown, 1962.

LISKA, GEORGE. *Europe Ascendant.* Baltimore, Md.: The Johns Hopkins Press, 1964.

LISKA, GEORGE. *Nations in Alliance.* Baltimore, Md.: The Johns Hopkins Press, 1962.

LOEWENBERG, GERHARD. *Parliament in the German Political System.* Ithaca, N.Y.: Cornell University Press, 1966.

LONG, FRANKLIN A. "Strategic Balance and the ABM," *Bulletin of the Atomic Scientists,* Dec. 1968.

LÖWENTHAL, RICHARD. "Der Einfluss Chinas auf die Entwicklung des Ost-West Konflikts in Europa," *Europa-Archiv,* 10/1967, pp. 339–350.

LUDZ, CHRISTIAN. *Parteielite im Wandel: Funktionsaufbau, Sozialstruktur und Ideologie der SED-Führung.* Cologne: Westdeutscher Verlag, 1968.

MC INNIS, EDGAR, RICHARD HISCOCKS, and ROBERT SPENCER. *The Shaping of Postwar Germany.* New York: Praeger, 1960.

MANDER, JOHN. *Berlin, Hostage for the West.* Baltimore, Md.: The Johns Hopkins Press, 1962.

MARTIN, LAURENCE W. "Ballistic Missile Defense and Europe," *Bulletin of the Atomic Scientists,* May 1967, pp. 42–46.

MENDERSHAUSEN, HORST. *Troop Stationing in Germany: Value and Cost.* Santa Monica, Calif.: RAND Corp. Memorandum RM-5881-PR, Dec. 1968.

MENDERSHAUSEN, HORST. "West Germany's Defense Problem," *Current History,* May 1968, pp. 268–274.

MERKL, PETER. *Germany, Yesterday and Tomorrow.* New York: Oxford University Press, 1965.

MERKL, PETER. *The Origin of the West German Republic.* New York: Oxford University Press, 1963.

MERRITT, RICHARD L. "A Transformed Crisis: The Berlin Wall," in Roy C. Macridis, ed. *Modern European Governments: Cases in Comparative Policy Making.* Englewood Cliffs, N.J.: Prentice-Hall, 1968.

MORGAN, R. P. "The Scope of German Foreign Policy," *The Yearbook of World Affairs,* 1966, pp. 78–105.

MORTON, LOUIS. "The Anti-Ballistic Missile: Some Political and Strategic Considerations," *Virginia Quarterly Review,* Winter 1966, pp. 28–42.

MOSELY, PHILIP E. "The United States and the East-West Detente: The Range of Choice," *Journal of International Affairs,* Vol. XXII, No. 1 (1968), pp. 5–15.

NAU, LUDWIG. "Die Sicherheitspolitik der Bundesregierung, II," *Frankfurter Hefte,* 2/1968, pp. 97–103.

NAU, LUDWIG. "Neue militärische Überlegungen in der Bundesrepublik," *Fankfurter Hefte,* 11/1968, pp. 743–746.

NERLICH, UWE. "Die nuklearen Dilemmas der Bundesrepublik Deutschland," *Europa-Archiv,* 17/1965, pp. 637–652.

NEUMANN, ERICH P. and ELISABETH NOELLE. *Antworten.* Allensbach am Bodensee: Verlag für Demoskopie, 1954.

NOELLE, ELISABETH. *Auskunft über die Parteien, Ergebnisse der Umfrage-Forschung in Deutschland.* Allensbach am Bodensee: Verlag für Demoskopie, 1955.

OECD Economic Surveys: France. OECD Publications, Paris, January 1968.

OECD Economic Surveys: Germany. OECD Publications, Paris, March 1967.

ORLIK I. and V. RAZMEROV. "European Security and Relations Between the Two Systems," *International Affairs* (Moscow), May 1967, pp. 3–8.

OSGOOD, ROBERT E. *NATO: The Entangling Alliance*. Chicago: University of Chicago Press, 1962.

PFALTZGRAFF, ROBERT L., JR. "Britain and the European Community: 1963–1967," *Orbis,* 12, 1/1968, pp. 87–120.

PRITZEL, KONSTANTIN. "Der Interzonenhandel," *Das Parlament,* B 48/67, Nov. 29, 1967.

PRYBYLA, JAN S. "The French Economy: Down the Up Staircase and Into the Market," *Current History,* Mar. 1968, pp. 135–142.

RANGER, ROBERT. "NATO's Reaction to Czechoslovakia: The Strategy of Ambiguous Response," *The World Today,* Jan. 1969, pp. 19–26.

RICHARDSON, JAMES L. *Germany and the Atlantic Alliance*. Cambridge, Mass.: Harvard University Press, 1966.

RICHARDSON, JAMES L. "Germany's Eastern Policy: Problems and Prospects," *The World Today,* Sept. 1968, pp. 375–386.

SCHACK, ALARD VON. "Zum nächsten Abschnitt deutscher Ostpolitik," *Aussenpolitik,* 19/2, Feb. 1968, pp. 81–89.

SCHILLING, JÜRGEN. "Der Euro-Staat—Noch immer die richtige Alternative für die Bundesrepublik?" *Frankfurter Hefte,* 4/1969, pp. 227–238.

SCHLESINGER, ARTHUR M. JR. *A Thousand Days*. Greenwich, Conn.: Fawcett Publications, Inc., 1967.

SCHRÖDER, GERHARD. "Germany Looks at Eastern Europe," *Foreign Affairs,* Oct. 1965, pp. 15–25.

SCHULZ, HANS-DIETER. "Moskaus wichtigster Partner: Die Stellung der 'DDR' im Ostblock," *Europa-Archiv,* 21/1964, pp. 785–794.

SCHUMACHER, KURT. "Die Staatsgewalt geht von den Besatzungsmächten aus." SPD pamphlet, n.d.

SCHWARZ, HANS-PETER, *Vom Reich zur Bundesrepublik, Deutschland im Widerstreit der aussenpolitischen Konzeptionen in den Jahren der Besatzungsherrschaft 1945–1949*. Neuwied-Berlin: Luchterhand, 1966.

SCHWARZKOPF, DIETRICH. "Die Idee des Gewaltverzichts: Ein Element der neuen Ostpolitik der Bundesrepublik," *Europa-Archiv,* 24/1967, pp. 893–900.

SECHER, HERBERT P. " 'Representative Democracy' or 'Chamber State': The Ambiguous Role of Interest Groups in Austrian Politics," *Western Political Quarterly,* XIII (1960) , pp. 890–909.

SEDIVY, JAROSLAV. "European Co-operation, European Security" *Literarni Noviny,* 25.ii.67., translated in *Czechoslovak Press Survey*. Munich: RFE Research, 1967.

SETHE, PAUL. *Zwischen Bonn und Moskau.* Frankfurt a. M.: Scheffler, 1956.

SHUB, ANATOLE. "Lessons of Czechoslovakia," *Foreign Affairs,* Jan. 1969, pp. 267–280.

SHULMAN, MARSHALL. "Europe Versus 'Detente,'" *Foreign Affairs,* Oct. 1965, pp. 389–402.

SMITH, JEAN EDWARD. *The Defense of Berlin.* Baltimore, Md.: The Johns Hopkins Press, 1963.

SMITH, JEAN EDWARD. "Two Germanies and Two Chinas," *The Reporter,* May 19, 1966, pp. 36–38.

SNYDER, GLENN H. *Deterrence and Defense.* Princeton, N.J.: Princeton University Press, 1961.

SOMMER, THEO. "Bonn Changes Course," *Foreign Affairs,* April 1967, pp. 477–491.

SOMMER, THEO. "Bonn's New Ostpolitik," *Journal of International Affairs,* Vol. XXII, No. 1 (1968), pp. 59–78.

SOMMER, THEO. "The Objectives of Germany" in Alastair Buchan, ed. *A World of Nuclear Powers?* Englewood Cliffs, N.J.: Prentice-Hall, 1966.

SPEIER, HANS. *German Rearmament and Atomic War.* Evanston, Ill.: Row, Peterson, 1957.

SPEIER, HANS, and W. PHILLIPS DAVISON, eds. *West German Leadership and Foreign Policy.* Evanston, Ill.: Row, Peterson, 1957.

STEHLE, HANSJAKOB. "Die blockierte Ostpolitik: Wechselwirkungen zwischen Bonns Bemühungen und Prager Reformkurs," *Die Zeit,* Dec. 10, 1968, p. 8.

STRAUSS, FRANZ-JOSEF. *The Grand Design: A European Solution to German Reunification.* New York: Praeger, 1966.

STRAUSS, FRANZ-JOSEF. *Herausforderung und Antwort.* Stuttgart: Seewald, 1968.

STUDNITZ, HANS-GEORG VON. *Bismarck in Bonn.* Stuttgart: Seewald, 1965.

SZAZ, ZOLTAN M. *Germany's Eastern Frontiers.* Chicago: Regnery, 1960.

TUDYKA, KURT P. "Die DDR im Kräftefeld des Ost-West-Konflikts," *Europa-Archiv,* 1/1966, pp. 16–27.

ULAM, ADAM. *Expansion and Coexistence.* New York: Praeger, 1968.

VALI, FERENC A. *The Quest for a United Germany.* Baltimore, Md.: The Johns Hopkins Press, 1967.

WAGNER, WOLFGANG. "Der Rückschlag der Bonner Politik in den arabischen Staaten," *Europa-Archiv,* 20/1965, pp. 359–370.

WAGNER, WOLFGANG. *Die Entstehung der Oder-Neisse Linie.* Stuttgart: Brentano, 1953.

WALLICH, HENRY C. *Mainsprings of the German Revival.* New Haven: Yale University Press, 1955.

WARSAW PACT POLITICAL COMMITTEE. "Declaration on the Strengthening of Peace and Security in Europe." Bucharest: Agerpress, 1966.

WATT, DONALD. "Germany," in Evan Luard, ed. *The Cold War: A Reappraisal.* New York: Praeger, 1964.

WETTIG, GERHARD. "Der Dialog zwischen SPD und SED in der kommunistischen Deutschland-Politik," *Das Parlament,* B 9/67, Mar. 1, 1967.

WETTIG, GERHARD. "Die europäische Sicherheit in der Politik des Ostblocks, 1966," *Osteuropa,* No. 2–3 (1967), pp. 106–111.

WETTIG, GERHARD. *Entmilitarisierung und Wiederbewaffnung in Deutschland, 1943–1955.* Munich: Oldenbourg, 1967.

WETTIG, GERHARD. "Moskau und die Grosse Koalition in Bonn," *Das Parlament,* B 10/68, Mar. 6, 1968.

WETTIG, GERHARD. "Soviet Policy on the Nonproliferation of Nuclear Weapons, 1966–1968," *Orbis,* 12, 4/1969, pp. 1058–1084.

WIESNER, JEROME B. "The Cold War Is Dead, But the Arms Race Rumbles On," *Bulletin of the Atomic Scientists,* June 1967, pp. 6–9.

WILDENMANN, RUDOLF. *Macht und Konsens als Problem der Innen- und Aussenpolitik.* Frankfurt a. M.: Athenäum Verlag, 1963.

WILLIS, F. ROY. *France, Germany, and the New Europe, 1945–1967.* Stanford, Calif.: Stanford University Press, 1968.

WILLIS, F. ROY. *The French in Germany, 1945–1949.* Stanford, Calif.: Stanford University Press, 1962.

WILLRICH, MASON. "West Germany's Pledge Not to Manufacture Nuclear Weapons," *Virginia Journal of International Law,* Vol. VII, No. 1 (Dec. 1966), pp. 91–100.

WOLFE, T. W. *Soviet Power and Europe: The Evolution of a Political-Military Posture, 1945–1964.* Santa Monica, Calif.: RAND Corp. Memorandum RM-5838-PR, Nov. 1968.

ZUNDEL, ROLF. "Das Ende der Doktrin?" *Die Zeit,* June 10, 1969, p. 6.

INDEX

70 71 72 73 7 6 5 4 3 2 1